Integrating Technology

Effective Tools for Collaboration

Shan Glandon

Library of Congress Cataloging-in-Publication Data

Published by Linworth Publishing, Inc.
480 East Wilson Bridge Road, Suite L
Worthington, Ohio 43085

Copyright © 2002 by Linworth Publishing, Inc.

All rights reserved. Reproduction of this book in whole or in part is prohibited without written permission of the author.

ISBN 1-58683-055-4
5 4 3 2 1

Table of Contents

About the Author vii
Introduction ix
List of Figures xv

Chapter 1   **Technology for Language Arts Units** 1
- Getting Informed: Are You Persuaded? 1
  - *Audience: Grades 4–8*
    - Getting Started 1
    - Looking at Advertisements 2
    - Developing an Advertisement 4
- Looking at Authors 7
  - *Audience: Grades 1–8*
    - About the Author 7
    - An Author Study for Younger Readers 9
    - An Author Study for Older Readers: A Literature Circles Approach ... 17
- Moving West: A Study of Pioneer Life 27
  - *Audience: Grades 4–8*
    - Literature Integration: Tall Tales: *The Wonderful Hay Tumble*, by Kathleen Harris 27
    - Literature Integration: Tall Tales: The Paul Bunyan Story 29
    - Literature Integration: Tall Tale Heroes 32
    - Literature Integration: Writing Original Tall Tales 37
    - Traveling the Oregon Trail 40
    - Traveling with Lewis and Clark 42

Chapter 2   **Technology for Math Units** 45
- Measurement: What Size Is It? 45
  - *Audience: Grades 2–4*
    - Introduction 45
    - Researching the Landmarks 46
    - Measuring and Developing a Scale 48
- Shadow Study 51
  - *Audience: Grades K–1*
    - Groundhog Facts 51
    - Shadow Hunt 53
    - Measuring Shadows 54
    - Predicting 55
- Shapes Are Everywhere 57
  - *Audience: Grades 4–8*
    - Can You Find It? 57
    - Tangrams 59
    - Finding Symmetry 60
    - Tesselations 61

Chapter 3   **Technology for Science Units** 63

Design Technology: Inventing 63
   Audience: Grades 3–8
- Thinking About Inventing: Introductory Lessons 63
- Inventors: Their Lives and Careers 66
- In the News: All About Inventing, Inventors, and Inventions 67
- Inventing 69

Insects in My Backyard 73
   Audience: Grades K–2
- Crickets 73
- Butterflies 75
- Structures 77
- Ladybugs 78
- A Celebration of Learning 79

Wetlands Exploration 81
   Audience: Grades 1–3
- A Walking Tour 81
- Discovering More 84
- Wild and Wonderful Wetlands 85
- Wetlands Couplets 86
- Exploring Wetlands 88
- Describing Our Wetlands 89

Chapter 4   Technology for Social Studies Units 91

Civil War Investigations 91
   Audience: Grades 6–8
- People of the Civil War 92
- Letters Home 94
- Causes of the Civil War 96
- Harriet Tubman 96
- The Abolitionists 97
- Newsletters to Families About the Unit 99

I Packed My Bag: Stories from Around the World 101
   Audience: Grades 1–3
- Getting Started 102
- Continuing the Travels 105
- *Tikki Tikki Tembo*, retold by Arlene Mosel 107
- *One Grain of Rice*, by Demi 108
- *The Cock, the Mouse, and the Little Red Hen*, a traditional tale illustrated by Graham Percy 109
- *The Paper Crane*, by Molly Bang 111
- *Strega Nona*, by Tomie dePaola 112
- *Stone Soup*, told by Marcia Brown 113
- *The Mitten*, adapted and translated by Jan Brett 115
- *The Lion's Whiskers*, by Nancy Raines Day 117
- *Why Mosquitoes Buzz in People's Ears*, retold by Verna Aardema 119
- *Bringing the Rain to Kapiti Plain*, retold by Verna Aardema 120
- *James and the Vine Puller*, a Brazilian folktale retold by Martha Bennett Stiles, illustrated by Larry Thomas; and *Panda and the Bunyips*, by

  Michael Foreman 121

If I Ran for President 125

 Audience: Grades 4–8

- The Contract Activity Packet 126
- The President's Job 130
- The President's Job II 131
- The President's Job III 138
- Leadership 138
- The Organization of the National Government 140
- The Election Process 140

Neighborhood Walk 143

 Audience: Grades 1–3

- Neighborhood Planning 145

Who Are We? Immigration in the United States 153

 Audience: Grades 4–8

- What Is an American? 153
- If You Were an Immigrant… 154
- *Land of Hope*: The Journey to America 155
- A New Situation 161

Chapter 5   **Technology Projects for the Class** 163

- Portfolios 163

 Audience: Grades 1–8

 Using *Hyperstudio* to create student portfolios

- Our Year in Pictures 165

 Audience: Grades K–8

 Using a slide show format to show the work of the class throughout the year

- Mother's Day Tea 166

 Audience: Grades 1–3

 Celebrating Mother's Day

- Reading Log 168

 Audience: Grades 1–8

 Supporting independent reading

- One-Page Learning Contracts 169

 Audience: Grades 1–8

 Differentiating learning assignments

About the Author

Shan Glandon is in her 15th year in education. She began as a media specialist at School 33 (Pre-K through 8th grade) in Buffalo, New York, and continued as a media specialist when she moved to Tulsa, Oklahoma, working at West Elementary and West Intermediate (K–6th grade) in the Jenks schools. About six years ago, Shan became a peer mentor in the district and began helping teachers in a variety of ways, i.e., creating and implementing integrated units, using multiple resources for instruction, increasing technology use in the classroom, developing authentic assessments, implementing the writing process and inquiry science investigations, improving questioning techniques, and differentiating instruction for diverse learners.

During the past two years as Elementary Curriculum Coordinator, she has continued to mentor teachers and also work at the district level supporting and implementing curriculum. She enjoys the ongoing connections with teachers and students and the challenge of teaching in many different curriculum areas. At the district level, she enjoys the opportunity to build vision and direction and to focus on "best practice" teaching.

Shan frequently offers workshops within her district and at Encylo-Media, the state conference held in Oklahoma City each September. She has received the 1994 Vision of Excellence Award for Jenks Public Schools and the 1988 Polly Clark Award for Outstanding Librarianship from the Oklahoma Library Association.

Introduction

In my role as a library media specialist and peer mentor for teachers, one of my responsibilities has been to help teachers integrate technology into daily lessons and activities. They took to heart the *National Educational Technology Standards for Teachers* and were interested in moving beyond textbooks and other traditional resources to learn how to incorporate multiple resources, authentic experiences and audiences, and technology into ongoing units of study. They also recognized the crucial role they play in developing students' technology skills for the 21st century and embraced the following beliefs:

- Skills for electronic information retrieval are critical in helping students evaluate the authority of the information, develop and combine effective keywords for searching, read and synthesize information (not print and hand in or cut and paste and use as is), and cite sources.
- Technology adds exciting variety to the options students can use to demonstrate understanding and learning, and close collaboration between the classroom and the library can help make those options an easy reality. The extra hands of the media specialist or the teacher and the ability to work in a lab setting give teachers and media specialists the flexibility they need in allowing time for production projects. Two facilitators can answer students' questions more quickly, solve problems more efficiently, and maximize time spent in developing a project. Banks of computers in the library and the classroom provide flexibility for individual and small-group project development as some students may be ready to begin production sooner than others in the classroom, or some students may need extra time to finish their projects.
- Computer simulations and other software programs provide exciting opportunities for problem solving and decision making. These opportunities can be whole-class participation with small-group, partner, or individual follow-up, or they can be set up as a center in the classroom or the media center.
- Global connections and awareness are developed through e-mail communication and Internet collaborations. Checking the mail can be a classroom helper job that is rotated during the unit or the school year. Ongoing collaborations with students and schools across the United States and the world bring authentic experiences to the classroom and mirror the world of work.
- Engaging, challenging lessons with opportunities for authentic assessments and ongoing communication with parents can be facilitated using technology resources. Establishing folders on the computer that store a variety of assessment rubrics and graphic organizers really helps in designing support materials for units. It's easy to make changes in a tool to tailor it to the needs of an activity or task. Slide shows, multimedia presentations, and original newspapers create the emphasis and pacing needed for a particular unit, grade level, or concept. Using technology smooths the time and effort needed to create newsletters and other communications with parents. It also is an easy way to keep track of the frequency of communication.

With these ideas in mind, it soon became apparent that we needed a tool to help with planning and organization for the use of technology in classroom activities and media center projects. The technology planning form used throughout this book was a natural outgrowth and became a friendly, easy-to-use visual tool for thinking about technology integration. It helped answer questions such as: How will students use technology? How will the teacher/media specialist use technology and model these skills for students? How will teachers integrate technology into the teaching and learning environment?

Purpose

Many teacher/library media specialist evaluation instruments include technology objectives. The planning form and the examples in the book help teachers and media specialists identify ways they already use technology and focus on ways to effectively and purposefully add technology, i.e., to facilitate management, to deliver more effective lessons, to build communication and collaboration opportunities, to develop exciting projects for students, and to provide variety and individual options. The form and the examples in the book provide a comprehensive way of thinking about technology integration and lower anxiety and frustration in thinking of technology as "just one more thing I have to learn and do and add."

The examples in the book reflect common units of study for kindergarten through eighth grades and show many different ways to incorporate technology and meet the standards listed in the *National Educational Standards for Students* and the *National Educational Technology Standards for Teachers* (International Society for Technology in Education, 2000). For more information on the complete text, visit <www.ISTE.org>. The activities in the units of study help students, teachers, and media specialists become proficient and responsible users of technology. Each area in the planning form supports the national standards. The four areas at the top of the form support standards for students, and the two areas at the bottom of the form address teacher standards.

Information retrieval assignments meet Standard 5 and give students experience with a wide range of electronic information sources so that they can navigate the Internet with purpose and confidence and collect and synthesize information from a variety of other databases.

Student productivity projects give students opportunities to use technology to demonstrate understanding, report learning, and enhance communication—experiences suggested by Standard 3.

Problem solving and decision making experiences using technology develop critical thinking skills as students explore exciting simulations and problem solving programs—a focus for Standard 6.

Communication and collaboration via online resources builds awareness of the world as a global community, provides mentoring opportunities, and increases peer-to-peer discussions and publishing—exciting experiences recommended in Standard 4.

The **teacher delivery of lessons** area on the planning form focuses on ways to develop the teacher's use of technology, scaffold learning for students, make lessons more exciting, and use multiple resources in units of study—goals of the standards for teachers.

An emphasis on technology for **classroom management** helps teachers ease the paperwork burden, implement flexible groups, monitor student progress more easily, build ongoing communication with parents, and develop a variety of assessment rubrics, as recommended in the standards for teachers.

A teacher or a media specialist does not need a million dollars to begin to integrate technology into units of study; much can be done with some basic tools, and the examples in the book are based on readily available hardware and software, such as the following:

1. Word processing, database, draw, spreadsheet
   Microsoft Office provides a standard package that includes Word, Excel, Outlook, and PowerPoint. *Appleworks 6* includes word processing, page layout, painting, spreadsheet, database, and presentation.
2. Scanner <www.epson.com/cgi-bin/Store/index.jsp>
   This Web site gives information about the Epson scanner that we prefer. It is user-friendly and manages a variety of image sources. Cost ranges from $150 to $500.
3. Digital camera <www.dpreview.com/reviews/specs.asp>
   This Web site gives information about the products of many companies. One camera that is both durable and easy to use is the *Sony Mavica*®. Pricing starts at $400.
4. Projection system
   Projection can be accomplished through an LCD panel, a connection to the television, or a projector. Projectors work well because the image is clearer and they are easy to connect and manipulate. Infocus projectors are a good buy.
5. Multimedia production: *Hyperstudio*, *Kid Pix*, *PowerPoint*
   Appleworks 6 from Apple Computer, Inc. <www.apple.com/appleworks/> offers a friendly, easy-to-use presentation component. It's a good beginning for novice users.
   Kid Pix Deluxe from The Learning Company <www.kidpix.com> offers a few more choices; students draw, write, record, and create slide shows with simple transitions.
   PowerPoint from Microsoft Corporation <www.microsoft.com/office/powerpoint> offers more complexity in terms of sounds and transitions.
   Hyperstudio 4 from Knowledge Adventure <www.hyperstudio.com> offers the most complexity.
6. Web design packages like *Netscape Composer*, *Home Page*, and *FrontPage Express* help teachers and students design their own Web pages.

A variety of software programs provide opportunities for problem solving and decision making. Some of these opportunities can be found via the Internet, and some are software programs that can be purchased through various vendors. As you browse the activities in the book, you will find location or order information for the recommended programs.

Content

Teachers and media specialists will find this book to be a helpful resource for integrating technology into daily routines and units of study. The suggested patterns of collaboration between the classroom and the library show different ways to link the work of the classroom with the work of the library. The collaborative nature of the examples supports the 10 "Learning and Teaching Principles of School Library Media Programs" outlined in *Information Power, Building Partnerships for Learning* (American Library Association, 1998) and makes the library media program an essential partner in the learning environment.

Most of the examples in the book are not complete units of study but are key activities within units where technology is effectively and purposefully integrated. Each unit example begins with a completed planning form showing the technology connections at a glance, an overview of the suggested activities for each unit, and grade level recommendations. The activities are then described in more detail. Each activity description includes technology goals, a suggested collaboration pattern between the teacher and the library media specialist, basic resources and preparation tasks, and an assignment description. Teachers and media specialists can use the activity examples as they are described in the book, or they can use them as springboards for their own ideas and ways of integrating technology.

The examples in the book show connections to four major content areas—language arts, math, science, and social studies—and also include whole class project ideas.

Three units are described for language arts. "Getting Informed: Are You Persuaded?" focuses on the world of advertising, and in the activity descriptions, students examine and analyze advertisements, identify and understand common techniques used in advertising, and produce original advertisements. "Looking at Authors" provides plans for pursuing an author study with younger students and one with older students. An author study lets students experience the body of work of the writer and engage in literary analysis discussions, comprehension tasks, and strategies for polishing their own writing craft. Activity descriptions in "Moving West: A Study of Pioneer Life" give suggestions for immersing students in the adventures of tall-tale heroes, researching and making presentations about tall-tale heroes, writing original tall tales, and posting them on the Web. Several literature connections are included in this unit.

There also are three math connections. Landmarks from around the world (i.e., the pyramids, the Great Wall, and the Eiffel Tower) are fascinating subjects for students to explore, and this is what they do in "Measurement: What Size Is It?" Activity descriptions focus on research strategies, techniques for helping students build scale models, and ways to tie the project to learning about measurement. "Shadow Study" activities describe ways to help students understand size concepts and positional words, i.e., big, bigger, biggest, short and tall, large and small, behind, and under. Activity descriptions in "Shapes Are Everywhere" share a variety of fun applications for creating products based on geometric shapes, i.e., tangrams, tesselations, and sculptures. Literature connections again are key components of these units.

Three science connections are included in the book. "Design Technology: Inventing" gives students opportunities to become inventors. Activities describe a process for learning about inventions (through a variety of literature), identifying invention ideas, developing invention ideas, and presenting and promoting them. The "Insects in My Backyard" unit describes literature experiences and science investigations that build understanding of the value of insects and awareness of the many kinds of insects. Wetlands are valuable habitats for the world. Through the "Wetlands Exploration" activities, students explore a wetlands habitat, research wetland habitats, prepare multimedia presentations, and share their findings in an ongoing collaboration with classrooms on the Web.

The five social studies units cover a variety of topics. The activity descriptions in "Civil War Investigations" provide a sequence of experiences that help students understand the causes and effects of the war, experience what it was like to be a soldier, and know important people and events of the period. In the "I Packed My Bag" unit, students use literature as springboards for developing beginning geography skills and becoming aware of customs and traditions from around the world. In the unit, "If I Ran for President," students explore the roles of the president, become an expert on the life and contributions of one of the presidents, and work in election committees to sponsor a school-wide election. Through the lessons and activities of "Neighborhood Walk," students visit (through literature) an imaginary neighborhood, explore their own neighborhoods, develop awareness of the variety of architecture in a neighborhood, build understanding of goods and services, and compare neighborhoods in other parts of the United States. The "Who Are We? Immigration in the United States" unit uses the novel *Land of Hope* by Joan Lowery Nixon to help students explore their own heritages, look at immigration patterns in the United States, and develop appreciation for the diversity of our country.

Several whole-class projects are suggested. The "Portfolios" project is an exciting and manageable way for students to create an ongoing record of their successes and growth areas. In creating the portfolio, students reflect on growth in each content area and share how they are developing as writers, mathematicians, historians, scientists, and readers. The computer portfolio is easy to revise and update, and students can take ownership of the process and invite family members to join them for lunch and a viewing of the portfolio. "Our Year in Pictures" is a wonderful way to celebrate the year and share with families highlights from the class. Students help in constructing a slide show (with captions) showing the activities and units from the year. Preparation of special cards and a slide show entitled "When I Grow Up" are highlights of the Mother's Day Tea project. Two other projects support ongoing management and learning: the reading log and the one-page learning contracts. The reading log provides a high interest way to help students read in a variety of genres. The one-page learning contracts provide ongoing, easy ways to differentiate learning and provide choices for students.

The computer is a tool that is most effectively integrated into ongoing units of study as an opportunity to enhance productivity, increase collaboration and communication, develop critical thinking, and speed information gathering. The units in the book are designed to provide engaging experiences for students and easy ways for integrating technology into daily activities and routines.

List of Figures

Figure 1.1	Getting Informed: Are You Persuaded? Unit: Technology Connections	xviii
Figure 1.1a	Getting Informed: Are You Persuaded? The Unit Activities at a Glance	1
Figure 1.2	Television Advertising	3
Figure 1.3	Assessment Rubric: Advertisements	4
Figure 1.4	Advertisement Planning Sheet	5
Figure 1.5	Sign-up: Product Pictures	5
Figure 1.6	Looking at Authors Unit: Technology Connections	6
Figure 1.6a	Looking at Authors, The Unit Activities at a Glance	7
Figure 1.7	Author Display	8
Figure 1.8	Reading Responses	9
Figure 1.9	Graphic Organizers: Reading	10–11
Figure 1.10	Reading Assessment	12
Figure 1.11	Comparison Chart: Author Study	13
Figure 1.12	Beginnings Information	13
Figure 1.13	Humor Web	14
Figure 1.14	Plot-line Drawing	14
Figure 1.15	Prewrite Brainstorming: Humorous Fiction	16
Figure 1.16	Sequence of Literature Circle Roles	19
Figure 1.17	Survival Skills Planner	19
Figure 1.18	Survival Scale	20
Figure 1.19	Examples of Conflict	21
Figure 1.20	Mistakes Chart	22
Figure 1.21	Post-reading Assessment Activities	23–25
Figure 1.22	Moving West: A Study of Pioneer Life Unit: Technology Connections	26
Figure 1.22a	Moving West: A Study in Pioneer Life, The Unit Activities at a Glance	27
Figure 1.23	Hay Tumble Story Page Template	28
Figure 1.24	Title and Introductory Pages	28
Figure 1.25	Evaluation Rubric: The Wonderful Hay Tumble	28
Figure 1.26	Brainstorming Web: Pioneer Farmer Challenges	29
Figure 1.27	Problem-solving Solution Grid	30
Figure 1.28	Story Line Graphic Organizer: Paul Bunyan	30
Figure 1.29	Evaluation Rubric: Paul Bunyan Stories	31
Figure 1.30	Note-taking Graphic Organizer	32
Figure 1.31	Evaluation Rubric: Tall-tale Heroes Research	33
Figure 1.32	Resume Template	34
Figure 1.33	Museum Plaque	37
Figure 1.34	Tall Tale Heroes Comparison Grid	38
Figure 1.35	Evaluation Rubric: Tall-tale Heroes Research	40
Figure 1.36	Assignment Requirements	42
Figure 1.37	Assessment Rubric	43
Figure 2.1	Measurement Unit: Technology Connections	44
Figure 2.1a	Measurement, The Unit Activities at a Glance	45
Figure 2.2	Scavenger Hunt Graphic Organizer	46
Figure 2.3	Research Graphic Organizer: Landmarks	47
Figure 2.4	Graph Paper	48
Figure 2.5	Shadow Study Unit: Technology Connections	50
Figure 2.5a	Shadow Study, The Unit Activities at a Glance	51

Figure 2.6	Groundhog Display	52
Figure 2.7	Assessment Checklist	52
Figure 2.8	Shadows Investigation	54
Figure 2.9	Shapes Are Everywhere Unit: Technology Connections	56
Figure 2.9a	Shapes Are Everywhere, The Unit Activities at a Glance	57
Figure 2.10	Hunt for Shapes Graphic Organizer	58
Figure 2.11	Hunt for Shapes Assessment Rubric	58
Figure 2.12	Scrapbook of Shapes	59
Figure 2.13	Tangram Recording Sheet	59
Figure 2.14	Tangram Storyboard Planning	59
Figure 2.15	Slide Show Template	60
Figure 3.1	Design Technology Unit: Technology Connections	62
Figure 3.1a	Design Technology: Inventing, The Unit Activities at a Glance	63
Figure 3.2	Bulletin Board Display: Inventors	66
Figure 3.3	Reporter Assignments	68
Figure 3.4	Inventors Journal	70
Figure 3.5	Assessment Checklist	70
Figure 3.6	Insects in My Backyard Unit: Technology Connections	72
Figure 3.6a	Insects in My Backyard, The Unit Activities at a Glance	73
Figure 3.7	Stationery Template	74
Figure 3.8	Reading Journal	74
Figure 3.9	Alphabet Page Template	75
Figure 3.10	Helpful and Harmful Insects	79
Figure 3.11	Invitation	79
Figure 3.12	Wetlands Exploration Unit: Technology Connections	80
Figure 3.12a	Wetlands Exploration, The Unit Activities at a Glance	81
Figure 3.13	Journal	82
Figure 3.14	Record-keeping Sheet for Camera Shots	82
Figure 3.15	Venn Comparison	83
Figure 3.16	KWHL Chart	83
Figure 3.17	Note-taking Graphic Organizer	86
Figure 3.18	Storyboard Planning Sheet	86
Figure 3.19	Wetlands Habitat Rubric	87
Figure 3.20	Couplets Brainstorming	88
Figure 4.1	Civil War Unit: Technology Connections	90
Figure 4.1a	Civil War, The Unit Activities at a Glance	91
Figure 4.2	Slide Show Storyboard Planner	92
Figure 4.3	Portfolio Template	92
Figure 4.4	Portfolio Cover Sheet: Civil War People Project	93
Figure 4.5	Artwork Record File	93
Figure 4.6	Assessment Rubric: People of the Civil War Slide Show	94
Figure 4.7	Storyboard Planning Example	95
Figure 4.8	Graphic Organizer: Notes from Letters Home	95
Figure 4.9	Harriet Tubman Information Packet	97
Figure 4.10	Acrostic Poem	97
Figure 4.11	Front Page: Abolitionists' Newspaper	98
Figure 4.12	Newspaper template	99
Figure 4.13	I Packed My Bag Unit: Technology Connections	100
Figure 4.13a	I Packed My Bag, The Unit Activities at a Glance	101
Figure 4.14	Mileage Chart	103
Figure 4.15	Continent Signs	104

Figure 4.16	Slide Show Template	105
Figure 4.17	Note from the Gingerbread man	106
Figure 4.18	Coat of Arms	107
Figure 4.19	Sinking and Floating Investigation Log	108
Figure 4.20	Job Charts	109
Figure 4.22	Conflict Resolution Poster	111
Figure 4.23	KWHL Chart	113
Figure 4.24	Note-taking Sheet	113
Figure 4.25	Prewrite Brainstorming Sheet	114
Figure 4.26	Cluster Web	114
Figure 4.27	Turkey Centerpiece	115
Figure 4.28	Heroes Chart	117
Figure 4.29	Extra Mile Award	117
Figure 4.30	Hero Characteristics	118
Figure 4.31	A Hero Is…	118
Figure 4.32	Riddle Display	119
Figure 4.33	Roles for the Drama	120
Figure 4.34	If i Ran for President Unit: Technology Connections	124
Figure 4.34a	If I Ran for President, The Unit Activities at a Glance	125
Figure 4.35	Contract Activity Packet	127
Figure 4.36	Roles of the President	138
Figure 4.37	Assessment Rubric: Presidents Letters	139
Figure 4.38	Leadership Graph	139
Figure 4.39	Leadership Definitions	140
Figure 4.40	Election Committee Responsibilities	141
Figure 4.41	Neighborhood Walk Unit: Technology Connections	142
Figure 4.41a	Neighborhood Walk, The Unit Activities at a Glance	143
Figure 4.42	*Roxaboxen* Acrostic Poem	144
Figure 4.43	Bridge Words	144
Figure 4.44	Response Chart	144
Figure 4.45	Changes Graph	146
Figure 4.46	Neighborhood Workshop Journal	147–149
Figure 4.47	Infrastructure Assignments	151
Figure 4.48	Building Assignments	151
Figure 4.49	Immigration Unit: Technology Connections	152
Figure 4.49a	Immigration, The Unit Activities at a Glance	153
Figure 4.50	I Am an American	154
Figure 4.51	Historical Fiction Characteristics	156
Figure 4.52	Interview Sheet	157
Figure 4.53	Immigration to America: Reasons	157
Figure 4.54	Note-taking Graphic Organizer	158
Figure 4.55	Family Heritages	158
Figure 4.56	Web Page Planning	160
Figure 5.1	Continuum Rating Sheet	164
Figure 5.2	Portfolio Template	165
Figure 5.3	When I Grow Up	167
Figure 5.4	Reading Log	168
Figure 5.5	Learning Contract Grid	169
Figure 5.6	Learning Contract Example	171
Figure 5.6b	Poetry Contract	172

Getting Informed: Are You Persuaded?		
Information Retrieval	**Student Productivity**	**Problem Solving and Decision Making**
Electronic encyclopedias, e.g., *Grolier's*, *World Book* Internet Web sites: **Coca Cola advertisements:** <http://memory.loc.gov/anmem/ccmphtml/colatime1.html>	Advertising posters	
		Communication and Collaboration
Teacher Delivery of Lessons		**Classroom Management**
Slide show of advertising examples Graphic organizer for television viewing Planning sheet		Assessment rubric for evaluating the advertisement posters

Figure 1.1 Getting Informed: Are You Persuaded? Unit: Technology Connections

Chapter 1

Technology for Language Arts Units

Unit 1: Getting Informed: Are You Persuaded?

Unit Objectives:
1. Write an editorial opinion letter/essay.
2. Identify the "hidden persuaders" used in advertising.
3. Create an advertisement.

Audience: Grades 4–8

Length of the Unit: 2 weeks

The Unit Activities at a Glance

Getting Started	Looking at Advertisements	Developing an Advertisement
Students look at editorials and write editorials.	Students learn about common advertising techniques and analyze ads for these techniques.	Students discuss television ads, listen to a guest speaker, and create original advertisements.

Figure 1.1a Getting Informed: Are You Persuaded? The Unit Activities at a Glance

■ Activity Focus: Getting Started

Technology Connection: Information Retrieval (ISTE-students 5), Teacher Delivery of Lessons (ISTE-teacher II-III)

Collaboration:
- Gathering research sources and topics for editorial opinions: Media specialist and teacher working together
- Introducing persuasive writing: Teacher

Resources: Print and electronic resources, e.g., magazines, Internet, other databases

Preparation Tasks:
- Gather editorials from a variety of newspapers or newsmagazines, i.e., the local newspaper, *USA Today*, *New York Times*, *Washington Post*, *Time*, or *Newsweek*.
- Prepare a list of topics for editorial opinions so that students have manageable ideas for the project.

Assignment Description:

Introduce editorial writing and talk about the purposes of editorial writing, i.e., to persuade (convince someone to think or act in a certain way), to promote (speak in support of a program or activity), to praise (comment on a positive action or recognize the efforts of an individual), to inform (to explain the positive and negative aspects of complex issues).

Look at a variety of editorials to identify their purposes and their structure. Develop a guidelines list for the structure of an editorial, i.e., identify the subject/issue in an engaging way, state your viewpoint (an experience, a quotation, a surprising statement, or a thesis statement), briefly explain the subject/issue, list facts/evidence that support your viewpoint, and conclude with a positive statement that summarizes and reinforces your best evidence.

Have students practice formulating viewpoint statements. Use these statements as examples and develop opposite viewpoints working together as a class.

1. Advertising informs us about new products and helps make the economy strong. What might the opposite viewpoint be?
2. Zoos contribute to the survival of the animal kingdom. What is the opposite viewpoint?

Now have students work with partners to write viewpoint statements for these topics: gun control, television viewing, pollution, homeless people, the existence of UFOs, and a higher age for receiving a driver's license.

Have students pick individual issues (recycling, capital punishment, bicycle paths, helmet safety, curfews, sports salaries, school uniforms), research the issue, take a viewpoint, and write an editorial about the issue. Editorials should be three paragraphs in length. The first paragraph should present the viewpoint in an engaging way and briefly explain the issue. The second paragraph should list facts and evidence that support the viewpoint, and the third paragraph should provide the concluding statements that reinforce the viewpoint and restate the key pieces of evidence. Paragraphs don't need to be lengthy—just a few key sentences that are direct and state the facts.

Have students share their editorials; then discuss what is most convincing in their writing.

■ Activity Focus: Looking at Advertisements

Technology Connection: Teacher Delivery of Lesson (ISTE-teacher II-III)

Collaboration:
- Developing the advertisements slide show: Media specialist and teacher working together
- Analyzing the Coca-Cola advertisements: Media specialist
- Looking at advertising: Teacher

Resources:
- Digital camera
- Projection system

Preparation Tasks:
- Use the digital camera to take pictures of a variety of advertisements and download them into a slide show on the computer.
- Bookmark the Web site <http://memory.loc.gov/ammem/ccmphtml/colatime1.html> (Coca-Cola advertisements) on computers in the media center.
- Create a graphic organizer for students to use as they view and analyze television advertising (see figure 1.2).

Product	Advertising Technique	Positive Features	Negative Features

Figure 1.2 Television Advertising

Assignment Description:
Introduce and discuss common advertising techniques:

1. The famous person. Advertisers select a well-known person, often a sports figure or a celebrity, and ask the person to endorse or promote the product.
2. The scientist. Advertisers use evidence from scientific studies in the promotion of the product e.g., nine out of ten dentists recommend (a brand of toothpaste) to fight tooth decay.
3. Success. Advertisers make the connection that use of the product brings success, happiness, adventure, or safety.
4. Glamour and Wealth. Advertisers go for "snob appeal" in promoting the product and create an image of wealth or beauty, e.g., many automobile advertisements.
5. Vague Statements. Advertisers make sweeping statements about the product, e.g., helps cure athlete's foot, more vitamins in each box.
6. Trustworthiness. Advertisers use a trustworthy figure (mother, elderly person, or friend) in the promotion of a product.
7. Join the Crowd. Advertisers create the impression that everyone is buying/using the product.
8. Flowery Language. Advertisers often use additional words and phrases that stretch the truth about products, e.g., a jumbo gallon, perfect results every time, giant economy size, gives you energy.

Brainstorm and list criteria for evaluating the effectiveness of an advertisement, e.g., engaging/catchy, convincing, colorful, clear, easy-to-understand message. Present the slide show advertisements and analyze their effectiveness, i.e., what appeals to students, what catches their eye, what they don't like. Identify any techniques that are used.

Access the American Memory Web site showing Coca-Cola advertisements since the soft drink was first introduced and sold. Have students work with partners in the media center and analyze the advertisements to identify techniques that have been used and to explore how the advertisements have remained the same and how they have changed throughout the years. Invite sharing and discussion.

At Home Connection: Have students select a late afternoon/evening television program and view and analyze the advertising during the program. Encourage them to use the graphic organizer (see Figure 1.2).

■ Activity Focus: Developing an Advertisement

Technology Connection: Student Productivity (ISTE-students 3), Classroom Management (ISTE-teacher IV-V)

Collaboration:
- Gathering newspaper and magazine resources: Media specialist and teacher working together
- Arranging a guest speaker: Media specialist
- Developing an assessment rubric: Teacher with media specialist assisting
- Creating the advertisements: Teacher and media specialist as co-facilitators
- Evaluating the advertisements: Teacher and media specialist working together

Resources:
- A variety of newspapers and magazines
- Guest speaker, e.g., art teacher sharing guidelines for designing posters, local advertising agency representative, a media advertising representative, a newspaper editor discussing how advertisements are created and involving students in creating an advertisement
- Drawing paper cut to bumper sticker format (5½" × 17"), enough for one per student
- Illustrating materials (markers, colored pencils, crayons)
- Projection system
- Color printer
- Scanner
- Digital camera
- Self-stick notes, so each student has enough to offer comments for each student in the class

Preparation Tasks:
- Develop an assessment rubric for evaluating the advertisements (see Figure 1.3). Make multiple copies and one transparency of the rubric.
- Develop a planning sheet for students to use as they create their original advertisements (see Figure 1.4). Make multiple copies and one transparency of the planning sheet.
- Connect a projection system to the computer so that students can see an introduction or a review of word processing choices for font and type sizes for the advertising copy information (slogans, descriptive information).

Name _____ Date _____

Advertisements will be evaluated using this rating scale:
3 - Exemplary 2 - Developing 1 - Attempted

_____ Showed careful craftsmanship
_____ Showed creativity
_____ Included colorful details
_____ Used descriptive words
_____ Included a catchy slogan/headline
_____ Named the product
_____ Met the deadline for the assignment

Figure 1.3 Assessment Rubric: Advertisements

Assignment Description:
Set the stage for students to create their own advertisements. Invite students to share the information they gathered by watching television advertising the night before. As they share information, tally and discuss the hidden persuaders they found. Listen to the guest speaker talk about design and layout. Using the newspaper and magazine resources, look at the slogans and headlines that

Advertisement Planning Sheet
Product:
Descriptive Words:
Slogan/catchy headline:
Hidden persuader (if any):
Rough Sketch:

Figure 1.4 Advertisement Planning Sheet

are used and analyze them for their effectiveness in terms of word choices, clarity, and directness. Evaluate the composition of the advertisements.

Distribute the drawing paper and the illustrating materials and have students design a bumper sticker in support of this viewpoint: Voting is an important job for a citizen. Invite students to share their bumper stickers and comment on effective slogans and composition.

Use the transparency to introduce the planning sheet (Figure 1.4) students will use to design their advertisements. Review each component: product name, descriptive words about the product that would make someone want to buy it, slogan or catchy headline, hidden persuader (if any) that students will use, rough sketch of the design of the advertisement, and their names somewhere in the advertisements as the creators. Display the assessment rubric (Figure 1.3) and review the descriptors so that students are clear about how the advertisements will be assessed.

Although students will be creating individual advertisements, encourage them to brainstorm with peers. Set up the room to encourage this interaction, e.g., have students work in groups at tables or rearrange the desks in groups of four or six. Circulate as students work, asking questions and giving guidance.

When most students have completed the plan for their advertisements, direct their attention to the computer screen and introduce/review word processing tips for selecting the format for printing (landscape or portrait), changing the paper size to legal ($8\frac{1}{2}$" × 14") and choosing fonts, type size, color, and style. Students who are more experienced with the computer may want directions for rotating and angling text; assure students that you will help with this as they work at the computer. Show students how to preview their work to see the overall design and arrangement.

Review the four options students have for adding pictures of the product: an original drawing of the product, a picture of the product from a magazine or other print source that can be scanned into the computer, a picture taken with a digital camera and downloaded into the computer, or a picture copied from an electronic source. Use the board to create a four-block sign-up for product illustration choices and ask students to place their names in the box of their choice (see Figure 1.5.). This is a helpful management tool for juggling camera and computer needs. Encourage students to show you a preview of their advertisements before printing a final copy on the color printer.

Have students present their advertisements to the class, and encourage students to use self-stick notes to offer positive comments about effective/appealing parts of the advertisements. When all the students have presented, leave the advertisements out (either at desks or tables, on the floor under the board, or propped in the board tray) and encourage students to distribute their "positive" comment self-stick notes on the advertisements. Give students time to read the comments from their peers. Evaluate the advertisements with the assessment rubric.

Original illustration	Importing
Digital camera	Scanning

Figure 1.5 Sign-up: Product Pictures

Technology for Language Arts Units

Looking at Authors

Information Retrieval	Student Productivity	Problem Solving and Decision Making
Electronic encyclopedias, e.g., *Grolier's, World Book*	Personal narrative stories	
		Communication and Collaboration
		E-mail to the author

Teacher Delivery of Lessons	Classroom Management
Graphic organizers for reading responses	Assessment rubrics for evaluating journal entries/fluency in reading
Chart—reading response prompts	
Comparison chart	Poster listing the literature circle role rotation
Prewrite brainstorming organizer	
Survival skills planner	Post-reading assessment choices
Transparency listing examples of conflict	
Internet sites: **Information for Ordering *Literature Circles* by Harvey Daniels:** <www.stenhouse.com> **Introduction to Literature Circles:** <www.sasked.gov.sk.ca/docs/mla/circle/intro.html>	

Figure 1.6 Looking at Authors Unit: Technology Connections

Unit 2: Looking at Authors

Unit Objectives:
1. Explore an author's style.
2. Enjoy the variety of stories written by the author.
3. Learn about the author.
4. Gain understanding of plot, setting, characters, and theme.
5. Practice and develop reading skills.

Audience: Grades 1–8

Length of the Unit: Variable, depending upon the age of the students and the lengths of the books

The Unit Activities at a Glance

About the Author	An Author Study for Younger Readers	Older Readers: A Literature Circle Approach
Students gather information about the author, develop a display, and e-mail the author.	The activity description provides an author study model unit based on humorous fiction stories by Cynthia Rylant and includes a writing connection.	The activity description provides a literature-circle-based reading unit based on survival stories by Gary Paulsen and includes pre- and post-reading activities.

Figure 1.6a Looking at Authors, The Unit Activities at a Glance

■ Activity Focus: About the Author

Technology Connection: Information Retrieval (ISTE-students 5), Communication and Collaboration (ISTE-students 4)

Collaboration:
- Identifying an author and gathering titles by the author: Media specialist and teacher in collaboration
- Learning about the author: Teacher

Resources:
- Author's Web site
- Multiple copies of titles written by the author

Preparation Tasks:
- Choose an author who has written a number of books; prepare booktalks on the titles.
- Locate and bookmark the author's Web site if one is available.

Assignment Description:

As students read books by the featured author, use the author's Web site or Web sites developed by the author's publisher (information and e-mail communication opportunities) to gain insight into the author's style/process of writing (handling writer's block, getting ideas, inspiration), to analyze how the author's environment affects his or her writing, and to see challenges in the author's life.

Brainstorm questions the students would ask if they could interview the author, i.e., questions about his or her life and writing. Divide the questions so that each student or student partnership has a question; have students access the author's Web site and read and browse the site to answer the question. Encourage students to find interesting ways to share what they have learned in designing a contribution to the author display. (see Figure 1.7.) (Teacher's note: For students just beginning to read, make arrangements with a class of older students to have them help the students gather information from the Web site. Emphasize to the older students that their role is to read the information and let the younger students manipulate the computer, take notes, and prepare their contributions for the author display.)

	(Author's name in a fun script)	
(Students' Contributions)	(Students' Contributions)	(Students' Contributions)

Figure 1.7 Author Display

At the close of the novel study, use the author's e-mail address to compose a class letter sharing the students' insights and experiences in reading the books. Students can work individually or with partners in composing their contributions to the letter.

Suggested authors include the following:

Young readers:

Frank Asch: <www.frankasch.com/>
Marc Brown: <www.pbs.org/wgbh/arthur/marc_brown/index.html>
Tomie dePaola: <www.bingley.com/MyWebPage.html>
Mem Fox: <www.memfox.net/intro.html>
Pat Hutchins: <www.titch.net/> (a Web site on one of her characters, Titch)
Ezra Jack Keats: <www.ezra-jack-keats.org/> (developed by the Ezra Jack Keats Foundation)
Bill Martin, Jr.: <www.tiill.com/authors.htm>
Leo Lionni: <http://coe.west.asu.edu/students/dcorley/authors/Lionni.htm> or
   <www.ci.shrewsbury.ma.us/Sps/Schools/Beal/Curriculum/media/Lionni/leolionni.html>
Laura Numeroff: <www.lauranumeroff.com/>
Don and Audrey Wood: <www.audreywood.com/>
Charlotte Zolotow: <www.ipl.org/youth/AskAuthor/Zolotow.html>
Other authors for young readers include Lois Ehlert, Arnold Lobel and Cynthia Rylant. Information about them is available on the Internet, but they do not have author sites.

Middle and older readers:

Avi: <www.avi-writer.com/>
Betsy Byars: <www.betsybyars.com/>
Jean George: <www.jeancraigheadgeorge.com/>

Johanna Hurwitz: <www.interkan.net/ravenstonepress/hurwitz.html>
Lois Lowry: <www.ipl.org/youth/AskAuthor/Lowry.html>
Phyllis Reynolds Naylor: <www.ipl.org/youth/AskAuthor/Naylor.html>
Joan Lowery Nixon: <http://members.aol.com/NikkiB5130/JNixon5130.htm> (site developed by her grandchild)
Katherine Paterson: <www.terabithia.com/bio.htm>
Gary Paulsen: <www.randomhouse.com/features/garypaulsen/>
Patricia Polacco: <www.patriciapolacco.com/>
Elvira Woodruff: <www.ewoodruff.com/>
Other authors include Eve Bunting, Karen Hesse, Willo Davis Roberts, and Zilpha Snyder. Information is available about these authors on the Internet, but they do not have specific Web sites.

■ Activity Focus: An Author Study for Younger Readers

Technology Connection: Teacher Delivery of Lesson (ISTE-teacher II-III)

Collaboration:
- Presenting booktalks on the titles in the author study: Media specialist
- Reading and responding: Teacher

Resources:
- Reading journals
- Multiple copies of titles written by the author you have chosen

Preparation Tasks:
- Prepare a variety of graphic organizers for students to use as they work with setting, plot, characters, and theme. (See Figure 1.9, pages 10–11.)
- Create a reading responses chart to hang in the classroom. (See Figure 1.8.)
- Create two assessment rubrics: one for journal responses and one for reading fluency. (See Figure 1.10, page 12.)
- Create a comparison chart on chart paper or butcher paper; make the chart long enough so that all the titles the students are reading by the author can be listed on the chart. Choose headings for the columns that fit what you will find in the stories. (See Figure 1.11, page 13, for an example based on humorous fiction stories by Cynthia Rylant.)
- Create a beginnings graphic organizer for students to use in the opening chapters of the stories. (See Figure 1.12, page 13.)

Responses to Reading

I noticed…
I wonder why…
I began to think of…
It seems like…
I can't really understand…
I can't believe…
I'm not sure…
I know the feeling…
I love the way…
I realized…
I was surprised…
I think…
If I were…
I wish…

Figure 1.8 Reading Responses

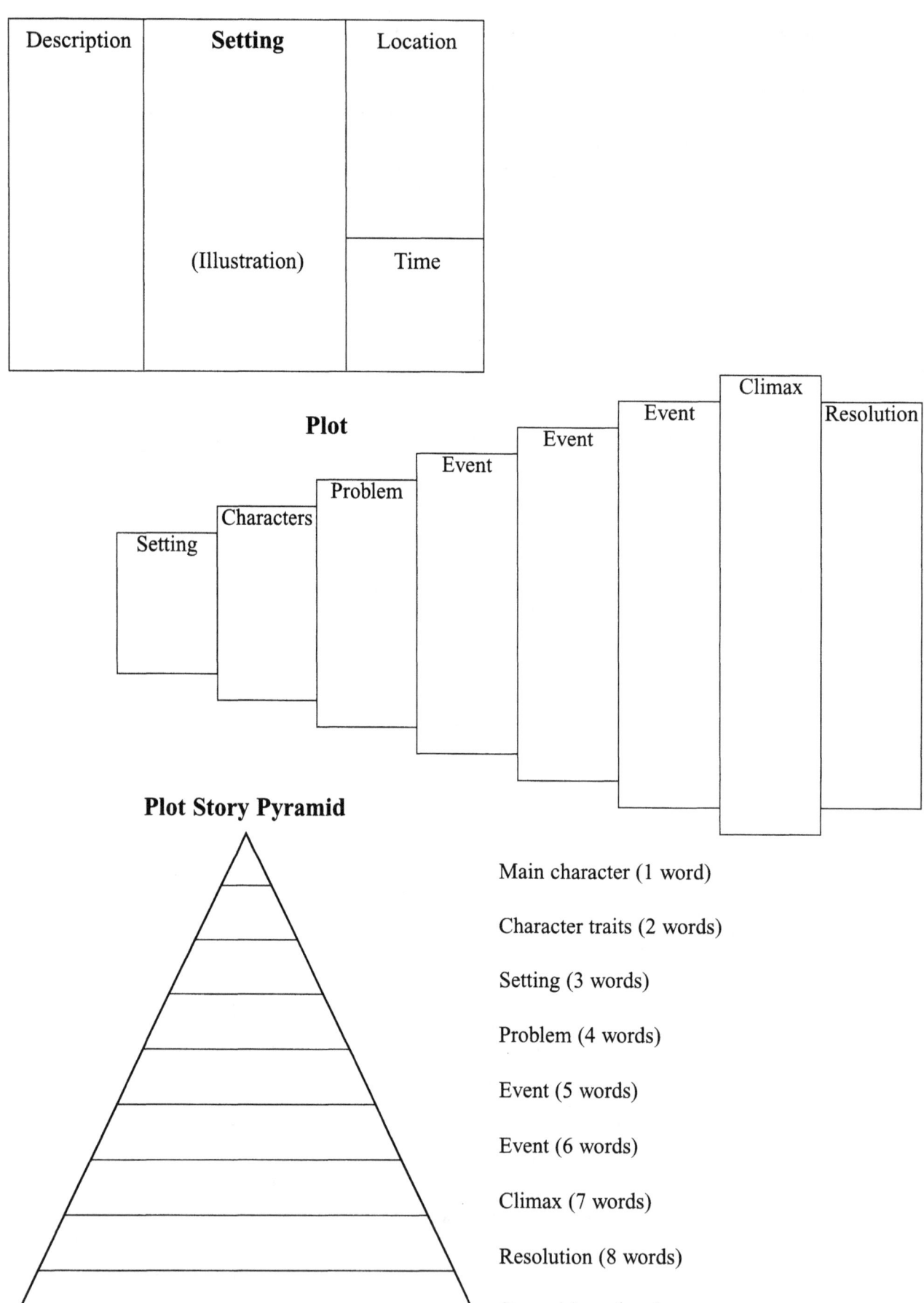

Figure 1.9 Graphic Organizers: Reading

Character Analysis

Action	Trait it reveals about the character

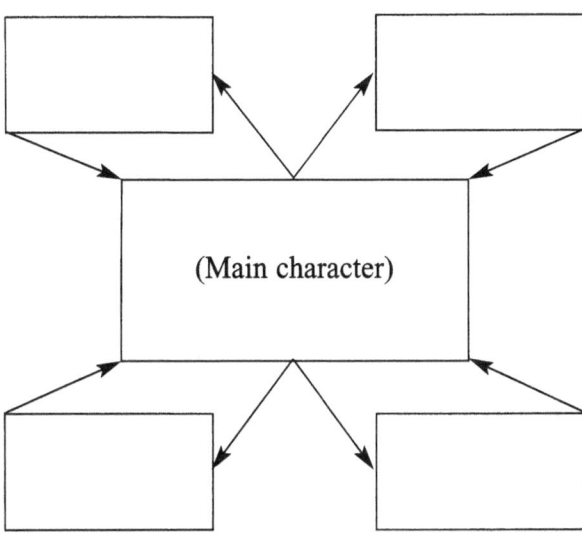

On the arrowed lines from the main character to the other character boxes, students record words and phrases describing how the main character feels about/relates to the other characters. On the arrowed lines from the other character boxes, students record words and phrases describing how the other characters view/relate to the main character.

Theme

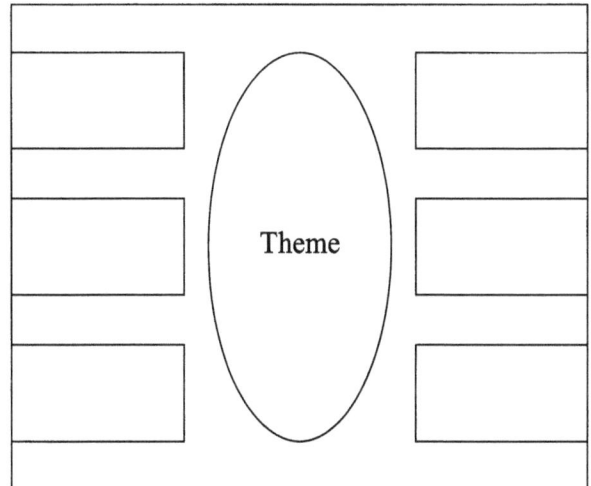

Students identify the theme for the story and use the boxes around the theme to record words and phrases from the author that support/verify the theme.

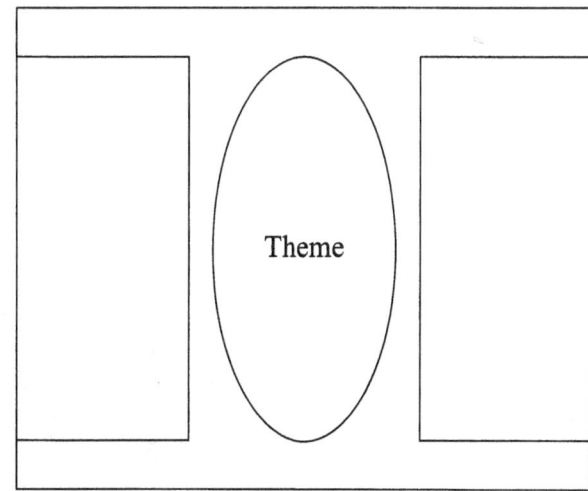

A variation for younger readers: Identify the theme and have students draw pictures of events in the story that support/verify the theme.

Figure 1.9 (cont'd) Graphic Organizers: Reading

Journal Entries

Entry 1	Entry 2	Entry 3
Entry 4	Entry 5	Entry 6
Entry 7	Entry 8	Entry 9
Entry 10	Entry 11	Entry 12

✓+ Use complete sentences; focus on the assignment, include lots of details and show thoughtful connections to the assignment.

✓ Some complete sentences, some focus on the assignment, missing some details

✓- Lacks sentence structure, missing assignment pieces, few details

Reading Fluency Assessment

Reading Inventory for _____ 2001–2002

Reads silently for sustained periods of time		
Acquiring	Developing	Demonstrated
Reads with fluency and expression		
Acquiring	Developing	Demonstrated
Self-corrects errors		
Acquiring	Developing	Demonstrated
Exhibits large sight vocabulary		
Acquiring	Developing	Demonstrated
Uses a variety of strategies to determine word meanings		
Acquiring	Developing	Demonstrated

Comments:

Figure 1.10 Reading Assessment

Survival Stories Comparison Chart

Stories	Characters	Setting	Problem	Survival Skills	Exciting Moments	Resolution

Humorous Fiction Comparison Chart

Stories	Characters	Setting	Problem	Most Humorous Moments	Most Exciting Moments

Figure 1.11 Comparison Chart: Author Study

Assignment Description:

Journals, the graphic organizers and assessment rubrics, and a daily routine for reading help students examine and enjoy the variety of stories written by the author, compare the stories in a number of ways, and study the style or craft of the author.

Develop a daily routine for reading the stories; one that works well for younger students includes these components:

Opening Discussion (5–8 minutes): Discussion activities could result from journal responses of the previous day, could be prediction sharing, or could be quick summaries of events so far.

The important characters are...

(Name the main characters and make sketches of them)

The setting of the story: The story takes place...

_____
_____

(Picture of the setting)

The problem in the story...

_____
_____
_____

Figure 1.12 Beginnings Information

Technology for Language Arts Units

Mini-lesson (10–15 minutes): The mini-lesson provides the focus for the day and targets literary analysis (character, plot, setting, theme, author's style) or reading skills (comprehension, mental pictures, predicting, asking questions).

Reading and Responding (30–40 minutes): Students read silently or with partners; responding activities give students opportunities to write in their reading journals, engage in discussion with peers, and work with the concepts/skills. Setting goals for this period facilitates management of the students and provides time for assessing and conferencing.

Here's an example using books from the Henry and Mudge series by Cynthia Rylant. The teacher used *Henry and Mudge and the Careful Cousin* to model the activities and skills students would apply to the Henry and Mudge titles they had selected for independent reading.

Day 1: Beginning the Novels

Opening Discussion: Develop a cluster web on humor. (See Figure 1.13.) Have students share with partners funny things that have happened in their lives, then record in journals keywords to describe the funny events.

Mini-lesson: Predicting: Introduce *Henry and Mudge and the Careful Cousin*. Predict the direction of the story based on the cover illustration and title. What is a careful cousin? What problems might her visit cause? Refer to the brainstorming web on humor, then pose this question: How will the author create humor in the book? Record the predictions on a class chart.

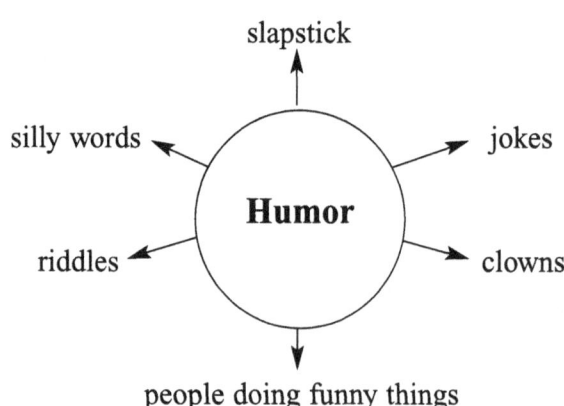

Figure 1.13 Humor Web

Reading and Responding: Read aloud the first chapter. Pause on page 11 and discuss the vocabulary word "frilly." What kind of dress is a frilly dress? Why would this worry Henry?

Finish the chapter and discuss the story. How do the illustrations and the words of the story on pages 6–9 show Henry's eagerness for the visit of his cousin? How does Mudge show his excitement? What are humorous moments in the chapter? Two of Annie's worries are relieved when she learns that Mudge does not bite and he doesn't jump on people...anymore. How will Henry solve the problem of Mudge's drooling? Introduce the reading responses chart and have students use their reading journals to respond to the first chapter.

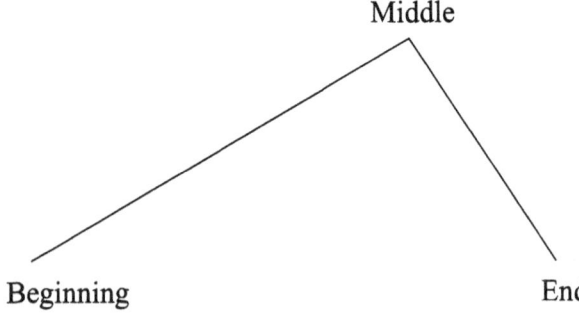

Figure 1.14 Plot-line Drawing

Day 2: Other Stories by C. Rylant

Opening Discussion: Use the board to make a plot-line drawing and explain as you draw, i.e., all stories have a beginning, a middle, and an end. (See Figure 1.14.) Discuss with students: What does an author try to do in the beginning of the story? Refocus question: What did we learn in the first chapter of *Henry and Mudge and the Careful Cousin*?

Teacher's note: As students share ideas they remember from the first chapter, help them see that the author introduces important characters (Henry, Mudge, Annie), the setting (Henry's house), and the purpose or problem of a story (Henry has been eagerly looking forward to Annie's visit; when she arrives in a frilly dress with shiny shoes and asks worried questions about Mudge, Henry begins to have second thoughts about her visit).

What happens in the middle of the story? (The climax or most exciting parts)

What happens at the end of the story? (Sometimes the problem is solved or the characters change.)

Mini-lesson: Selecting Books for Independent Reading: The teacher takes his or her students to the media center to hear the booktalk and has students select Henry and Mudge titles for independent reading. After returning to the classroom, the teacher has students predict the directions of their stories based on cover illustrations and titles. Introduce the "beginnings" illustrating sheet. (See Figure 1.12 on page 13.) Students should use the first chapters of their books to illustrate and name main characters, to illustrate and describe the setting, and to state the purpose or problem of the story.

Reading and Responding: Set goals for reading time, e.g., read Chapter 1, use a journal to respond to the chapter using one of the reading response starters or one of your own. Then use the "beginning" illustration form to draw and write about the characters, setting, and purpose/problem in the story.

Ongoing Assessment: Use the reading fluency assessment and invite several students (one at a time) to read aloud. (See Figure 1.10 on page 12.)

Day 3: Comparing

Opening Discussion: Display the comparison chart and have students show their "beginnings" illustrations and share information from their stories. As they share, record the information in the first four columns of the chart (title, characters, setting, and problem). Comment on the imagination of Ms. Rylant as students look at the differences in the stories.

Mini-lesson: Vocabulary: Return to *Henry and Mudge and the Careful Cousin*; reread pages 14 and 15. Refresh students' memories about the story. Turn the page and discuss the chapter title with the students: Annie Turns Pink. How do students interpret this chapter title? What does it mean to "turn pink"? What are situations that cause someone to "turn pink"? What will cause Annie to "turn pink"? What causes students to "turn pink" with embarrassment?

Reading and Responding: Read aloud Chapter 2. Discuss: How would you feel if you were in Henry's shoes? Annie's shoes? What would you try now if you were Henry? What was humorous in this chapter? Refocus question: What made you laugh during this chapter? How do the illustrations add to the humor? Have students use one of the journal response starters and respond to the reading.

Day 4: Back to the Other **Henry and Mudge** *Stories*

Opening Discussion: Just for fun, play charades to dramatize Mudge's behaviors. Give students time to think a moment; then invite volunteers to act out a behavior (wagging his tail, rolling over, drooling, barking in excitement, chewing on a stick, sniffing things in the yard, eating a flower, learning not to jump up on people, shaking the water from his body after a rain storm or a swim, growling, sleeping, eating, or lapping water).

Mini-lesson: Setting Purposes for Reading: Have students read Chapter 2 titles and discuss their meanings. For example, in *Henry and Mudge and the Happy Cat*, Chapter 2 is titled "A Good Mother," and the illustrations show the cat in the closet and in the bathtub playing with a dripping faucet. Questions that come to mind include: Who is the good mother? (Henry's mom? the stray cat? Mudge, even though Mudge is a he?) Does this mean that the stray cat will have kittens?

Reading and Responding: Have students make predictions about the directions of their stories and set goals for independent reading, i.e., read, respond, draw a picture showing how the chapter title connects to the events of the story, and write a one-sentence summary about the connection.

Ongoing Assessment: Use the reading fluency assessment and invite several students (one at a time) to read aloud.

Preparation for a Writing Project: Create a story idea brainstorming form to help students collect ideas for personal narrative humorous fiction pieces. (See Figure 1.15.) Make multiple copies of the

Humorous Moment	Humorous Moment
Title:	Title
Humorous Moment	Humorous Moment
Title:	Title

Figure 1.15 Prewrite Brainstorming: Humorous Fiction

form, enough for one per student and make a transparency of the form. Prepare for the lesson by thinking of four humorous moments in your own life and how you would sketch these story ideas and title them.

Day 5: Chapter 3, **Henry and Mudge and the Careful Cousin**

Opening Discussion: Write the word "climax" on the board, and discuss how authors build excitement in their stories. Reread page 29 in the Careful Cousin book and focus on the last sentence ("This was going to be a very long visit.") as you turn the page and discuss the chapter title, "Zam!" Pose these questions for discussion: What will happen next? How will Henry survive Annie's visit? What would you do if you were in Henry's shoes?

Reading and Responding: Read Chapter 3 aloud. Discuss: What changes caused Henry's reaction at the end of the story: "They both couldn't wait to see her again." What helped Annie change? What is the message of the story? How would students describe and illustrate the climax of this story? (As they share and decide on the climax of the story, add this description to the comparing chart begun in an earlier lesson.)

Mini-lesson: Collecting Ideas for Writing: Display the transparency of the story idea brainstorming form. (See Figure 1.15.) Use it to sketch and give titles to humorous story ideas from your own life. Encourage students to think of two story ideas from their own lives and sketch and title them. Examples include Chewing on Toes (The picture showed a baby crawling to chew on an adult's toes) and The Missing Chair (The picture showed a child thinking the chair was there, but missing it).

At Home Connection: Have students discuss other humorous story ideas with family members.

Day 6: Chapter 3, The Other Stories

Opening Discussion: Invite students to share one of their illustrations of a humorous moment from their own lives.

Mini-lesson: Setting Purposes for Reading: Have students read Chapter 3 titles and discuss their meanings. For example, in *Henry and Mudge and the Big Test*, Chapter 3 is titled "The Big Test," and the illustrations show Henry trying to train Mudge. Questions that come to mind include: Will Henry succeed? Will Mudge fail "The Big Test"? What will happen during "The Big Test"?

Reading and Responding: Have students make predictions about the directions of their stories and set goals for independent reading, responding, illustrating the climax of the story, and brainstorming ideas for their own humorous moments writing projects.

Ongoing Assessment: Use the reading fluency assessment and invite several students (one at a time) to read aloud.

At Home Connection: Encourage students to find a joke or a riddle to share during the next day's lesson.

Day 7: Chapter 3, The Other Stories, continued
Share your joke/riddle and invite students to share their jokes/riddles. Discuss what makes humorous fiction so enjoyable. Finish the comparison chart as students share humorous moments from their stories.

Continuing Lessons: Focus the continuing lessons in these two areas:

1. Writing personal narrative humorous fiction pieces, using the writing process.
   Prewriting: Collecting Details: Have students narrow to one idea in their prewrite brainstorming and use a cluster web to collect details about the experience: Who was involved? Where did it happen? What happened? What else happened?
   Rough Drafting: Involve students in a mini-lesson on paragraph structure and focus on effective topic sentences.
   Rough Drafting: Details: Have students continue to write their humorous fiction narratives by adding supporting detail and closing sentences.
   Revision: Read students' narratives and select one or two revision areas based on students' writing, e.g., sentence structure (run-ons, fragments), enhancing details (adjectives, verbs, descriptive phrases), and making the topic sentence engaging.
   Editing: Focus on correcting ending punctuation, capitalization, and spelling errors. Break the tasks into manageable pieces by focusing on capitalization one day, punctuation another day, and spelling a third day.
   Publishing: Have students publish their narratives, e.g., a slide show or a book.
2. Exchanging Henry and Mudge stories and continuing to read about their adventures. Teacher's note: The comparison chart and the discussions will spark tremendous interest in Rylant's books, and students will be eager to exchange titles and read more.

■ Activity Focus: An Author Study for Older Readers: A Literature Circle Approach

Technology Connection: Teacher Delivery of Lesson (ISTE-teacher II-III)

Collaboration:
- Presenting booktalks on the titles in the author study: Media specialist
- Reading and responding: Teacher

Resources:
- Reading journals
- Multiple copies of titles written by the author you have chosen

Preparation Tasks:

- Prepare a variety of graphic organizers for students to use as they work with setting, plot, characters, and theme. (See Figure 1.9.)
- Create a reading responses chart to hang in the classroom. (See Figure 1.8.)
- Create two assessment rubrics: one for journal responses and one for reading fluency. (See Figure 1.10.)
- Create a comparison chart on chart paper or butcher paper; make the chart long enough so that all the titles the students are reading by the author can be listed on the chart. Choose headings for the columns that fit what you will find in the stories. (See Figure 1.11 for an example based on survival stories by Gary Paulsen.)
- Create a beginnings graphic organizer for students to use in the opening chapters of the stories. (See Figure 1.12.)

Assignment Description:

Journals, the graphic organizers and assessment rubrics, and a daily routine for reading help students examine and enjoy the variety of stories written by the author, compare the stories in a number of ways, and study the style or craft of the author.

Introduce the concept of literature circles and develop a daily routine for reading the stories. Literature circles (described by Harvey Daniels in his book, *Literature Circles*, originally published in 1994 by Stenhouse Publishers in York, Maine, now in a second edition) are small groups of students who meet regularly to discuss and respond to books they are reading. Each day that the student groups meet, students take on specific roles for the discussion time. Roles help students take turns and involve leading discussions, analyzing vocabulary, developing summaries, revisiting parts of the text, and making connections. For more information, see <www.stenhouse.com> (information about the second edition of the book and ordering information) and <www.sasked.gov.sk.ca/docs/mla/circle/intro.html> (an introduction to literature circles).

The key to effective implementation of the literature circles experience is careful introduction of the roles and practice in the roles. Select a short novel or a series of picture books (not necessarily by the author you will be studying, but books that are well written and offer good discussion possibilities). *Sarah, Plain and Tall* by Patricia MacLachlan is a good novel, and stories by Chris Van Allsburg are good picture book choices.

Use the board to write the title of the role you are introducing (connector), and describe and list the responsibilities for the job. The connector taps into students' prior knowledge and invites discussions that encourage students to personalize the events and characters of the story, e.g., I have a cousin who is just like (character) in the story, so I can understand how irritating he/she is; that event reminds me of the time…; this book is just like (name another book); I've read other books by this author and she/he always uses (name some common thread in the stories).

Connector Job Responsibilities

1. Use small self-stick notes to mark possible places in the reading that spark connections.
2. Select two passages from the story and write the page numbers for the selections.
3. Write short summaries identifying the key points of your connection memories.
4. Develop two questions that will encourage "connections" sharing when the literature circle meets.
5. Read aloud from the novel or picture book you have chosen and model the process of the job.
6. Use the self-stick notes to mark possible passages. Show the students how to use their journals to record their preparation for the role. Each journal entry should follow this format:
   Date: Date the entry

Role: List the role
Role Preparation: Writing that completes the role for the day, i.e., discussion questions, connection comments, an illustration and keywords from the passage, text pages for rereading, and the reasons for the selections.
Assigned reading pages: Pages that need to be read before the next literature circle meets.

Gather students in a large circle, reread one of the selected "connections" passages, share your connection, and invite sharing around the circle with your question. If a student wishes to pass, allow that decision. Reread your second passage, share your connection, and invite responses in the circle.

Repeat this process as you introduce each role. When all of the roles have been introduced and practiced once, use subsequent chapters to gain additional practice with the roles. Continue to remind students about the responsibilities of the job (be specific), how to set up and record information in their journals, and how to set goals for the number of pages to read. Vary the way students read (silently, with partners) and share their writing (in groups of three, in groups of four, whole-class circle). Once or twice during the introduction of the roles, "fish bowl" a literature circle process, i.e., invite three students to join you in a literature circle, each having prepared a different role. Take the lead as discussion director and pose your discussion questions. Have the illustrator share next, then the connector, and finally the passage picker. Set goals for the assigned reading for the next literature circle and confirm the roles students will prepare. When the author study actually begins, it is helpful to create a roles poster to remind students of the sequence for rotation. (See Figure 1.16.)

Literature Circle Roles
1. Discussion Director
2. Illustrator
3. Connector
4. Passage Picker

Figure 1.16 Sequence of Literature Circle Roles

Five Basic Survival Skills
Fire
Shelter
Signaling
Food and Water
First Aid

Figure 1.17 Survival Skills Planner

Here is an example of an author study unit using these titles by Gary Paulsen: *Hatchet, River, Brian's Winter, Island,* and *The Voyage of Frog.*

Pre-Reading Experience: In this activity, focus on tapping into the students' prior knowledge/understanding of survival and survival skills. Prepare for the experience by creating a survival skills planner; make a transparency and multiple copies of the planner, enough for one per student. (See Figure 1.17.)

Begin by discussing this acronym: **S.T.O.P.** (sit, think, observe, plan). Introduce the "Five Basic Survival Skills" brainstorming sheet (see Figure 1.17) and pose these questions: Why are these basic to survival? Why are they important? How do they help? Give students thinking time and ask them to list some ideas.

Describe the survival situation students face: We have been discussing survival tools and skills. You will soon need these skills and tools because you are about to enter an island wilderness for a 30-day adventure in the outdoors. In preparation for this adventure, your group must create a survival kit, but your survival kit is limited to six items, based on the five skills listed on the planning sheet. What will you take? (Teacher's note: Before breaking into small groups, give students time to ask questions about the assignment and be clear about how they are to proceed.)

Have students work in their cooperative groups and create survival kits for their island stay. Circulate as they work, giving encouragement, posing additional questions, and listening to their discussions. Have groups select reporters to share the items in the survival kits. Encourage explanations as each group shares its kit. List the items as they are shared, then invite discussion of similarities and differences among the groups.

Reading the Books: Set up a routine where students read, respond, and engage in class discussion one day and participate in literature circles the following day.

Day 1: Getting Started. Use the cover illustrations and title to make predictions about the stories and set purposes for reading. Introduce the beginnings graphic organizer (see Figure 1.12) and set goals for reading Chapter 1, e.g., read Chapter 1, complete the "beginnings" graphic organizer to illustrate the setting, main characters, and problem in the story, use the reading response starters or one of your own to reflect on Chapter 1, make a prediction about the direction of the story. To conclude the reading for the day, refer students to the comparison chart and complete the information for the settings of the stories; then discuss similarities and differences.

Day 2: Literature Circles. Review the literature circle jobs and have students complete job preparations and meet in their literature circle groups. List goals on the board so that students are clear about the process to be followed, e.g., complete preparation for students' literature circle roles, meet in literature circles, set goals for the next meeting of literature circles (number of pages to be read, role for the day), reflect on the reading and make a new prediction for the story. Circulate as students prepare for circles and as they meet in circles. Unless there is an urgent problem, be a quiet observer and listener, making notes about successes and challenges you observe in the group meetings. Close the reading experience by sharing some of your literature circles process observations, focusing on the successes you have seen. In addressing problems that may have arisen (fooling around, not listening to each other, arguing), pick one to address, and ask students to propose solutions that would work.

Day 3: Author's Craft. Begin the third day of reading with a discussion on how Mr. Paulsen builds tension and suspense in his writing. What words and phrases really make the reader feel the uncertainty of the main character's situation? Draw a rating scale on the board. (See Figure 1.18.) Have students rate the main character's chances of survival based on this point in the stories. Set goals and have students read the pages assigned in the previous day's literature circle groups. When students have completed reading for the day, revisit the survival discussion to see if the main characters' situations have changed.

Survival Scale				
None	Slim	Possible	Probable	Sure Thing
1	2	3	4	5

Figure 1.18 Survival Scale

Day 4: Meeting in Literature Circles Again. As a pre-reading experience, have students select passages in their stories that show Mr. Paulsen's wonderful descriptions, and draw pictures based on the descriptions. Have students complete their preparations for literature circles, and then meet in their circles. Encourage the illustrators to invite sharing of the drawings created in the opening of the lesson: "What are descriptive passages you enjoyed and why?" At the close of literature circles, focus on the character column in the comparison chart and record information about them: How would you describe the personalities of the characters? What survival skills are evident in the characters' actions?

Day 5: Evidence of Conflict. Write "conflict" on the board and begin a discussion about conflict. How would students define conflict? Why does an author include conflict in a story? Display the transparency that lists different kinds of conflict (see Figure 1.19) and discuss each kind. Help students think of examples of the different kinds of conflict, and share examples from their stories.

Internal: overactive imagination, fear, lack of confidence, worry

External-nature: lost in a forest/at sea, caught in a storm, stuck in the mountains

External-society: truancy from school, lying and cheating, stealing

External-person: anger at a friend, jealousy, disagreement with a parent

External Conflict	External Conflict
Person Against Person A character has a problem with one or more of the characters.	**Person Against Nature** A character is in conflict with some element of nature—bitter cold, extreme heat, a storm.
External Conflict	**Internal Conflict**
Person Against Society A character has a problem with society.	**Person Against Self** A character struggles against herself/himself, trying to decide what to do about some problem.

Figure 1.19 Examples of Conflict

Have students read silently or with partners. Set goals to accommodate varying speeds of reading, e.g., students who finish early can add to the author display. Encourage students to use self-stick notes to mark places where they see examples of internal or external conflict, then write about the examples in their journals using this format:

Kind of conflict (internal or external):
Page number in the book:
Explanation of why this event in the book is an example of internal or external conflict:

Day 6: Literature Circles. Close the period by completing the "exciting moments" column in the comparison chart, and record and discuss examples from each group. Have students reflect on and journal about "exciting moments" in their lives. Invite sharing among partners if students feel comfortable sharing their experiences.

Day 7: Turning Points. Begin a discussion to help students understand how the phrase "turning point" can be applied to a story. Images that may help include a tug of war and a fork in the road. A tug of war begins with an even give-and-take motion (ask a student to participate with you in this give-and-take motion). At some point, one side begins to have an advantage (let the student take the advantage). Then at a crucial moment the momentum begins to swing toward one side. Invite students to share decisive experiences in their lives that they would consider turning points.

Set goals for reading that focus on character analysis, e.g., meeting with a partner and discussing a problem faced by the main character, identifying a "turning point" in the development of the main character's survival skills. Invite sharing to close the reading period.

Day 8: Literature Circles. Have students complete their preparations for literature circles, then meet in their circles. Conclude by revisiting the "exciting moments" column in the comparison chart and record "turning point" examples from each group.

Take time at this point in the author study to develop post-reading assessment choices. Develop a focus for the activities, e.g., character analysis and development of a variety of levels of choices in terms of depth and complexity of thinking and open-endedness of directions. (See Figure 1.21 on pages 23–25 for some examples.)

Day 9: Character Figures. Have students meet in their literature circles to explore characterization and develop a graphic display of the character's actions, words, and feelings. Give each group a long sheet of butcher paper and a variety of illustrating materials, e.g., markers, crayons, and colored pencils.

List these guidelines on the board or on an overhead transparency:

- Select one student in the group and have him/her lie on the butcher paper while another student in the group traces the outline of the body.
- Draw facial features that best portray the looks and feelings of the main character in the novel.
- Draw a heart on the character's chest and write inside it the things that the main character loves.
- Lightly pencil in a spine; then write the character's main goal within that shape.
- Write or draw pictures on the hands that illustrate actions of the character.
- Select two quotes that reveal how the character views himself/herself. Record these on either side of the character's head.
- Use the legs to add other pictures that tell about the main character.
- Use the descriptions of the author or the group's mental pictures from the author's words and add clothing details to the character; be careful not to hide the other pictures and information.

Give students time to divide the responsibilities of the assignment so that each student makes a contribution. Display the figures when they are completed and have students explain the reasons for their choices.

Day 10: Literature Circles. At the close of the period, focus on the setting and problem columns in the comparison chart. What information would students add to the chart? How have things changed or stayed the same in the stories?

Day 11: Mistakes. Take a poll of the students in response to this question: Are mistakes good or bad? Discuss students' reasoning and ideas. Record their responses in a two-column chart on the board. (See Figure 1.20.) Have students write briefly about mistakes in their own lives that brought learning/changes in behavior/new insights.

Introduce the post-reading choices and encourage students to let you know their choices as soon as possible. Have students read silently or with partners, then analyze the main characters' learning. "Which mistakes brought the best learning or the biggest change in behavior? Why? Write about this mistake and the reasons that you chose it." Invite sharing about the main characters, the mistakes they have made, and how they have learned from these mistakes.

Plan an outdoor location for Day 13. (Teacher's note: Observing nature and using what occurs in the natural world are important skills for Paulsen's characters. Choose a location with lots of hidden depth.)

Are Mistakes...	
Good	Bad

Figure 1.20 Mistakes Chart

Mural

A dynamic character is one who changes during the story. Select four events in the story that show how the main character grows and changes. Design a mural illustrating these four events; write captions for each picture that describe how the character is changing. Create a title for the mural and give yourself credit for its design, e.g., "Mural designed by (your name)."

Evaluation criteria:
Illustrations
1. Illustrations show how the character is changing during the events of the story.
2. Illustrations show careful construction (neatness) and planning.
3. Illustrations are colorful and filled with detail.

Captions
1. Captions are thoughtfully written and show understanding of the character.
2. Captions describe how the character is changing during the events of the story.
3. Captions use correct grammar, spelling, punctuation, and capitalization.
4. Captions are easy to read (best handwriting).

Other requirements
1. The mural is titled and signed by the student.
2. The project is completed by the assignment due date.

Poem

In a good piece of writing, the characters come alive. We feel like we know them; we care about them, and they become part of who we are. Write a "free verse" poem about the main character that not only shares what happens to him/her in the story but also describes his/her feelings and thoughts. Create a brainstorming web to begin collecting details about the character.

Use these guidelines when you begin to write the poem:
1. Make each line build a mental picture in the reader's mind.
2. Use your web ideas to create each line; think about some combination of these ideas from your web. The requirements are: two feeling lines, two looks lines, three action lines, one speaking line.
3. Use/add these techniques to make a more effective poem:
   - Simile makes a comparison using "like" or "as."
     Example: Fear gripped his body, making him freeze like a statue.
   - Alliteration is the repetition of consonant sounds at the beginning of words.
     Example: Bright blue sky, sun slowly sinking
4. Remember that a free verse poem is just that—it does not have to rhyme!

Evaluation criteria:
1. The character brainstorming web is thorough and complete; it includes examples from the book.
2. The poem follows the guidelines for writing "free verse" poetry.
3. The lines of the poem are thoughtfully written and show understanding of the character.
4. The poem uses correct grammar, spelling, punctuation, and capitalization.
5. The poem is easy to read (best handwriting).
6. The poem is titled and signed by the student.
7. The project is completed by the assignment due date.

Figure 1.21 Post-reading Assessment Activities (continued on page 24)

Map

Make a map of the setting of the story. Be sure to include all the places main the character uses/visits during the story. Label the map to show the experiences encountered by the main character.

Here's an example from *Hatchet*:
- The Crash: The plane crashes and sinks.
- Safety: Brian crawls from the water and rests against a small tree.
- The Ledge: Brian finds shelter and builds a shelter screen.
- The Bear: Brian encounters a black bear while eating raspberries. He runs away in a panic.

Evaluation criteria:
1. The brainstorming list is thorough and detailed.
2. The map is carefully constructed and uses the ideas on the brainstorming list to show lots of details.
3. The map is colorful.
4. The map includes a legend, a title, and the student's name.
5. The map labels tell the story of Brian's survival and rescue.
6. The map labels use correct grammar, spelling, punctuation, and capitalization.
7. The map labels are written in my best handwriting or typed.
8. The project is completed by the assignment due date.

Interview

Stories are about what happens to characters. Stories are also about what happens inside these characters—thoughts, dreams, and feelings. Stage an interview with the main character. The interviewer's questions should help the audience learn about the main character's experiences and understand his/her thoughts and feelings during the experiences of the story.

Plan the interview:
1. Write the interview questions. Phrase your questions so that the answers are more than a "yes" or a "no."
2. Plan the answers so that you can really "take on" the personality of the main character and answer the questions in ways he/she would.
3. Invite a peer to act as the interviewer. He/she will ask the interview questions.
4. Plan an engaging introduction and closing.
5. Rehearse! Rehearse! Rehearse!

Evaluation criteria:
1. The interview questions were open-ended and invited lots of response.
2. The interview responses were thoughtful and revealed the main character's personality and how he/she survived in the wilderness.
3. The interview had an engaging introduction and closing.
4. The interview was well-rehearsed.
5. The interview demonstrated the following skills:
   - We looked at the audience.
   - We spoke loudly and clearly.
   - We spoke in a slow, natural tone and looked at our notes only when we needed reminders.
   - We used clear, correct language. We did not use slang or sounds like ah, dah, or um.
6. The project was completed by the assignment due date.

Figure 1.21 (cont'd) Post-reading Assessment Activities (continued on page 25)

> **Poster**
>
> Create a poster that shows the struggles of the main character.
>
> 1. Start by drawing and coloring a portrait of the character.
> 2. Make a list of the challenges faced by the character and successful solutions. You must have at least six challenges and successful solutions.
> 3. Find a creative way to show these ideas on the poster, e.g., drawing, real objects, papier-mache.
> 4. Plan and rehearse an interesting way to share the poster with the class.
>
> Evaluation criteria:
> 1. The brainstorming list is thorough and detailed.
> 2. The brainstorming list includes challenges and successful solutions.
> 3. The poster is carefully constructed and uses the ideas on the brainstorming list to show lots of details.
> 4. The poster is colorful.
> 5. The poster includes a title and the student's name.
> 6. The presentation of the poster to the class was interesting and engaging.
> 7. The presentation shared the challenges of the wilderness and Brian's solutions to these challenges.
> 8. The project was completed by the assignment due date.

Figure 1.21 (cont'd) Post-reading Assessment Activities

Day 12: Literature Circles.
Day 13: Setting: Observing Nature. Walk to the outdoor location. Have students bring journals, sketch paper, copies of their books, and pencils for sketching. Ask students to sketch a view in the outdoor location and to "look with the main character's eye." What are the hidden features? (For example, if they are sketching a tree, if they look closer they might see a trail of ants, sap running, a bird on a branch, a nest, or a walking stick insect.) Encourage them to look deeply at the view and to include some "hidden picture" images. Have students share their drawings and talk about how they trained their eyes to really see. What hidden picture images have they included in the drawings? Display the drawings.

Have students read the pages set by their literature circle groups.

Day 14: Literature Circles.
Day 15: Patience. Begin a discussion on patience: Why is patience a virtue? What are situations where it is absolutely necessary? What are situations faced by the main characters in the stories where patience was required? Have students read silently or with partners, and then work on their post-reading activity.
Day 15: Literature Circles, Closing Meeting. Complete literature circle time by reflecting on the four roles students completed during the author study. Think about successes, challenges, and enjoyment. Have students compose an e-mail letter to the author sharing their enjoyment and thoughts about the books. Have students make finishing touches on their final products.
Day 16: Post-reading Presentations. Set up the post-reading final products and tour the display. Invite sharing by each student. Have students evaluate their final products.

Moving West: Tall Tale Literature

Information Retrieval	Student Productivity	Problem Solving and Decision Making
Electronic encyclopedias, e,g., *Grolier's*, *World Book* Internet Web site: **Zip Code Information:** <www.usps.gov>	Resume for a tall-tale figure Museum plaque Original tall tale *Kidspiration* for prewrite brainstorming	*Oregon Trail: Pioneer Adventures* (The Learning Company) *Mapmakers' Toolkit* (Tom Snyder Productions)
		Communication and Collaboration
		Internet Web site: **Publishing the Original Tall Tales:** <www.ih.k12.oh.us.esapanites>

Teacher Delivery of Lessons	Classroom Management
The Wonderful Hay Tumble story page template and title/introductory pages Solution grid poster for creative problem solving exercise Comparison grid poster Note taking graphic organizers	Assessment rubrics for evaluating the story page contributions for *The Wonderful Hay Tumble*, the Paul Bunyan story project, research products on tall tale heroes, and the original tall tales

Figure 1.22 Moving West: A Study of Pioneer Life Unit: Technology Connections

Unit 3: Moving West: A Study of Pioneer Life

Unit Objectives:
1. Build knowledge and awareness of tall-tale heroes and their adventures.
2. Develop story-writing skills.
3. Build understanding of the challenges and hardships faced by pioneer families.

Audience: Grades 4–8

Length of the Unit: 4 weeks

The Unit Activities at a Glance

Tall Tales: *The Wonderful Hay Tumble*, by Kathleen Harris	Literature Integration: Tall Tales: The Paul Bunyan Story	Literature Integration: Tall-Tale Heroes
Students listen to the story, identify characteristics of tall tale stories, create new pages for the story (if it continued), and discuss the legacy of pioneer farmers.	Students listen to the story and use the creative problem solving process to help Paul conquer a blizzard. They also work in teams to prepare storytelling presentations and discuss the value of teamwork in pioneer times.	Students research tall tale heroes and present their findings in a resume/interview or a museum display.
Literature Integration: Writing Original Tall Tales	**Traveling the Oregon Trail**	**Traveling with Lewis and Clark**
Students use *Kidspiration* to collect ideas for writing original tall tales. They use the writing process to write and publish the stories.	Students use the computer simulation *Oregon Trail* to experience the challenges faced by the pioneers in moving West.	Students use *Mapmakers' Toolkit* to illustrate the travels of Lewis and Clark.

Figure 1.22a Moving West: A Study in Pioneer Life, The Unit Activities at a Glance

■ Activity Focus: Literature Integration: Tall Tales:
The Wonderful Hay Tumble, by Kathleen M. Harris

Technology Connection: Teacher Delivery of Lessons, Classroom Management (ISTE-teacher II-V)

Collaboration:
- Sharing the story: Media specialist with teacher participating
- Directing the art project: Teacher
- Completing and presenting the book: Media specialist with teacher participating

- Journal reflecting and discussing: Teacher with media specialist participating
- Evaluation rubric: Students, teacher, and media specialist

Resources: *The Wonderful Hay Tumble*, by Kathleen M. Harris (New York: Morrow/Avon, 1988)

Preparation Tasks:
- Create a story page template for students to use as they design and show other accomplishments of the "hay tumble." (See Figure 1.23.) The students use the left side of the template to illustrate the approach of the hay tumble and the problem it faces and the right side of the template to show the accomplishment of the hay tumble. Students complete the story starter on the left side and add their own solution text on the right side.
- Use a word processing program to create title and introductory pages. Have a student create an illustration for the title page. (See Figure 1.24.)
- Use a word processing program to create an evaluation rubric for the "hay tumble" art project and the journal reflection about the heritage of pioneer farmers. Once you have this rubric created, you can reuse the format for subsequent activities in the unit, building consistency and familiarity for students and parents. (See Figure 1.25.)

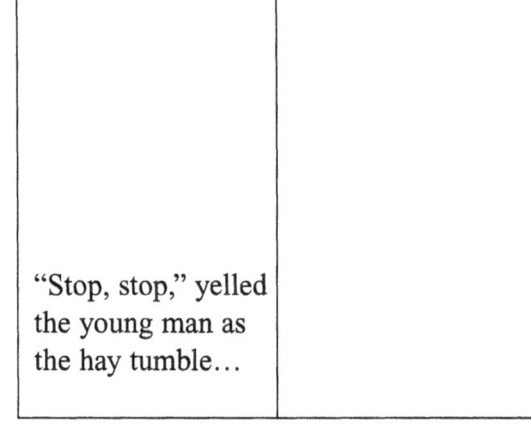

Figure 1.23 Hay Tumble Story Page Template

| The Wonderful Hay Tumble…the story continues

Written and Illustrated by the students in
Ms. Jones' class
West Elementary
2002 | A long time ago when farming was the main occupation in Vermont, there lived a poor young man. He was so poor that all he and his wife could afford was a farm high up in the hills in the town of Mansfield…a farm filled with rocks. He and his wife worked from sunup to sundown but nothing went right…until the day of the wonderful hay tumble… |

Figure 1.24 Title and Introductory Pages

The Work of the Wonderful Hay Tumble Continues: An Evaluation Rubric

Activity Description: In their study of pioneer days, students have been exploring the life of a pioneer farmer…looking at fact and fiction. After listening to *The Wonderful Hay Tumble*, a tall tale by Kathleen Harris, students worked with partners to create and illustrate new pages for the story. Their pages used hyperbole (exaggeration) and humor to show how a hay tumble could tackle some of the challenges faced by pioneer farmers. At the conclusion of the activity, students were asked to reflect on the contributions of pioneer farmers.

Activity Rating Scale: The art project and journal reflection and discussion were evaluated using this rating scale:

- ✔+   Exemplary
- ✔   Progressing
- ✔-   Emerging

Student	Teacher	
Story Idea		
		Shows original thought.
		Connects to the life of a farmer.
Artwork		
		Shows careful construction.
		Shows evidence of planning.
		Shows attention to color and details.
Text		
		Follows the pattern established in the book.
		Shows appropriate use of hyperbole (exaggeration).
		Shows attention to spelling, capitalization, and punctuation.
Journal Reflection		
		Demonstrates understanding of the life of pioneer farmers.

Figure 1.25 Evaluation Rubric: The Wonderful Hay Tumble

Assignment Description:

Introduce the story by brainstorming challenges faced by pioneer farmers. (See Figure 1.26.) Show the cover of the book and invite discussion about the challenges faced by the farmer in this story (based on the cover illustration). Speculate about the title of the story: What is a hay tumble? Why is it called the "wonderful" hay tumble? Remind students of the characteristics of a tall tale (hero/heroine, difficult job, use of exaggeration and humor, originated in pioneer and frontier days as stories to entertain and make light of difficult situations) and ask them to notice details in the story that prove that this story is a tall tale.

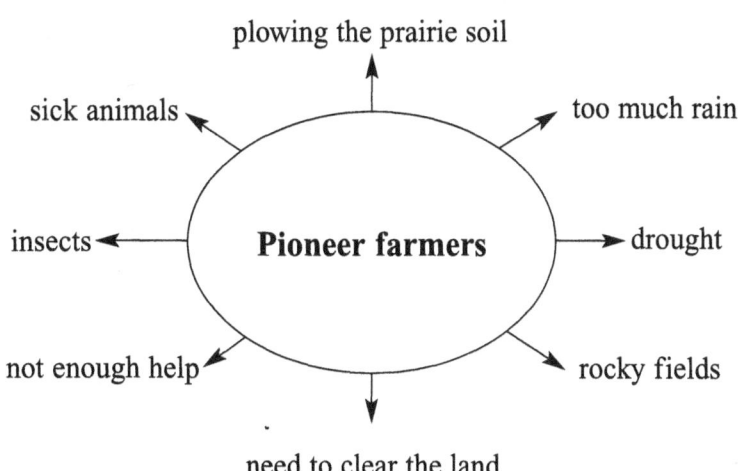

Figure 1.26 Brainstorming Web: Pioneer Farmer Challenges

Share and discuss the story. How did the hay tumble change the lives of the poor man and his wife? What evidence tells the reader that this is a tall tale? What are examples of hyperbole (exaggeration, a key element of tall tales) in the story?

Introduce the art project and have students work with partners and brainstorm ideas for new pages if the story were to continue. What other tasks could the hay tumble accomplish? What other jobs might the hay tumble manage? (Some ideas if students are stumped: shear the sheep and bag the wool ready for market, gather the eggs in the hen house and place them in baskets, milk the cows and fill the jugs and churn some butter, shell the peas and make them ready for dinner and canning, paint the barn a bright red, twist through the house and wash and fold the laundry, scrub the dishes, and clean the house.)

Encourage students to develop rough sketches to plan their pages, then complete final drawings using the story page templates. (See Figure 1.23.) As students write the text that accompanies their illustrations, have them use the story starter on the template and follow the patterns in the book. Gather the pages into a book and present the book to the class.

Journal Reflection and Discussion: What is the example set by pioneer farmers and why is this important as part of our heritage?

■ Activity Focus: Literature Integration: Tall Tales: The Paul Bunyan story

Technology Connection: Student Productivity (ISTE-students 3), Teacher Delivery of Lessons, Classroom Management (ISTE-teacher II-V)

Collaboration:
- Sharing the story: Media specialist and teacher as co-facilitators
- Storytelling project: Media specialist and teacher as co-facilitators
- Information sources: Media specialist

- Developing the stories: Teacher
- Presentations: Media specialist and teacher as audience members
- Evaluation rubric: Students, teacher, and media specialist

Resources:
- *Paul Bunyan,* by Steven Kellogg (New York: Morrow/Avon, 1993)
- Transparency markers in a variety of colors, one color per team
- Other stories about Paul Bunyan, enough for one per team of three students:
  - *The Bunyans,* by Audrey Wood, illustrated by David Shannon (New York: Blue Sky Press, ©1996)
  - *Moon Trouble,* by M.C. Helldorfer, illustrated by Jonathan Hunt (New York: Bradbury Press, ©1994)
  - *Ol' Paul, the Mighty Logger: Being a True Account of the Seemingly Incredible Exploits and Inventions of the Great Paul Bunyan,* profusely illustrated with drawings made at the scene by the author, Glen Rounds (New York: Holiday House, 1976)
  - *The Morning the Sun Refused to Rise: An Original Paul Bunyan Tale,* written and illustrated by Glen Rounds (New York: Holiday House, 1984)
- Transparencies, enough for one per team
- Overhead projector

Preparation Tasks:
- Create a problem solving solution grid. (See Figure 1.27.) To determine the number of proposed solutions you will have, divide the class into teams of four to five students. Enlarge the grid to poster size using a poster maker; laminate the poster so that it can be used again.

Solution Ideas	The blizzard stops.	Babe is happy.	The crew can go back to work.	Hyperbole (exaggeration) used in the solution.
Team 1				
Team 2				
Team 3				
Team 4				
Team 5				

Figure 1.27 Problem-solving Solution Grid

- Create a story line graphic organizer for the students to use when they are reading and summarizing stories about Paul Bunyan and planning their storytelling presentations. (See Figure 1.28.)
- Open the rubric created for *The Wonderful Hay Tumble* activity. Use "Save As" and rename the file for the new rubric, e.g., Rubric-Bunyan activity. Revise the activity description to fit the Paul Bunyan project, and revise the evaluation descriptors for the new project. Make multiple copies and a transparency of the rubric. (See Figure 1.29.)

Story Sources Information:			
Story Summary	**Ideas for Our Presentation to the Class**		
Setting	Art for the transparency		
Characters	Roles	Student Actors	Unique Features
Problem			
Solution			

Figure 1.28 Story Line Graphic Organizer: Paul Bunyan

Paul Bunyan Stories: An Evaluation Rubric

Activity Description: In their study of pioneer days, students have been exploring teamwork—how pioneer families and communities worked together as they traveled westward and settled the Midwest and the West. Paul Bunyan was a legendary figure of this time, and his adventures across the United States show examples of teamwork. Students worked in teams to create a solution for the blizzard faced by Paul and his crew, and they also worked together in their storytelling presentations.

Activity Rating Scale: The art project and journal reflection and discussion were evaluated using this rating scale:

✔+   Exemplary
✔   Progressing
✔-   Emerging

Student	Teacher	
CPS Solution Development		
		Shows respect for the ideas of each team member.
Transparency		
		Shows careful construction.
		Shows evidence of planning.
		Shows attention to color and details.
		Identifies the setting and an important idea from the story.
Storytelling Presentation		
		Begins in an engaging way.
		Follows a sequence.
		Includes a role for each team member.
		Demonstrates the unique features of the characters.
		Concludes in an engaging way.
		Demonstrates skill in public speaking: eye contact, expression, volume.

Figure 1.29 Evaluation Rubric: Paul Bunyan Stories

Assignment Description:

As a fun way to focus on teamwork, have students work in small groups and use charades/creative dramatics to demonstrate an activity that requires teamwork, e.g., riding a bicycle built for two, playing tennis, sharing a family meal, building a sand castle. Discuss behaviors that help in teamwork situations and behaviors that get in the way.

Introduce and share the story of *Paul Bunyan* by Steven Kellogg. Stop midway through the story on the page that reads "Babe was so depressed"; don't finish the sentence. Begin creative problem solving with the students.

1. Identify the situation: A blizzard has struck and stopped the seasons of spring, summer, and fall. Babe is depressed, and the crew cannot work; in fact, they are hibernating.
2. Identify the facts of the situation: Students should do this, but ideas you might expect include Paul Bunyan has sunglasses and an axe, he cuts timber into lumber, he's tall and strong and inventive, two cooks and nine lumbermen work for him, and this is a tall tale and can have tall (exaggerated) solutions.
3. Identify the problem: Problem statements begin in this way: How might Paul Bunyan…? Invite suggestions and discussion and refine the problem statement until it reflects the situation of the story, e.g., How might Paul Bunyan stop the blizzard, make Babe happy, and get his crew back to work again?
4. Brainstorm solution ideas: Display the problem solving grid (see Figure 1.27) and review the criteria for the solution. Have students work in teams to brainstorm solutions for the problem, encouraging them to take advantage of the materials/ideas listed in the fact-finding stage and to be respectful of each team member's solution proposal. One student should be a recorder and write the final proposed solution of the team.

5. Evaluate solutions for their effectiveness: As student teams share their proposed solutions, summarize and record key points of the solution on the grid. Rate each solution, using a 3-to-1 scale; 3 would be a very effective solution, and 1 would indicate a not-very-effective solution.

Read the rest of the story and compare the students' solutions with the solution developed by Mr. Kellogg. Discuss: How did Paul and his crew and Babe work as a team? Why is teamwork an important skill?

Introduce the storytelling project. Students will work in teams of three, select and read another story about Paul Bunyan, and use the story line graphic organizer (see Figure 1.28) to summarize and plan their storytelling presentations. Each team will develop a colorful transparency that will be displayed during the presentation; the transparency should give clues to the setting and an important idea from the story read by the team. Display the evaluation rubric and review the criteria for the storytelling presentation.

Journal Reflection: What is teamwork and why is it an important characteristic of pioneer life in America?

■ Activity Focus: Literature Integration: Tall Tale Heroes

Technology Connection: Information Retrieval (ISTE-students 5), Student Productivity (ISTE-students 3), Teacher Delivery of Lesson (ISTE-teacher II-III)

Collaboration:
- Introducing the project, selecting topics, searching for information, taking notes, preparing a bibliography: Media specialist with teacher assisting
- Preparing the products: Media specialist with teacher assisting
- Presentations: Media specialist and teacher as audience members
- Evaluation rubric: Students, teacher, and media specialist

Resources:
- Electronic (encyclopedia and Internet) and print sources for researching
- Internet site: <www.usps.gov>
- Illustrating materials (crayons, colored pencils, poster paints)

Name	Tall-tale Hero:
Identify his/her job:	
Identify distinctive companions or clothing or articles associated with the character.	
Describe the looks of the character.	
Summarize important details about the accomplishments and adventures of the character. Continue on the reverse side of the paper if you need more room.	
Source 1	
Source 2	

Figure 1.30 Note-taking Graphic Organizer

32 Integrating Technology: Effective Tools

- Access to white butcher paper (Note: Students who choose the art project will create life-size models of their heroes by tracing outlines of themselves.)

Preparation Tasks:
- Bookmark the zip codes site so that students can easily find zip codes for their tall tale hero resumes. At the index page for the post office, click on "Find Zip Codes," then scroll down to the bottom of the next page to "City/State Zip Codes."
- Create a note-taking graphic organizer for students to use as they gather information about their tall tale heroes. (See Figure 1.30.) Make multiple copies and a transparency of the form to use when you introduce and model the note-taking process.
- Create a resume template for students choosing the resume as the final product for reporting their tall tale research information. (See Figure 1.32.) In designing the template, use the landscape view and set one-half-inch (0.5") margins on all sides. Create three columns for the trifold, and organize the template according to the example in Figure 1.32. The students access the template and add information and artwork about their heroes. Print copies of the template for students to use as storyboard planning sheets; this will help them use their computer time wisely and efficiently. Make a transparency of each page to use in explaining the product requirements.
- Open the rubric file used for a previous tall tale project. (See Figure 1.31.) Use "Save As" and rename the file, then revise the rubric to fit the new activity. Make multiple copies and a transparency of the rubric.

Assignment Description: Students research tall tale heroes and choose one of the products as a way to present their findings to the class.

Tall Tale Heroes: An Evaluation Rubric

Activity Description: During their studies of pioneer days in America, students have also been reading and studying tall tale literature—stories told to entertain and make light of difficult challenges and jobs. In this activity, students researched tall tale heroes and presented their learning through art (a museum exhibit) or writing (a resume for today's job world).

Activity Rating Scale: The art project and journal reflection and discussion were evaluated using this rating scale:

- ✔+ Exemplary
- ✔   Progressing
- ✔- Emerging

Student	Teacher	
Research		
		Used at least two resources, one print and one electronic.
		Cited the sources.
		Used the graphic organizer.
		Related information in my own words.
		Included lots of details.
Product		
		Showed careful craftsmanship (neatness, color, composition).
		Included lots of research information.
		Showed attention to revision: correct grammar, vivid language, complete sentences, clear organization.
		Showed attention to editing: spelling, capitalization, punctuation.
Presentation		
		Used eye contact.
		Spoke clearly using appropriate volume.
		Spoke with expression.
		Included a creative beginning and ending.
		Showed preparation and rehearsal.

Figure 1.31 Evaluation Rubric: Tall-tale Heroes Research

Address	**Sources of Information**	**Hero's Name**
Type the address information in this space. Be sure to have an accurate zip code.	Use this space to type your bibliography of sources.	
Social Security #	*(Place a graphic in this space.)*	*(Place a graphic in this space.)*
Type the social security number in this space.		
Telephone	Resume developed and designed by:	
Type the telephone number in this space. Be sure to have an accurate area code.	(Type your name in this space.) 2002	Use this space to type a catchy slogan about the hero.

Accomplishments	**Address**	**Accomplishments**
Use this space to tell about one adventure and/or accomplishment. Select and story that illustrates one of the abilities you listed in the center column.	Use this space to list the skills and abilities of your hero. Create symbols to add color and excitement to the list, e.g., if your hero is courageous, make a red heart; if your hero is strong, draw or import and barbell; if your hero is inventive, include a lightbulb.	*(Place a graphic in this space.)*
(Place a graphic in this space.)	**References**	Use this space to tell a third adventure and/or accomplishment. Select a story that illustrates one of the abilities you listed in the center column.
	List two references for your hero in this space. The references can be people from your research about your hero or other tall tale heroes who might know your character. Be sure to include addresses with accurate zip codes and telephone numbers with accurate area codes.	

Figure 1.32 Resume Template

Product Choice 1

What would happen if your tall tale hero lived today?

Where would your hero work?

What kind of job would your hero seek?

Prepare a resume that advertises the skills and experience your hero brings to the job he/she is seeking. In your presentation to the class, role play an interview scene and share your talents and skills through this interview process. You may invite a peer to role play the interviewer, but you must dramatize the tall-tale hero.

Product Choice 2

The living history museum is developing an exhibit on tall tale heroes in American history. Use your research information to create a realistic life-size figure of your tall tale hero and write an information plaque that would be displayed near your figure. In your presentation to the class, pretend that you are a museum docent and share information and stories about your hero. Be creative and entertaining.

Assignment Notes:

To introduce the research project, display the graphic organizer for note taking and model its use. Use the information students know about Paul Bunyan.

1. Name: Your name
2. Tall tale hero: Paul Bunyan
3. Job: Lumberjack
4. Distinctive companions or clothing or articles: Babe, his blue ox, and his trusty axe
5. Description: Very tall, broad-shouldered, brown hair, bearded, wears lumberjack clothes (plaid shirts) and big boots
6. Accomplishments and/or adventures: Encourage students to think in terms of character traits and skills, e.g., Paul believed in teamwork. He gathered the best in the field, and his team included Sour Dough Slim, the seven Hackett brothers, and, of course, his faithful blue ox, Babe. Paul worked hard. His footsteps created the Great Lakes. His axe carved out the Grand Canyon and cleared some of the land ready for pioneer farmers. He also built the Appalachian Mountains when he tussled with the Gumbero. He was inventive. His crew members lashed bacon to their feet and skated across the griddle to help make breakfast for everyone. Paul put his wagon on wheels to make travel across the prairie easier.

Show students how to cite their sources using the final two lines of the form, and remind them that they need to find information in an electronic source and a print source.

Give details about each of the product choices. Display the outer page of the resume template and talk through the requirements as though you had selected the assignment; complete the information as you talk. Again, use Paul Bunyan as your hero.

Address, social security number, telephone number

This is "creative" information based on the life of the hero. In thinking about Paul Bunyan's adventures and stories, his permanent address could be in Minnesota. In looking on a map of Minnesota, a city might be Duluth because it's in the north, surrounded by lots of forestland.

(Show students how to access the Internet site for locating zip codes and how to enter the city and state and find a zip code for the city.) Based on this imagining, Paul's address could be Paul Bunyan, 220 Northern Forest Road, Duluth, Minnesota 55806. Social security numbers have 9 numbers, so here's one that might be assigned to Paul: 425-00-4325. In checking the phone book, the area code for Duluth, Minnesota is 218; a fun number for Paul could be 281-22-TREES.

Sources of information and credits
List the sources from the note-taking sheet and enter your name in the credits space. Since Paul was a lumberjack, quickly sketch a row of pine trees to add color to this portion of the resume.

Hero's name, graphic, slogan
Paul Bunyan's name goes in this space, and students should select a picture of the hero; a good one for Paul might be one of him standing with his best friend, Babe. To create a slogan for the model, have students work with partners and quickly think of fun slogans for Paul. Record one of the suggestions in the appropriate space. (Some ideas: *The Greatest Lumberjack of All* or *No Tree Is Too Tall!*)

Display the inner page of the resume and continue explaining the requirements:

Abilities and references
The students should analyze their notes about the accomplishments and adventures of the hero to identify skills and abilities that would work well in today's job market. A list of skills for Paul Bunyan might include leadership, perseverance, inventiveness, logging, and carving. List these ideas in the "abilities" space in the center column. Quickly sketch colorful symbols that might accompany the abilities, e.g., a George Washington silhouette for leadership, a mountain for perseverance, a light bulb for inventiveness, and a hammer and chisel for logging and carving skills.

Resumes always have references from people who know the hero and could recommend him/her for a job. In Paul's case, one reference might be given by a Hackett brother: Jim Hackett, 224 Log Street, Duluth, Minnesota 55806; Telephone: 218-222-LOGS. Another reference might come from Paul's parents: John and Mary Bunyan, 56 Elm Street, Portland, Maine 04107; Telephone: 207-345-2249. Remember that the zip codes and area codes are the only real parts of the references.

Accomplishments and graphics
Students should use the left column to add summaries of adventures that support the hero's skills and a graphic. Selection of his crew and the story about pancakes for breakfast and skating on the griddle would be good examples to illustrate Paul's leadership skill. The illustration could be a drawing showing the faces of the crew members. The right column could tell about his accomplishments, e.g., the Grand Canyon, the Appalachian Mountains, and the Great Lakes. The graphic could be a map of the United States marked with the locations of the accomplishments.

Continue talking about the final requirement for the resume and share an idea for how you might present the resume to the class, e.g., Paul Bunyan could interview for a job with a fence company. Some questions the interviewer might ask: What experiences prepare you for this job? Have you ever worked on a team? How will you handle the weather changes in an outdoor job like fencing? Whom may we call for references?

Discuss the requirements of the second product choice, the living history museum display. Begin by asking students if they have visited a museum and what exhibits they have seen. Hold up a long sheet of butcher paper and ask for a student volunteer. Have the student lie on his/her back on the paper and quickly trace an outline of the student. Hold up the outline and ask students how they would turn this figure into Paul Bunyan, i.e., clothes, boots, hair, his axe. Remind students to use careful craftsmanship in adding color and details and in cutting out the figure. Use a blank overhead transparency and talk about the information plaque that should accompany the display. Design the plaque as you talk. See Figure 1.33 for an example. The plaque should include this opening information (just like a real plaque in a museum): Title of the piece (Paul Bunyan), date the figure was produced (ca. 2001), the artist (the student's name), his/her nationality and birth year (Henry Jones, American, 1992–), the medium used in creating the life-size figure (tempera on paper), the dimensions of the figure (62" × 25"), and an imaginary museum name and location (The Jones [teacher's name] Gallery, Tulsa). The rest of the plaque should tell the story of Paul Bunyan based on the student's research notes and should conclude with two citations that show sources for the information. Remind students that the information must be typed and displayed in a creative way, e.g., pasted and shellacked onto a thin piece of wood, surrounded by a border of pine trees, imprinted with a picture of Babe. Pretend to be a museum docent and model how you would present the information about the hero.

> **Paul Bunyan**
> ca. 2001
>
> Henry Jones, American, 1992–
> Tempera on paper
> 62" × 25"
>
> The Jones Gallery, Tulsa
>
> Paul was an amazing lumberjack. Even as a baby in Maine, he was unusual, weighing in at 100 pounds and measuring 32 inches. Paul was so big that he rattled the earth when he crawled. He needed lots of food as a growing boy, and he's now taller than a Redwood and twice as strong.
>
> He owns a logging company, and he and his crew and his best friend, Babe, can be found traveling the United States chopping wood, building mountains, digging canals and lakes, and carving the Grand Canyon.
>
> When they carved the Grand Canyon, it was so hot that the land dried and cracked. His crew couldn't find anything to eat, and Babe bawled every day because he was so hungry. Paul knew he had to do something! He started walking, returning to the corn fields of Iowa. He gathered bushels of that ripe corn and returned to the Southwest, just in time. When that corn hit the hot sun of the desert, it exploded into buckets and buckets of popcorn, and the crew ate to their hearts' content.
>
> Written by Henry Jones from information found in a book by Steven Kellogg and an article in *World Book Multimedia*.

Figure 1.33 Museum Plaque

Assignment Topics:

Pecos Bill	Joe Magarac	Johnny Appleseed
Mike Fink	Mose	Febold Feboldson
McBroom	Gib Morgan	John Henry
Sam Patch	Stormalong	Sally Ann Thunder
Windwagon Smith	Davy Crockett	Ann Whirlwind Crockett

■ Activity Focus: Literature Integration: Writing Original Tall Tales

Technology Connection: Student Productivity (ISTE-students 3), Communication and Collaboration (ISTE-students 4)

Collaboration:
- Story writing: Teacher
- Web page posting: Teacher

Resources:
- *Kidspiration.* Inspiration Software, Inc. (7412 SW Beaverton Hillsdale Highway, Suite 102, Portland, Oregon 97225-2167. Telephone: 1-503-297-3004. Web site: <www.inspiration.com>.)
- Projection system

Preparation Tasks:
- Create a comparison grid of the tall-tale heroes and the challenges/tasks they faced. (See Figure 1.34.) Use the first column to list the tall-tale heroes students researched and reported through resumes or museum displays, the second column to briefly summarize the problems faced by the heroes, and the third column to list examples of hyperbole from the solutions to the problems. Enlarge the grid to poster size using a poster maker; laminate the poster so that it can be used again. An easy way to post students' original tall tales is to access the class Web page created by students at the Web site <www.ih.k12.oh.us/esapanites>. Bookmark this site to use as a source for other original tall tales and as a site for submitting your students' original stories. If you have trouble accessing the site, do a search using the keywords "Mrs. Apanites."

Heroes	Problems	Hyperbole (exaggeration)

Figure 1.34 Tall Tale Heroes Comparison Grid

- *Kidspiration* is a neat brainstorming program that can be used in multiple ways for many subject areas, e.g., prewriting, concept mapping, character webs, cause-and-effect analysis, Web site planning, lesson planning. In this lesson, it is an exciting tool for students to use as they brainstorm ideas for their original tall tales. If you don't have a network version that can be used in a computer lab setting and accessed by all the students, set up the program as a center in the classroom, connect the computer to a presentation system, and introduce it to the students during the beginning lesson on writing a tall tale. Students can work individually or with partners to complete their prewriting brainstorming; then they can change the web to an outline format and print copies of their outlines for the rough-drafting stage of the writing process. The outlines really help the students organize their stories into coherent sequences that reflect definite beginnings, middles, and ends: setting, hero/heroes, challenge, solutions (through hyperbole and invention). Create a template brainstorming web: hero/heroes, challenge, hyperbole.
- Once the template is created, use the "Save As a Template" choice in the file menu and name the template, "My Tall Tale." The new template is stored in the templates file of the program; when students access the template the first time, it opens as an "untitled" document. They must then save the document as their own prewriting file, e.g., John's tall tale, Suzanne's tall tale.
- Make an overhead transparency of the story, "A Farmer's Dilemma."

A Farmer's Dilemma

One day a farmer began noticing that the weather was changing, and he was worried. It had been fine all during the spring when he was planting the fields. But now, trouble seemed to be coming. Every day he'd scratch his head and look at the sky and then at his fields—and back to the sky and back to the fields. Each day the sun seemed to have trouble shining brightly. And the clouds…well, they grew and grew in the sky and got lower and lower. Some days it felt like he could reach up and touch those clouds. Trouble was, those clouds not only blocked the sun but also never gave any rain. They just kept growing darker and darker and lower and lower until pretty soon it was so dark not even the sun could make any light.

The farmer was really worried then. It was almost mid-summer, and his crops were barely ankle high. No sun and no rain and such puny crops—what could he do?

One thing he had noticed as the sun disappeared, the lightning bugs seemed to be out all the time, not just at night. Now if he could just think of a way to use all that light…"by Jove, I've got it. I'll let those chickens loose and get them eating all those lightning bugs." Well, that's what he did. Those chickens ate so many lightning bugs that pretty soon they gave off enough light that he could hang them in the fields. Well, that fooled those crops, and they began to grow and grow and grow, reaching for the light.

The second problem wasn't so easy to solve. This one needed a partner, so he consulted his wife. "Wife, I've finally gotten those crops growing and reaching for the light, but what am I going to do about no rain?" His wife looked up at the sky, but she didn't have to look far because the clouds were so low. She studied and studied those clouds and then reached up and grabbed a cloud and began to squeeze it together. Pretty soon, a gusher of rain poured from that cloud. She turned to her husband and said, "I've thought of a solution. Hitch up the tractor." She went into the house and returned carrying an enormous bag with small holes poked into it. They attached it to the tractor, filled it with clouds, and slowly moved into the fields. As the tractor traveled through the crops, they took turns squeezing the bag and refilling it with clouds. Water poured through the holes onto the thirsty plants, and the plants began to stand up straight and tall. After the farmer and his wife had traveled through most of the field, they began to notice that the dark didn't seem so dark. Now that the crops were standing tall and growing by leaps and bounds, they decided to continue using the clouds to create the new pond they had always wanted in the north field. Soon, the sun was shining bright as day.

- Open the rubric file used for a previous tall-tale project. (See Figure 1.35 on page 40.) Use "Save As" and rename the file, then revise the rubric to fit the writing project. Make multiple copies and a transparency of the rubric.

Assignment Description:

Prepare students for writing original tall tales. Display the comparison chart (Figure 1.34) and list the tall-tale heroes students researched. Discuss and add information in the challenge and

Original Tall Tales: An Evaluation Rubric

Activity Description: After reading and researching tall-tale heroes, students developed their own tall-tale heroes and used the writing process to create original tall-tale stories.

Activity Rating Scale: The art project and journal reflection and discussion were evaluated using this rating scale:

✔+   Exemplary
✔   Progressing
✔-   Emerging

Student	Teacher	
Organization		
		Showed evidence of a strong beginning, middle, and end.
		Showed evidence of an easy flow of ideas (sequenced and logical).
Product		
		Focused on the topic (an extraordinary hero).
		Included supporting details (described the hero's challenge).
		Showed originality and imagination.
		Showed effective use of hyperbole (exaggeration).
Conventions		
		Used complete sentences.
		Showed variety in sentence lengths.
		Used effective word choices.
		Showed evidence of correct grammar.
		Showed attention to mechanics (spelling, capitalization, punctuation).

Figure 1.35 Evaluation Rubric: Tall-tale Heroes Research

hyperbole columns. Share the tall tale, "A Farmer's Dilemma." Use the *Kidspiration* template to discuss the story and demonstrate its use as a prewriting strategy. Show students how to click in the boxes to add their own ideas and how to use the "rapid fire" tool for adding new boxes to the web. Display the transparency of the story so that students have a reference for discussion. Once the details have been entered, show students how to print the information in outline form. (Click on the outline tool and print the brainstorming ideas.) They will use the outlines as guides for drafting their stories.

Schedule computer lab time and allow students to access the class Web page you bookmarked <www.ih.k12.oh.us/esapanites> to read some of the tall tales submitted by students from around the United States. Give students time to preview their ideas with partners, i.e., orally tell their story ideas. Display the evaluation rubric (see Figure 1.35) and review the criteria for assessment of the tall tale. Set up a schedule for the center in the classroom or reserve time in the computer lab for the whole class to work at once on their prewriting step.

Follow the steps of the writing process (rough drafting, revising, editing, and publishing) to complete the stories. Have students share their tall tales, and show them how to submit their tales to the bookmarked Web page. The easiest way to transfer a tale is to open a student's file and select and copy the story. Open the site, go to the page "Submit a Tall Tale," paste the story, and click on "Submit."

■ Activity Focus: Traveling the Oregon Trail

Technology Connection: Problem Solving and Decision Making (ISTE-students 6)

Collaboration: Introducing the Activity: Teacher

Resources:

- *Daily Life in a Covered Wagon*, by Paul Erickson (Washington, DC: The Preservation Press, 1994)
- *The Oregon Trail: Pioneer Adventures*, 4th edition. The Learning Company, 1 Athenaeum Street, Cambridge, Massachusetts 01242. Telephone: 1-800-227-5609. Web site: <www.learningco.com>. Price information: $39.95. (Teacher's note: Read the information packet that accompanies the CD-ROM to familiarize yourself with the program, its options, and the sequence of the journey.)
- Projection system

Assignment Description:

Make a two-column chart on the board; label one column "go" and the other "stay." Pose this question: If you lived in pioneer times, why would you move west or make the decision to stay in the East? Divide the class into two groups; one group will brainstorm reasons why moving west is an opportunity not to be missed, and the other group will brainstorm reasons to stay home in the East. Give students time to meet and compile their lists, then invite discussion and debate. Take a vote and let each student decide whether to travel or stay home.

Introduce and share some of the story (*Daily Life in a Covered Wagon*), e.g., for those of you who chose to travel west, here's what you might experience; for those of you who chose to stay home in the East, here's what you missed. (Teacher's note: The book is too long to read in one sitting. Pages from the book that are effective introductions to the *Oregon Trail* program include the following: pages 4–5: an introduction to the time period and an interesting map; the first column on page 6: an introduction to the Larkin family; page 8 and a review of the picture on page 9: the wagon; pages 10–11: inside the wagon; and pages 20–21: landmarks on the trail.) Discuss the story using these questions: How did pioneers prepare for the journey? What were important supplies? What challenges did pioneers face on the trail? How did they survive? If you were putting together a wagon train, whom would you include?

Introduce *Oregon Trail*, and travel the trail together. Choose a skill level (beginner, challenger or expert), select the people who will travel in your wagon train, and outfit your wagon. As you travel the trail and make decisions, show students how to click on the various icons to fish, hunt, rest, and look in the guidebook; check supplies, health and morale; and check the map for the status of the journey. The guidebook is filled with valuable tips for traveling the trail and can help students make decisions e.g., crossing rivers safely, avoiding dangers, having enough food, and traveling up and down mountains.

Assign partners or allow students to choose partners, and set up a schedule for the center. Show students how to save their journeys; students can return to saved games and pick up where they left off. When students "settle," have them make notes on a separate piece of paper about the results of their decision making. The computer will give them an analysis of their decisions, e.g., the overall health and morale of the people, the supplies they still have at the end of the trail, and their prospects for the future.

After all student partnerships have completed their journeys and analyzed their experiences, have students rate their journeys as very successful, somewhat successful, or unsuccessful, and explain why. Invite sharing and discussion.

■ Activity Focus: Traveling with Lewis and Clark

Technology Connection: Problem Solving and Decision Making (ISTE-students 6)

Collaboration:
- Gathering resources: Media specialist
- Introducing the center and demonstrating the software: Teacher
- Evaluating the maps: Teacher

Resources:
- *Sacagawea*, by Judith St. George (New York: G. P. Putnam's Sons, 1997)
- *Mapmakers Toolkit*. Tom Snyder Productions (80 Coolidge Hill Road, Watertown, Massachusetts 02472. Telephone: 1-800-342-0236. Web site: <www.tomsnyder.com>)
- Projection system

Preparation Tasks:
- Preview the *Mapmaker's Toolkit* software and identify the features you want to demonstrate to students.
- Develop an assignment description card that lists the requirements of the project. (See Figure 1.36.)
- Identify student partnerships.
- Gather a variety of resources on Lewis and Clark and their journey, i.e., *Lewis and Clark*, by R. Conrad Stein (New York: Children's Press, 1997), *The Incredible Journey of Lewis and Clark*, by Rhoda Blumberg (New York: Lathrop, 1987).
- Develop a rubric for assessing the maps. (See Figure 1.37.)

On the Trail with Lewis and Clark

As we read the story of *Sacagawea* and complete our research investigations, use *Mapmakers' Toolkit* and create your own visual record showing highlights from the long journey of Meriweather Lewis and William Clark. use the boxes to check off the assignments you have completed.

- ❏ Identify and describe the starting point of the journey.
- ❏ Label the rivers they traveled. Add descriptive details for two of the rivers.
- ❏ Describe and mark the locations of two weather experiences on the journey.
- ❏ Describe and mark the locations of two experiences with native American peoples.
- ❏ Describe foods found and provided by Sacagawea.
- ❏ Identify four or five animals sighted on the journey.
- ❏ Locate and describe four or five geographic landforms seen on the journey.
- ❏ Locate and describe three or four highlights of the journey.

Figure 1.36 Assignment Requirements

Assignment Description:
Set up *Mapmakers Toolkit* as a center in the classroom and create a rotating schedule for students during the weeks of the pioneer unit. Introduce the software and demonstrate its features, and review the assignment requirements. Use *Sacagawea* by Judith St. George as a read-aloud. Have students use information from the read-aloud and information gathered from other resources in the center to create maps showing the route taken by Lewis and Clark in their exploration of the land of the Louisiana Purchase. The custom features of the program (color, geographic details, text descriptions, and symbols) can be used to show the geography of the land and highlight experiences during the two-year journey.

Assignment requirements for the map might include the following:

1. Identify and describe the starting point of the journey.
2. Label the rivers they traveled. Add descriptive details for two of the rivers.
3. Describe and mark the location of two weather experiences on the journey.
4. Describe and mark the location of two experiences with Native American peoples.
5. Describe foods found and provided by Sacagawea.
6. Identify four or five animals sighted on the journey.
7. Locate and describe four or five geographic landforms seen on the journey, e.g., grasslands, mountains, hills, and plateaus.
8. Locate and describe three or four highlights of the journey, e.g., winter camp at Fort Mandan, crossing the Rocky Mountains, sighting the Pacific Ocean.

On the Trail with Lewis and Clark

Students used research resources, our reading of the novel *Sacagawea* by St. George, and *Mapmakers Toolkit* to create a visual record showing highlights of the long journey of Meriweather Lewis and William Clark.

Maps were evaluated using this rating scale:

3	Exemplary	Map is carefully designed and shows proficient use of the custom features of the program.
		Information requirements are clearly labeled and explained in depth.
		Information details illustrate significant highlights of the journey.
		Assignment is completed by the due date.
2	Developing	Map design shows some use of the custom features of the program; some parts of the map may be confusing.
		Some information requirements are labeled and explained in depth.
		Information details illustrate highlights of the journey; some may not be significant.
		Assignment is completed by the due date.
1	Emerging	Map design shows limited understanding of the assignment and the program.
		Some information requirements are missing.
		Information lacks detail and significance.
		Assignment is not ready by the due date.

Figure 1.37 Assessment Rubric

Measurement: What Size Is It?

Information Retrieval	Student Productivity	Problem Solving and Decision Making
Electronic encyclopedias, e.g., *Grolier's*, *World Book* Internet sites: **Great Buildings:** <www.greatbuildings.com> **Great Buildings and Structures:** <http://architecture.about.com/cs/greatbuildings/>		
		Communication and Collaboration

Teacher Delivery of Lessons	Classroom Management
Scavenger hunt graphic organizer Research graphic organizer Graph paper	

Figure 2.1 Measurement Unit: Technology Connections

Chapter 2

Technology for Math Units

Unit 1: Measurement: What Size Is It?

Unit Objectives:
1. Measure objects using standard and nonstandard units of measurement.
2. Make conversions among standard units for measuring length.
3. Convert measurements to a scale model.

Audience: Grades 2–4

Length of the Unit: 2 weeks

The Unit Activities at a Glance

Introduction	Researching the Monuments	Measuring and Developing a Scale
Students listen to *Ben's Dream* by Chris Van Allsburg and complete a scavenger hunt naming monuments of the world. An art extension lets them explore Van Allsburg's illustrating technique with line, light, and shadow	Students work with partners and research favorite monuments.	Students work with scale and then construct scale models of their monuments.

Figure 2.1a Measurement, The Unit Activities at a Glance

■ Activity Focus: Introduction

Technology Connection: Teacher Delivery of Lessons (ISTE-teacher II-III)

Collaboration:
- Lessons on measurement: Teacher
- Sharing the story: Media specialist
- Scavenger hunt: Media specialist and teacher as co-facilitators

Resources:
- *Ben's Dream*, story and pictures by Chris Van Allsburg (Boston: Houghton Mifflin, 1982)
- Drawing paper
- Pens and pencils

Preparation Tasks:
- Prepare a scavenger hunt graphic organizer. (See Figure 2.2.)
- Prior to beginning the landmarks research, spend time (at least a week) working with measurement using the activities and tasks suggested in the textbook.

Assignment Description:
- Share and discuss the story.
- Introduce the scavenger hunt graphic organizer and have students spend time hunting for the names of the landmarks and identifying other interesting landmarks from around the world.
- Share the results of the scavenger hunt and list the landmarks on chart paper. Brainstorm other landmarks/monuments/noteworthy structures the students have found e.g., Washington Monument and Lincoln Memorial. Add other landmarks from around the world, e.g., Pharos of Alexandria (ancient lighthouse), Hanging Gardens of Babylon, and Machu Picchu.

Traveling the Globe with Ben and Margaret	
Location	Landmark
New York, New York	
London, England	
Paris, France	
Pisa, Italy	
Athens, Greece	
Giza, Egypt	
Moscow, Russia	
Agra, India	
Northern China	
Black Hills, South Dakota	
Other landmarks Ben might have visited if the story continued:	

Figure 2.2 Scavenger Hunt Graphic Organizer

Art Extension:

Set up a center so students can explore and experiment with the line art from the book. Provide pens, pencils, and drawing paper, and encourage students to revisit Mr. Van Allsburg's illustrations, noting the textures created by the lines, and the light and shadow in each illustration. Then have students draw their own scenes using line art.

■ Activity Focus: Researching the Landmarks

Technology Connection: Information Retrieval (ISTE-students 5), Teacher Delivery of Lessons (ISTE-teacher II-III)

Collaboration: Researching: Media specialist with teacher assisting

Resources: Print and electronic resources, i.e., books, encyclopedias, Internet sites, other databases

Preparation Tasks:
- Bookmark these Web sites: <www.greatbuildings.com> and <http://architecture.about.com/cs/great buildings/>.
- Create a graphic organizer for students to use as they research and take notes about the landmarks. Make multiple copies, enough for one per student; also make transparencies of the organizer. (See Figure 2.3.)

Assignment Description:

Have students work with a partner to choose and research a landmark. Introduce the research assignment by displaying the transparency of the note-taking graphic organizer and reviewing the information requirements students should complete. Brainstorm resources that will help students find information; access the two Web sites and show students how to locate information about their landmarks. Encourage students to be detailed and thorough in their note taking because they will be creating three-dimensional models of the landmarks. Suggested research topics include the following:

1. Statue of Liberty, New York City, New York
2. Big Ben, London, England
3. Eiffel Tower, Paris, France
4. Mt. Rushmore, Black Hills, South Dakota
5. Leaning Tower of Pisa, Pisa, Italy
6. Acropolis, Athens, Greece
7. Taj Mahal, Agra, India
8. The Great Sphinx, Giza, Egypt
9. Washington Monument, Washington, DC
10. Pharos of Alexandria, Alexandria, Egypt
11. The Hanging Gardens of Babylon, near modern day Baghdad, Iraq
12. Lincoln Memorial, Washington, DC
13. The Great Wall of China, northern China (Teacher's note: It will be difficult for the students to build the entire wall at an accurate scale because the wall is 1,500 miles long. Students who take on this assignment could build a one-mile segment of the wall and use a map of the United States to show how far a student would have to travel in the United States to travel the length of the wall.)

Student:

Landmark:

Structure of the Landmark

A. Size
  1 _____
  2 _____

B. Shape
  1 _____
  2 _____

C. Other Interesting Facts
  1 _____
  2 _____
  3 _____

History of the Landmark

A. Builder
  1 _____
  2 _____

B. Reasons for the Landmark
  1 _____
  2 _____

C. Location
  1 _____
  2 _____

D. Other Interesting Facts
  1 _____
  2 _____
  3 _____
  4 _____

Figure 2.3 Research Graphic Organizer: Landmarks

■ Activity Focus: Measuring and Developing a Scale

Technology Connection: Teacher Delivery of Lessons (ISTE-teacher II-III)

Collaboration: Measuring and developing a scale: Teacher

Resources:
- Masking tape
- Measuring tools, e.g., rulers, yard/meter sticks

Preparation Tasks: Create graph paper (either in inches or centimeters) for the students to use as they transfer their actual landmark sizes to scale-model sizes. Make multiple copies, enough for several copies per student partnership. (See Figure 2.4.)

Assignment Description:

Using a scale of 50 feet : 1 inch, have students figure the heights of their landmarks, then mark the heights in an open space (hallway, playground, gym, or cafeteria) to show the comparative heights of the various landmarks. Distribute the graph paper and set up some measurement guidelines to remind students of the scale, i.e., one inch equals 50 feet, $\frac{1}{4}$ inch equals $12\frac{1}{2}$ feet, $\frac{1}{2}$ inch equals 25 feet, $\frac{3}{4}$ inch equals $37\frac{1}{2}$ feet. Help students use their research measurements to draw scale pictures of the landmarks and plan the materials they will use to build the monuments, e.g., cardboard, Legos, sugar cubes, butcher paper, boxes.

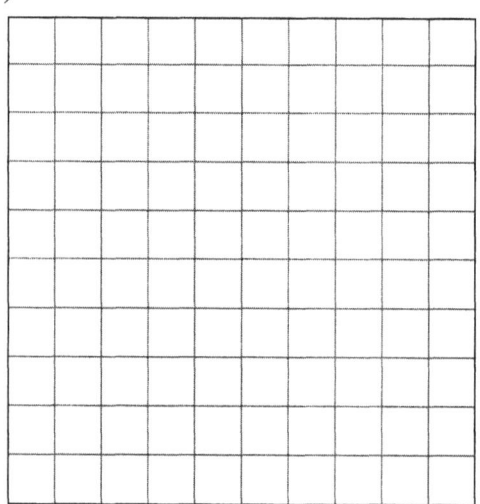

Figure 2.4 Graph Paper

Have students pick one feature of their landmarks and use nonstandard measurements (their body lengths, chairs, or books) to show that feature.

As students construct their landmarks, continue to focus on measurement lessons, using activities and tasks from the textbook. Have students develop information cards to place beside their landmarks. Invite other classes to tour the display.

Shadow Study		
Information Retrieval	**Student Productivity**	**Problem Solving and Decision Making**
Internet sites: **Groundhog Information:** <www-ed.fnal.gov/entry_exhibits/woodchuck/woodchuck.html>	Slide Show: What Makes a Shadow?	Graphing
		Communication and Collaboration
		Global Schoolhouse Project, Lightspan Network: <www.lightspan.com/corporate/pages/lsnetwork.asp?_prod=LS&_nav=n1_lsnetwork>
Teacher Delivery of Lessons		**Classroom Management**
Internet sites: **Sounds of the Groundhog:** <www.hoghaven.com> **Stormfax Almanac:** <www.stprmfax.com/ghogday.htm> Shadow investigation sheet		Assessment checklist

Figure 2.5 Shadow Study Unit: Technology Connections

Unit 2: Shadow Study

Unit Objectives:
1. Explore size concepts and understand positional words, e.g., big, bigger, biggest, short, tall, large, small, behind, and under.
2. Investigate shadows, i.e., what makes a shadow and how shadows change.

Audience: Grades K–1

Length of the Unit: 1 week

The Unit Activities at a Glance

Groundhog Facts	Shadow Hunt
Students listen to a Groundhog Day story, brainstorm questions for research, and work with partners to find answers to their questions. Students also explore making shadows.	Students listen to a story, then go on a shadow hunt on the school grounds. Shadow pictures are gathered into a class slide show.
Measuring Shadows	**Predicting**
Students complete a shadows investigation and make comparisons among the shadows.	Students participate in an e-mail collaborative project through the Global Schoolhouse site. They also share groundhog facts, make predictions for Groundhog Day, and discuss results from previous years.

Figure 2.5a Shadow Study, The Unit Activities at a Glance

■ Activity Focus: Groundhog Facts

Technology Connection: Information Retrieval (ISTE-students 5), Teacher Delivery of Lesson, Classroom Management (ISTE-teacher II-V)

Collaboration:
- Researching the groundhog: Media specialist
- Introducing the legend: Teacher

Resources:
- A story about Groundhog Day, e.g., *Geoffrey Groundhog Predicts the Weather*, by Bruce Koscielniak (Boston: Houghton Mifflin, 1995)
- *Shadowgraphs Anyone Can Make* (Philadelphia: Running Press)
- Overhead projector projected onto a bare wall

- Large sheets of butcher paper
- Markers
- A variety of objects, e.g., three crayons in different lengths, mittens or gloves in three different sizes, or puzzle pieces that represent three sizes

Preparation Tasks:

- Create a Groundhog Day display. Enlarge a picture of a groundhog. To the left of the groundhog, hang a piece of chart paper titled "Groundhog Facts." To the right of the groundhog, hang chart paper, and restate the legend of the groundhog: The groundhog hibernates all winter. February 2 is the day he awakens and comes out of his hole. The legend says that if he sees his shadow, there will be six more weeks of winter. If he doesn't see his shadow, spring is just around the corner. Below the groundhog, hang another piece of chart paper divided into two columns: "Yes, he will see his shadow" and "No, he will not see his shadow." (See Figure 2.6.)

Figure 2.6 Groundhog Display

- Bookmark these Web sites: <www.hoghaven.com/> (sounds of the groundhog; it's really fun) and <www.ed.fnal.gov/entry_exhibits/woodchuck/woodchuck.html> (groundhog information). Create a checklist to assess students' understanding of size concepts and positional words. (See Figure 2.7.)

Students	Big, Bigger, Biggest	Short, Tall	Large, Small	Behind, Under

Figure 2.7 Assessment Checklist

Assignment Description (a week before Groundhog Day, February 2):

Introduce and share the story. Pause on page 29 after reading the *Daily Gazette* headlines and articles, and discuss how Geoffrey solved the problem of the prediction. What did he do to finally make a prediction? Share the rest of the story.

Direct students' attention to the groundhog display. Read and discuss the legend, e.g., can a groundhog really predict spring or more winter? List questions that students have, e.g., how did the legend get started? Does the prediction always come true?

Access the groundhog sounds Web site and play some of the sounds. Explain the research facts assignment; students will work with partners and go to the media center to find one interesting fact about groundhogs or the legend of the groundhog. They can record their facts through pictures and through words and pictures. (Teacher's note: Effective pairings for this task would be a more fluent reader/writer with a less fluent reader/writer.)

Also explain that in a few days the class will be making their own predictions about the groundhog and his shadow and recording their predictions in the two-column chart in the display.

Explore making shadows with the students. Pose this question: What causes a shadow? Turn off the lights in the room and project the light source against a bare wall. Have students stand in front of the light source and have fun making different kinds of shadows, e.g., tall shadows, short shadows, moving shadows, animal shadows (see some of the examples in *Shadowgraphs*). After students have experimented for a while, introduce the concepts of big, bigger, and biggest. Hang a sheet of butcher paper on the wall and ask for three volunteers to create shadows that represent these sizes. Draw around the shadows and label them. Choose one of your objects and display the three different sizes on the projector. Draw around the objects and ask students to label their sizes. Repeat the process with the other objects. Use the assessment checklist to make notes on students' understanding of the concept.

■ Activity Focus: Shadow Hunt

Technology Connection: Student Productivity (ISTE-students 3)

Collaboration:
- Looking for shadows: Teachers
- Sharing the shadows we found: Media specialist

Resources:
- *What Makes a Shadow?* by Clyde Bulla, illustrated by June Otani (New York: HarperCollins, 1994)
- Flashlight
- Sketching paper
- Pencils
- Clipboards (Teacher's note: The clipboard makes an easy drawing surface and helps students manage their papers.)
- Slide show software, i.e., *AppleWorks*, *PowerPoint*

Preparation Tasks: Create a slide show template for students to add their shadow pictures, and sentences or phrases about the pictures.

Assignment Description (need a sunny day or at least a day with some sun):
To create interest in the story, explore making shadows with a flashlight and student volunteers. Share and discuss the story, *What Makes a Shadow?* Where did students in the story find shadows in the neighborhood and on the playground? How did students make the final shadow in the book (an elephant)? Seek volunteers and try to duplicate the shadow.

Go on a shadow hunt on the school grounds; have students bring pencils, sketching paper, and clipboards. Encourage students to select unusual shadows and make illustrations of the objects and their shadows. Circulate as students work and use the checklist (see Figure 2.7) to assess understanding of the size concepts and the positional words. Share the shadow pictures and tally all the shadows students found. Have students save their pictures because they will be using them to create a class slide show, What Makes a Shadow?

Developing the Slide Show:
Have students work in small groups in the media center creating their slides for the shadow show. Present the show to the class when it is finished.

■ Activity Focus: Measuring Shadows

Technology Connection: Problem Solving and Decision Making (ISTE-students 6), Teacher Delivery of Lesson (ISTE-teacher II-III)

Collaboration: Measuring our shadows: Teacher

Resources:
- chalk
- measuring tools, i.e., rulers, yard/meter sticks
- spreadsheet, i.e., *Microsoft Excel*, *AppleWorks*

Preparation Tasks: Create a shadows investigation sheet. (See Figure 2.8.)

Assignment Description:
Choose a sunny day and an outside location on a sidewalk or parking surface. Use chalk if the surface is clear of snow; use rulers if snow covers the surface. Plan three measurement times: morning, noon, and afternoon. Have students work with partners and measure their shadows. Have one partner stand still while the other partner marks the beginning and end of the shadow, using the chalk or the rulers. Measure the shadow and record the measurement on the investigation sheet. Repeat the process with the other partner.

Student		Date
Shadows Investigation		
	My Shadow	My Partner's Shadow
Morning		
Noon		
Afternoon		

Figure 2.8 Shadows Investigation

Return to the classroom and discuss the results. Who had the shortest shadow? tallest shadow? smallest shadow? largest shadow? Have students meet in groups of three and order their shadow lengths in terms of big, bigger, and biggest. Use the assessment checklist to make notes about students' levels of understanding for these concepts.

Return to the measurement site at noon and in the afternoon, and repeat the process of measuring the shadows. Make comparisons among the shadows. When were the shadows at their tallest? shortest?

Enter the results on a spreadsheet and make graphs of the information, e.g., morning tallest to shortest shadows, noontime smallest to largest shadows, afternoon percentages of shadows that were big, bigger, and biggest (pie graph), partnership graphs, and groups of three graphs.

■ Activity Focus: Predicting

Technology Connection: Communication and Collaboration (ISTE-students 4)

Collaboration:
- Project posting with *Global Schoolhouse*: Media specialist and teacher
- Tallying and sharing the predictions: Media specialist and teacher

Resources: *Gregory's Shadow*, by Don Freeman (New York: Viking, 2000)

Preparation Tasks:
- Several weeks before beginning the unit, access *Global Schoolhouse* on the Lightspan Network <www.lightspan.com/corporate/pages/lsnetwork.asp?_prod=LS&_nav=n1_lsnetwork>, and register an online project for communication and collaboration with other students/classrooms across the United States. At the *Global Schoolhouse* page, click on "Project Registry," then select "add your project." Follow the online directions to register your project. Information requirements for project registry include the following details: Project Information: Author (name and e-mail address), title, beginning and ending dates, brief summary; Project Details: Level (beginning), curriculum area/s (math), full description of the project, objectives; Project Registration Information: e-mail address, registration acceptance dates, number of classrooms, age range, target audience, additional registration information, if needed. For this unit, share the legend of the groundhog, and invite students/classrooms to make predictions about whether the groundhog will see a shadow.
- Bookmark the Web site <www.stormfax.com/ghogday.htm> (Stormfax Almanac listing Groundhog Day shadow/no shadow results from 1887 to the present).

Assignment Description:

On February 1, return to the groundhog display and have students share the facts they have gathered. Ask students to predict what they think will happen with the groundhog's shadow on the next day. Record their predictions in the two columns. Discuss the results and ask students to share what they based their predictions on. Record the predictions from the participating classrooms and compose a letter to each participant sharing the prediction results from all the classrooms. Access the Web site (Stormfax Almanac) and look at the results through the years. Share the story by Don Freeman.

Shapes Are Everywhere

Information Retrieval	Student Productivity	Problem Solving and Decision Making
Internet sites: **Tessellation (Historical and Geographical Connections:** <www.mathforum.org/sum95/suzanne/tess.intro.html>	Slide Show: Looking at Symmetry Creating original tessellations	Internet site: **Tangram Puzzles** <http://standards.nctm.org/document/eexamples/chap4/4.4index.htm#applet>
		Communication and Collaboration

Teacher Delivery of Lessons	Classroom Management
Internet sites: **Encyclopedia of Art:** <http://artcyclopedia.com> **Directions for Making Tangrams:** <http://mathforum.org/trscavo/tangrams/construct.html> "Hunt for Shapes" graphic organizer Tangram design forms Story planning graphic organizer	Assessment rubric for evaluating the "Hunt for Shapes" scrapbooks

Figure 2.9 Shapes Are Everywhere Unit: Technology Connections

Unit 3: Shapes Are Everywhere

Unit Objectives:
1. Recognize and define a variety of geometric shapes, e.g., circles, triangles, quadrilaterals, and polygons.
2. Draw lines of symmetry in two-dimensional geometric figures.
3. Recognize and describe patterns in the real world.
4. Discover, describe, create, and extend a wide variety of patterns.

Audience: Grades 4–8

Length of the Unit: 2 weeks

The Unit Activities at a Glance

Can You Find It?	Tangrams
Students look for geometric shapes in the environment and create scrapbooks of examples.	Students complete a variety of activities using tangrams, i.e., an initial exploration, a book of tangram designs, tangram puzzles, tangram storytelling.
Finding Symmetry	**Tessellations**
Students complete a variety of activities exploring symmetry, i.e., a fact or fable slide show, ink/paintblot illustrations, folded designs, alphabet designs.	Students view the work of M.C. Escher, create their own tessellations, and investigate historical and geographic connections with tessellations.

Figure 2.9a Shapes Are Everywhere, The Unit Activities at a Glance

■ Activity Focus: Can You Find It?

Technology Connection: Student Productivity (ISTE-students 3), Teacher Delivery of Lesson, Classroom Management (ISTE-teacher II–V)

Collaboration:
- Slide show: Media specialist and teacher working together
- Introducing the project: Teacher and media specialist working together

Resources: Digital camera

Preparation Tasks:
- Use colorful poster board to make a variety of geometric shapes: circle, oval, square, triangle, rectangle, and hexagon.

Technology for Math Units 57

- Create a slide show showing artwork based on geometric shapes. (Some artists to study include Pablo Picasso, Max Ernst, and Georges Braque. Scan prints by the artists or search the Internet for examples of their art. (A great site for art prints is <http://artcyclopedia.com/>. The index page offers a search component that allows you to search by artist's name, movement, medium, or nationality.)
- Create a graphic organizer for the "hunt for shapes" activity. Make multiple copies of the page (enough for eight to ten per student) and a transparency. (See Figure 2.10.)
- Create a rubric to assess the "hunt for shapes" scrapbook. (See Figure 2.11.)

Location:
(Picture, rubbing, sample, sketch of the example)
Caption

Figure 2.10 Hunt for Shapes Graphic Organizer

Assignment Description:

Display and identify the shapes, and ask students to locate examples of the shapes in the classroom, e.g., circular clock or rectangles of the tables/desks. Introduce the slide show and slowly preview the slides, pausing to identify the geometric shapes and to discuss how they are used to build the images.

Introduce the "hunt for shapes" activity. Students will search the environment for use of basic geometric shapes, e.g., fabric, rugs, brick walls, and artwork. They should find eight to ten examples and record them on the graphic organizer sheets, creating a scrapbook of patterns and shapes. Distribute the graphic organizer and use the transparency to show how to record the examples the students find:

Location: Where they found the example.

Example box: A digital camera picture, a sketch by the student, a piece of the example (fabric square, carpet sample), a rubbing. (Teacher's note: You can require at least one digital camera picture so that students gain experience in using the camera and downloading and printing the image.)

Caption box: A question or short description to focus the viewer's attention on the shape that is used, e.g., How many triangles can you find in the picture?

When students have gathered their examples, bind the pages into scrapbooks (See Figure 2.12 on page 59), display them, and have students present and talk about their favorite examples from their searches.

"Hunt for Shapes" Assessment Rubric

Scale:
- 3 Clearly communicated ideas and all the required information.
- 2 Communicated ideas and the information; may have confusing or missing pieces.
- 1 Ideas and information are vague and/or incomplete.

	Student	Teacher
1. Chose effective examples that demonstrated understanding of the assignment.		
2. Identified the location for each example.		
3. Created an interesting caption for each example.		
4. Used appropriate conventions in writing the caption (grammar, spelling, punctuation, capitalization).		
5. Demonstrated careful craftsmanship in developing and placing the example.		
6. Created the final scrapbook.		
7. Developed a short presentation telling about favorite examples.		
8. Met the deadlines for the assignment.		
Totals:		

Comments:

Figure 2.11 Hunt for Shapes Assessment Rubric

■ Activity Focus: Tangrams

Technology Connection: Problem Solving and Decision Making (ISTE-students 6), Teacher Delivery of Lesson (ISTE-teacher II-III)

Collaboration:
- Working with tangrams: Teacher
- Selecting literature for tangram stories: Media specialist

Resources: *Grandfather Tang's Story: A Tale Told with Tangrams*, by Ann Tompert, illustrated by Robert Parker (New York: Crown, 1990)

The Hunt for Shapes

Produced by Jeremy

2001–2002

Figure 2.12 Scrapbook of Shapes

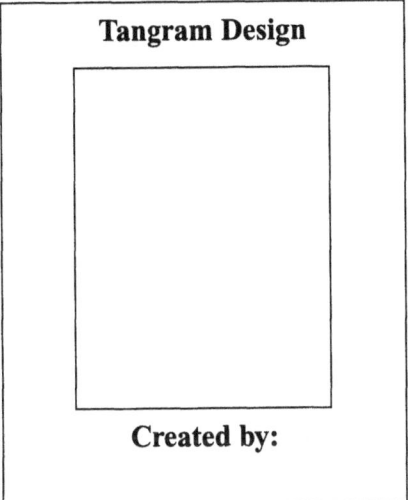

Figure 2.13 Tangram Recording Sheet

Preparation Tasks:
- Access the math forum Web site <http://mathforum.org/trscavo/tangrams/construct.html>, download the directions for making tangram sets, and make sets of tangrams for students to use during the lessons. Store the sets in zippered bags.
- Create a tangram design recording sheet for students to use as they manipulate the tangrams and make their own shapes. (See Figure 2.13.)
- Bookmark the Tangram puzzle site at <http://standards.nctm.org/document/eexamples/chap4/4.4/index.htm#applet>.
- Create a storyboard planning sheet for students to use as they prepare their tangram story presentations. (See Figure 2.14.)

Activity Descriptions:

Exploring with Tangrams: Distribute the tangram sets to the students, identify the shapes that are found in each set, and make size comparisons among the shapes. Use the overhead projector to manipulate the tangrams into designs and patterns, making sure that the tangrams touch but do not overlap.

A Book of Tangram Designs: Have students work with partners and the tangrams to create a class book of shape puzzles. When partners have created their shape, they should trace the outline of the shape on one of the recording sheets, provide an answer key, and then slip both into the notebook of designs. (Teacher's note: Use a loose-leaf notebook and print the recording sheets on three-hole paper so that students can easily insert their designs into the notebook.)

Tangram Puzzles: Set up the puzzles activity as a center. Select one of the puzzles and show students how to manipulate the shapes to construct the puzzle.

Telling Tales: Share the book *Grandfather Tang's Story*, and closely examine the illustrations to study the shapes created from the tangrams. Have students work in small groups to create their own tangram stories. Students can write original tales, or they can browse the media center and select a folktale, e.g., *Three Little Pigs*, *The Little Red*

Students:	
Story:	
Text	Figures
Scene 1: (Text from the story)	(Figure that will be shown)
Scene 2:	
Scene 3:	
Scene 4:	
Scene 5:	

Figure 2.14 Tangram Storyboard Planning

Technology for Math Units

Hen, or *The Fool of the World and the Flying Ship*; a fable, "The Tortoise and the Hare" or "The Fox and the Grapes"; or a picture book, e.g., a book by Leo Lionni, Eric Carle, or Frank Asch; and create tangram versions of the story. Encourage students to keep the shape requirements simple and easy to manage, e.g. a pig, a wolf, or a house for the *Three Little Pigs* and a flying ship and three people for *The Fool of the World*. Show students how to use the storyboard planner to develop their presentations. (See Figure 2.14.)

■ Activity Focus: Finding Symmetry

Technology Connection: Student Productivity (ISTE-students 3)

Collaboration:
- Creating the slide show: Media specialist
- Introducing symmetry: Teacher and media specialist as co-facilitators

Resources:
- Slide show program, e.g., *AppleWorks*, *Microsoft PowerPoint*
- Typing paper, enough for several sheets per students
- Tempera paint or ink
- Scissors
- Illustrating materials, e.g., markers, crayons, colored pencils

Figure 2.15 Slide Show Template

Preparation Tasks:
Create a slide show template for students to record their examples of symmetry. Each student will use two slides. The first will be a picture of the object with a statement at the bottom, i.e., Fact or Fable: A (object) is symmetrical; the second slide will reveal the truth. However, the template will be one slide because the students will copy and paste their first slide so that they don't have to redraw the object. (See Figure 2.15.)

Assignment Description:
Introduce the concept of symmetry. Use a sheet of paper to make a snowflake and invite suggestions for cutouts from the students. Make the snowflake, then unfold it and talk about the concept of symmetry. Engage students in a variety of experiences in creating symmetry:

Ink/paint blots: Fold a sheet of paper in half, open it and drop paint/ink on one side and fold and smooth the paper again. Open the paper again to see the designs.
Simple designs: Fold a new sheet of paper in half and cut a simple shape on the fold. Open the paper to see the design.
Alphabet design: Work with a partner, select a letter of the alphabet that has symmetry (A, H, I, M, O, T, V, W, X, Y), and use your bodies to demonstrate the letter for the class.

Introduce the slide show project. Students will search for examples of symmetry at school, at home, and in the community. Then they will draw the object on the first slide and complete the fact/fable statement. Show students how to copy and paste the slide for a second picture, how to change the fact/fable statement, and how to add lines of symmetry to the object.

■ Activity Focus: Tesselations

Technology Connection: Student Productivity (ISTE-students 3)

Collaboration:
- Gathering resources: Media specialist
- Introducing the lesson: Teacher
- Using the computer to design tessellations: Teacher and media specialist as co-facilitators

Resources:
- Paint program or multimedia program, e.g., *AppleWorks*, *Kid Pix*, *HyperStudio*
- Typing paper
- Math journals, e.g., spiral notebooks, folders with inserted paper devoted to math notes and reflections
- Projection system

Preparation Tasks:
- Gather materials on M.C. Escher. Several of his pieces show repeating figures and will be interesting opportunities for analysis for the students. The art encyclopedia online <http://artcyclpedia.com> has some good examples. Search by artist's name and when the results are displayed, access the National Gallery of Art in Washington, DC. There are several interesting examples in the collection.
- Use cardboard to make a variety of shape templates, e.g., equilateral triangles, squares, and hexagons.
- Bookmark the Web site <www.mathforum.org/sum95/suzanne/tess.intro.html> (tessellation tutorials). Preview the design tutorials to select one that students will follow when they work in the computer lab and design their own tessellations.
- Arrange time in the computer lab for students to work on their designs.

Assignment Description:
Access the Web site and use the "What Is a Tessellation?" information to begin the lesson. Pose this question to students: What is a tessellation? Take students through the information and examples on regular tessellations (skipping the angle measurement portion), naming conventions, and semi-regular tessellations.

Share and discuss information about M.C. Escher; then have students work with partners and the cardboard templates to design a regular or semi-regular tessellation. Share and discuss the designs.

Use the computer lab, introduce the paint program, and show students how to make a geometric shape; then copy and paste it to tessellate the design. Have students experiment with the shapes and create their own tesselations. Print the finished designs. Have students present their work to the class, and then create a display of the designs.

Historical and Geographical Connections: Have students work with partners and investigate historical and geographical connections for tessellations and tilings. Have partners choose an area of the world (from the choices on the Web site <www.mathforum.org/sum95/suzanne/tess.intro.html>) and explore the information and examples to prepare a report for the class. Encourage students to use their math journals to record the information and examples they gather.

Ongoing Work:
Bookmark the tessellations tutorial Web site as a center in the classroom and give students time to create other tessellations. They will be eager to continue the computer lab experience.

Design Technology: Inventing

Information Retrieval	Student Productivity	Problem Solving and Decision Making
Electronic encyclopedias, e.g., *Grolier's*, *World Book* Internet sites: **Inventors Hall of Fame:** <www.invent.org/book/book-text/indexbyname.html>	Newspaper on Inventing	Internet Site: **Leonardo's Mysterious Machinery:** <www.mos.org/sln/Leonardo/>
		Communication and Collaboration
		Global Schoolhouse Project, Lightspan Company: <www.lightspan.com/corporate/pages/lsnetwork.asp?_prod=LS&_nav=n1_lsnetwork>

Teacher Delivery of Lessons	Classroom Management
Internet sites: **Exploravision Projects:** <www.toshiba.com/tai/exploravision/> **What Can You Do with a Pencil?:** <www.noogenesis.com/inventing/pencil/pencil_page/html> **Design Challenges from Leonardo:** <www.mos.org/sln/Leonardo/> **3M Design Process:** <http://mustang.coled.umn.edu/inventing/Inventing.html> **Alexander Graham Bell's Science Notebooks Online:** <http://memory.loc.gov/ammem/bellhtml/bellhome.html> Inventor's Journal	Assessment rubrics for evaluating newspaper contributions and inventor reports.

Figure 3.1 Design Technology Unit: Technology Connections

Chapter 3

Technology for Science Units

Unit 1: Design Technology Connection: Inventing

Unit Objectives:
1. Develop awareness of inventors and their accomplishments.
2. Use a design process and work as an inventor.

Audience: Grades 3–8

Length of the Unit: 4 weeks

The Unit Activities at a Glance

Thinking About Inventing: Introductory Lessons	Inventors: Their Lives and Careers
Students participate in a variety of activities to spark creativity and prepare for inventing, i.e., first attempts at inventing, reports from history, changes for the future, Leonardo's design challenge.	Students listen to a story, then go on a shadow hunt on the school grounds. Shadow pictures are gathered into a class slide show.
In the News: All About Inventing, Inventors, and Inventions	**Inventing**
Students create a newspaper about inventing.	Students invent something using a 4-step process.

Figure 3.1a Design Technology: Inventing, The Unit Activities at a Glance

■ Activity Focus: Thinking About Inventing: Introductory Lessons

Technology Connection: Problem Solving and Decision Making (ISTE-students 6), Communication and Collaboration (ISTE-students 4), Teacher Delivery of Lessons (ISTE-teacher II–III)

Collaboration:
- Brainstorming and discussion: Teacher
- Gathering resources for reading: Media specialist
- Posting a project with *Global Schoolhouse*: Media specialist and teacher

Resources:
- Projection system
- *The Fortunate Fortunes,* by Nathan Aaeseng (Minneapolis: Lerner, 1989)
- *Midstream Changes*, by Nathan Aaeseng (Minneapolis: Lerner, 1990)
- *The Problem Solvers*, by Nathan Aaeseng (Minneapolis: Lerner, 1989)
- *The Rejects*, by Nathan Aaeseng (Minneapolis: Lerner, 1989)
- *The Unsung Heroes*, by Nathan Aaeseng (Minneapolis: Lerner, 1989)
- *Steven Caney's Invention Book,* by Steven Caney (New York: Workman Publishing, 1985)
- Creative thinking supplies: To help students begin the inventing process, gather a variety of examples of inventions that can be used as springboards for discussion and for imagining, e.g., a toilet seat, a belt, a backpack, a backpack on wheels, roller skates and roller blades, and a rake.
- Paper strips: Use 8½" × 14" typing paper and cut it in half lengthwise so that you have strips measuring 4¼" × 14", enough for two strips per student.

Preparation Tasks:
- Bookmark these sites:
  - <www.mos.org/sln/Leonardo/ >
  - <www.toshiba.com/tai/exploravision/>
  - <www.noogenesis.com/inventing/pencil/pencil_page.html>
- Access *Global Schoolhouse* on the Lightspan Network <www.lightspan.com/corporate/pages/lsnetwork.asp?_prod=LS&_nav=n1_lsnetwork> and register an online project for communication and collaboration with other students/classrooms across the United States. At the *Global Schoolhouse* page, click on "Project Registry," and then select "add your project." Follow the online directions to register your project. Information requirements for project registry include the following details: Project Information: Author (name and e-mail address), title, beginning and ending dates, brief summary; Project Details: Level (beginning), curriculum areas (social studies, science, technology), full description of the project, objectives; Project Registration Information: e-mail address, registration acceptance dates, number of classrooms, age range, target audience, and additional registration information if needed.
- For this unit, invite students/classrooms to contribute illustrations and explanations showing inventions that would allow humans to perform skills that animals have. Participants should identify animals that have skills they wish they had, then make sketches of inventions that would allow them to perform those skills. Participants also should include brief explanations of the inventions that identify the animals and their skills, and describe the inventions and how they work. When students are ready to share their work, they should send the illustrations and the explanations via e-mail. Set up a slide show template (using *AppleWorks*, *PowerPoint*, or another program) so that the illustrations and explanations can be downloaded into this display format for easy viewing and reading. Also, set up a spreadsheet so that students can record the animals and desired skills selected by participating students/classrooms.
- Gather multiple copies of the Nathan Aaeseng books listed in the resources section. The ideal is one copy per student, but if that is not possible, students can partner-read. Students will read from these during the introductory lessons.

- Access the pencil site listed above and prepare some of the pencil examples listed on the Web site. (Teacher's note: If you have trouble accessing the site, search using the keywords "pencil inventions.")

Assignment Descriptions:

Thinking About Inventing: Have students work with partners to make lists of everything in the classroom that had to be invented. Have students join another partnership and combine their lists into one. Repeat this process. Share and display the lists.

Introduce Leonardo da Vinci and focus on his work as an inventor. Access the home page you have bookmarked <www.mos.org/sln/Leonardo/>, go to the Inventors Workshop, and share the information. Click on Leonardo's Mysterious Machinery; have students work in small groups to identify the purposes of the machines that are illustrated in each picture. In sharing their choices, students should provide reasons that are based on analysis of the drawings. Discuss how the accuracy of the drawings helped in identifying the purposes of the machinery.

Have students choose animals that have skills they wish they had; then have students make sketches of inventions that would allow them to perform those skills. Encourage students to include descriptions of how the inventions work. Share the *Global Schoolhouse* collaboration opportunity and set up a schedule for students to check for responses, download attachments (illustrations and explanations), communicate with participating students/classrooms, and record information in the spreadsheet.

Gathering Ideas: Write these quotes on the board, "Necessity is the mother of invention" and "Invention flourishes most in times of war." Engage students in a discussion about the two quotes. Continue the discussion, focusing on this question: Where do inventors get their ideas? (Some inventors get their ideas by accident, as a result of observation, to solve a problem or fill a need, because of tinkering, or as an extension of a previous invention.) What do you think?

Access the "Exploravision" project sponsored by Toshiba, and review some of the winning projects. Discuss the needs or reasons for these inventions. Where did these inventors get their ideas?

Divide the class into five groups and assign one of the Aaeseng books to each group. Groups should browse their books, select featured inventors/invention stories, read the stories, and prepare posters sharing the information they discovered. Posters should show the invention, name the inventor (if possible), describe challenges/difficulties faced by the inventor, and identify how the invention occurred. Present posters to the class. Continue to have students read in the books. Give sustained silent reading time during the school day and encourage students to continue reading during and after school time.

Into the Future: Display the belt, then buckle it around a stack of books, and sling them over your shoulder. Discuss with students inventions that improve the way we carry our school materials. Show them the backpack and the backpack on wheels. Brainstorm how the backpack will look in the future.

Access the pencil Web site and take students through the questions and examples. Pause before sharing the answers/responses on the Web site so that students have opportunities to brainstorm and discuss. Vary the ways students respond to the ideas, e.g., share with a partner, brainstorm in a small group and report to the class, or discuss as a whole class.

Distribute the strips of paper and have students fold the strips into four sections. Show the toilet seat and have students make rough sketches of the toilet seat in the second section of their papers. Explain that toilet seats used to be made from wood and did not have lids. Draw a quick sketch of this in the first section. Ask students to imagine improvements in the toilet seats of the future and to draw pictures in the third and fourth sections. Invite sharing and tally the suggestions in a chart on the board.

Share collaboration illustrations and explanations from the Global Schoolhouse project.

Working on a Design: Write these words on the board, "Old items, New uses"; then pose the question: How many different ways can you think of to use a paper plate? Give students thinking time, then invite sharing and list their ideas on the board.

Access the Leonardo Web site, and share and discuss the suggested design challenges (be inventive). Have students select one of the design challenges, either from Leonardo's challenges or from the modern challenges, and work with partners to sketch inventions that would solve the challenges. Have students share their designs and explain how the inventions meet the challenges.

■ Activity Focus: Inventors: Their Lives and Careers

Technology Connection: Information Retrieval (ISTE-students 5)

Collaboration:
- Researching: Media specialist working with small groups of students from the classroom
- Developing the product: Teacher
- Presenting to the class: Teacher
- Evaluating: Teacher and media specialist together

Resources:
- Print and electronic resources for researching, e.g.., books, encyclopedias, Internet, other databases
- Inventors Hall of Fame Web site: <www.invent.org/book/book-text/indexbyname.html>
- Index cards, larger size, enough for five per student

Preparation Tasks:
- Bookmark the "Inventors Hall of Fame" Web site on several computers in the media center <www.invent.org/book/book-text/indexbyname.html> (Inventors Hall of Fame).
- Prepare a bulletin board display for the research results. (See Figure 3.2.)

Assignment Description:
Pick an inventor and tell about his or her inventions. Use index cards to report your research findings.

Card 1: The name of the inventor

Card 2: The century in which the inventor worked, e.g., 1600s, 1800s, or 2000s. Often, the inventor was born in one century but made his or her discoveries in another century. Students should list the century in which the invention was made.

Card 3: The invention: make a drawing of the invention and label it.

Inventors and Their Accomplishments

	Inventor	Inventor	Inventor	Inventor
The Century				
The Invention				
It's a Fact				
Did You Know?				

Figure 3.2 Bulletin Board Display: Inventors

Card 4: Summary of interesting facts learned about the inventor, e.g., challenges and unusual jobs or experiences.

Card 5: Explanation of how this inventor's idea has made our lives better or easier.

Assignment Notes:

Access the "Inventors Hall of Fame" Web site; show students how to browse the site to select an inventor and to read the entry to gather information for the bulletin board display. Although the Web site entries will not give students all the information they need, show students how to read and sort through the information for its possibilities. Identify the information that still needs to be gathered, and brainstorm other sources, e.g., a picture of the invention or more biographical facts. Using markers, show students how to complete their index cards so that they are eye-catching and easy to read on the bulletin board.

Create a schedule for small groups of students to conduct research in the media center. Once the index cards are completed, show students how to post them on the bulletin board display. When the display is complete, take a tour and have each student share information about his or her inventor.

■ Activity Focus: In the News: All About Inventing, Inventors, and Inventions

Technology Connection: Information Retrieval (ISTE-students 5), Student Productivity (ISTE-students 3)

Collaboration:
- Introducing the project and gathering information: Media specialist with teacher participating
- Writing the news articles/developing the art entries: Teacher
- Typing the articles and scanning the artwork: Teacher and media specialist together in the computer lab
- Creating the newspaper: Media specialist
- Evaluation rubric: Students, teacher, media specialist

Resources:
- Print and electronic resources for researching, e.g., books, encyclopedias, Internet, other databases
- Newspapers (Save the newspaper for several days so that students will have a variety of sources to examine as they begin writing their news articles.)
- Word-processing program, e.g., *AppleWorks*
- Scanner

Preparation Tasks:
- Create a list of reporter assignments for the newspaper. (See Figure 3.3 on page 68.)
- Make overhead transparencies of the reporter assignments, the sample news article "Women Have Always Been Inventors," and one or two short articles from the local newspaper.
- Set up a schedule for research and development of the newspaper.
- Reserve computer lab time so that students can type their news articles and scan their artwork.

Who Is the Greatest Inventor?

Read about famous inventors and what they invented. Prepare a survey and ask other students and teachers who they choose as the greatest inventors. Tally the votes and write about the results of your survey.

Invention
Write a poem describing your understanding of invention. Use the letters of the word to write your poem:
I
N
V
E
N
T
I
O
N

Who Invented Ordinary Things?

Choose two ordinary objects that have been invented and write a newspaper article telling who, what, when, where, why, and how they were invented. Illustrate your article.

Invention Chains

Inventions often happen in chains. One discovery or invention makes the next one possible. Choose an invention and trace its history. Make a time line showing its development.

How Does It Work?

Pick an invention and tell how it works through diagrams and description.

Worst and Best Inventions?

Read about and brainstorm a list of inventions that have been very significant for mankind. Prepare a survey and ask other students and teachers to identify what they think is the worst invention and the best invention. Tally the votes and write about the results of your survey.

Is Necessity the Mother of Invention?

Inventions often take place because of a need or a problem. Make a list of inventions and identify the need or problem that preceded the invention. For example, a way to travel in a skyscraper without having to climb stairs is an elevator.

Who Are the Women Inventors?

Write a book review on *Mothers of Invention: From the Bra to the Bomb: Forgotten Women and Their Unforgettable Ideas*, by Ethlie Vare. Tell about some of these women and what they invented.

Believe It or Not?

Make a list of fun, informational facts about inventions, using the *Guinness Book of World Records* or other trivia books.

The Invention Cartoon

Work with a partner to create a cartoon strip on inventing.

What's in a Patent?

Research the history of the patent and write an informational article for the New Inventor: When did patenting begin, what is a patent, and how do you get one?

Figure 3.3 Reporter Assignments

Assignment Description:
Students choose assignments and create a newspaper about inventors, inventions, and inventing. Give students instruction in developing news articles and writing interesting headlines.

Women Have Always Been Inventors

by Erin Huven

Mothers of Invention by Ethlie Vare tells the true stories behind many of the things we use today and gives credit to the many female inventors in history. Hertha Ayrton helped save the lives of thousands of soldiers during World War 1 with her invention of the anti-gas fan. Bette Nesmith Grahman invented *Liquid Paper* because she was a terrible typist. She brought white paint to work to white out her mistakes, then set about improving her discovery. She read and talked to a few people and set up a laboratory in her kitchen. Her garage became a bottling factory; eventually she sold her *Liquid Paper* and became a millionaire. Mellita Bentz was another forgotten inventor. She got so sick and tired of bitter-tasting coffee that she took a piece of blotting paper and put it in the bottom of a pot that she had punched holes in. She put the coffee grounds on the paper and let the water flow through them. The rest is history. This solved the problem of bitter-tasting coffee and began the era of drip coffee. Her husband helped her make more of these pots and they called them Mellita's Coffee. These are just two of the inventors whose stories are told in the book *Mothers of Invention: From the Bra to the Bomb: Forgotten Women and Their Unforgettable Ideas*, by Ethlie Vare; William Morrow & Co., 1988. This book reminds us of the many women behind the everyday inventions and discoveries that have changed our lives.

■ Activity Focus: Inventing

Technology Connection: Teacher Delivery of Lessons, Classroom Management (ISTE-teacher II-V)

Collaboration:
- Gathering invention idea resources: Media specialist
- Facilitating the invention process: Teacher
- Promoting the Invention Fair: Parents, students, teacher, media specialist
- Sponsoring the Invention Fair: Teacher and media specialist

Resources: A variety of magazines that feature invention ideas, e.g., *National Geographic World*, *Odyssey*, and *Owl*

Preparation Tasks:

- Access the 3M Web site <http://mustang.coled.umn.edu/inventing/Inventing.html> and review the four steps—scout, wizard, critic, and trailblazer—and decide on the helpful hints for students you will use from the Web site. Create an inventors journal for students to use as they make their inventions. (See Figure 3.4 for suggested journal pages.)
- Bookmark the Alexander Graham Bell Web site <http://memory.loc.gov/ammem/bellhtml/bellhome.html> (interesting family papers and examples from his science notebooks).

Inventor's Journal

Journal pages 1–3: gathering ideas	Journal page 4: my best ideas	Journal page 5: my solution grid	Journal page 6: my proposed invention	Journal page 7: my design	Journal page 8: selling my design

Figure 3.4 Inventors Journal

Assignment Description:

Set up or distribute the inventing journals. Review each step of the process and have students begin with the idea-gathering stage. Use suggestions from the 3M Web site listed under the "scout" step; give students two to three days to gather ideas. Access the Alexander Graham Bell site and show students selected pages from his notebook to model recording ideas in the students' journals. Encourage them to visit with family members and other adults.

Use pages 4 and 5 in the journal to narrow the ideas to one selection. Have students list their six to eight best ideas on page 4, then create a solution grid on page 5. (See Figure 3.5 for a sample grid.) Brainstorm criteria for the grid, e.g., expense, time, danger, and do it myself. Use a scale of 1 (challenging), 3 (okay), and 5 (no problem) to rate each idea. Select the idea that receives the most points.

Have students use pages 6 and 7 in the journal to describe and design the invention. In describing the invention, students should address these questions: What is the invention? Who

Solution Grid

Ideas	Criterion 1	Criterion 2	Criterion 3	Criterion 4	Total Score

Figure 3.5 Assessment Checklist

Integrating Technology: Effective Tools for Collaboration

will use the invention? How will it be used? When? Where? Have students use page 7 in the journal to illustrate the features of the invention and identify the materials used in the design. Students can use after-school hours to make the invention.

Once the invention models are made and at school, have students use page 8 in their journals to plan promotion campaigns for their inventions. Use the "trailblazer" guidelines from the 3M Web site to guide their thinking and brainstorming: product, price, promotion, and place. Sponsor an Invention Fair. Invite family members and other guests. Set up the inventions, have copies of the newspaper available, and create a display showing the animal skills inventions drawings and graph from the *Global Schoolhouse* collaboration.

Insects in My Backyard		
Information Retrieval	**Student Productivity**	**Problem Solving and Decision Making**
Internet Web sites: **Butterfly Gardens:** <www.uky.edu/Agriculture/Entomology/entfacts/misc/ef006.htm> **Frequently Asked Questions:** <www.mesc.usgs.gov/butterfly/butterflyfaq.html>	Slide Show: Our Favorite Insect Books	
		Communication and Collaboration
		Letter to Eric Carle through his Web site: eric-carle.com
Teacher Delivery of Lessons		**Classroom Management**
Internet Web sites: **More About Crickets:** <www.pca.state.mn.us/kids/c-september.html> **Insect Anatomy:** <www.bijlmakers.com> **Ladybug Information:** <www.enchantedlearning.com/subjects/insects/Ladybug.shtml> Reading Journal Alphabet book pages		Assessment rubrics for evaluating A to Z book contributions and the slide show contributions Letter to families **Awesome Clipart for Kids:** <www.awesomeclipartforkids.com/> **Web Clip Art:** <http://webclipart.tqn.com/internet/webclipart/msub64.htm> Celebration of learning invitation

Figure 3.6 Insects in My Backyard Unit: Technology Connections

Unit 2: Insects in My Backyard

Unit Objectives:
1. Gain skill in these science processes: observing, classifying, and experimenting.
2. Develop understanding of key concepts in science, i.e., insects have a cycle of life, an insect's body helps it survive, some insects are helpful, and some insects are harmful.

Audience: Grades K–2

Length of the Unit: 3 weeks

The Unit Activities at a Glance

Crickets	Butterflies
Students create a habitat for crickets, choose books for independent reading, research questions about crickets, and develop a class slide show.	Students create a butterfly habitat, research questions about butterflies, and develop an A to Z butterfly book.

Structures	Ladybugs	A Celebration of Learning
Students learn an insect's body parts and create imaginary insects.	Students learn about ladybugs, create a ladybug habitat, listen to a story by Eric Carle, compose a letter to Carle, and create original puppet shows.	Students plan a celebration, and invite families to share in the products and learning from the unit.

Figure 3.6a Insects in My Backyard, The Unit Activities at a Glance

■ Activity Focus: Crickets

Technology Connection: Student Productivity (ISTE-students 3), Teacher Delivery of Lessons, Classroom Management (ISTE-teacher II-V)

Collaboration:
- Introducing and observing the crickets: Teacher
- Gathering resources for reading: Media specialist
- Creating the slide show: Media specialist with teacher assisting

Resources:
- *The Very Quiet Cricket,* by Eric Carle (Philomel, 1990)
- A variety of books about insects, enough for one per student
- Projection system
- Crickets (check in the telephone book for a local supplier; look under pet supplies)

- habitat containers: three or four plastic tanks with lids or two aquaria with lids
- sand in small containers
- crumbled paper or parts of egg cartons
- small plastic lids fitted with pieces of sponge (water for the crickets)
- foods: moist carrot, apple or potato, powdered cereal, bread crumbs

Preparation Tasks:
- Use a word processing program to create a stationery template that you can use throughout the year as you write letters to parents. Many clip art Web sites offer fun choices; some favorites include <www.awesomeclipartforkids.com/> (Awesome Clipart for Kids) and <http://webclipart.tqn.com/internet/webclipart/msub64.htm> (click on "school and school related"). (See Figure 3.7 for an example.) Develop a letter to parents explaining the activities of the insects unit.
- Gather a variety of insect books for students to use for independent reading. Prepare booktalks on the titles.
- Use a word processing program to create a response journal for students to use as they read their insect books. (See Figure 3.8.) Print and bind multiple copies, enough for one per student.

Figure 3.7 Stationery Template

Reading Journal

Reading Journal (Picture drawn by child) Name:	Title of My Book: Author of My Book:	My favorite part...	My second favorite part...	I learned...	I think...

Figure 3.8 Reading Journal

- Bookmark the Web sites <www.pca.state.mn.us/kids/c-september.html> for an interesting source of information about crickets. Arrange for research buddies, if needed, i.e., older students who can help students read the information.
- Set up a slide show template for students to use as they illustrate scenes from their favorite insect books. A template lets students begin immediately on their artwork without worrying about margins and setup details.

Assignment Descriptions:

The Cricket's Habitat: Show the container of crickets and have students participate in creating a habitat for the crickets. Have students make observations and draw pictures of the crickets, e.g., in the habitat, using its legs, and searching for food.

Introduce and read the story. Discuss how the cricket's body helps it survive. Travel to the media center to hear booktalks and to choose insect books for independent reading. Introduce the reading journal (see Figure 3.8) and have students write their names and draw pictures on the covers. Review the pages in the journal and discuss what students will be recording, i.e., title and author of the book on page 2, illustrations of two favorite parts of the story, writing about facts they learned, and writing about what they think about insects now that they have read the book. If students need assistance with the writing parts of the journal, make this an at-home connection activity and encourage students to dictate their ideas to a family member.

More About Insects: A Slide Show: Begin with a KWL (What we know, what we want to know, what we learned) brainstorming about crickets. What do we know from our observations and from the story we read? (List those ideas under "Know.") What questions do we have? (List those questions under "Want.")

Access the bookmarked Web site, and browse the information together as a class to see if you can find answers to the students' questions. Dramatize parts of the information or take time to observe the live crickets in their habitats to help students make connections to the information. Add information to the "Learned" column after reviewing the information.

Introduce the slide show template and show students how to draw scenes from their books. Set up a schedule with the media center so that students can work in small groups creating the slide show. This could be a center activity, and students should take their books and their reading journals to the library when they work on the slide show. (Teacher's note: When all the slides are created, put the show together and schedule a time for a class viewing. Continue to have the show available for students to browse on their own time.)

■ Activity Focus: Butterflies

Technology Connection: Information Retrieval (ISTE-students 5)

Collaboration:
- Introducing and observing caterpillars: Teacher
- Completing A to Z butterfly research: Media specialist with teacher assisting

Resources:
- *The Very Hungry Caterpillar*, by Eric Carle (Philomel, 1969)
- Butterfly caterpillars (available from Carolina Biological Supply Company, 2700 York Road, Burlington, North Carolina 27215. Telephone: 1-800-227-1150. Web site: <www.carolina.com/>)
- Habitat container: a plastic box with a lid or an aquarium with a lid
- Caterpillar foods, i.e., plants from the Mallow family, sage, dandelion
- Musical selection that will help students float like butterflies

Preparation Tasks:
- Create alphabet pages for the A to Z butterfly book. (See figure 3.9.)

Figure 3.9 Alphabet Page Template

- Use these topic headings for each letter of the alphabet:

All Kinds	Butterflies	Caterpillars
Dust	Endangered	Food
Growing a Caterpillar	Homes	Into a Butterfly
Just as Fun	Know the Time	Life Cycle
Moths	Names	On the Wing: Flying
Pollinator	Quite an Insect	Rain
Sleep	Talking	Unusual Facts
Very Pretty	Wings	X Marks the Spot: Favorite Flowers
Yea	Zipping Around	

- Create slips of paper listing the topic headings and the question numbers (from the Frequently Asked Questions Web site) that give information about the topic.

All Kinds, Question 2	Butterflies, Questions 1 and 3
Caterpillars, Questions 15, 20, 35, 39, 40	Dust, Question 24
Endangered, Question 9	Food, Questions 17 and 18
Growing a Caterpillar, Question 11	Homes, Question 5
Into a Butterfly, Questions 16 and 23	Just as Fun, Any Question, open topic
Know the Time, Question 38	Life Cycle, Question 4
Moths, Questions 1 and 3	Names, Question 30
On the Wing: Flying, Questions 22 and 26	Pollinator, Question 42
Quite an Insect, Any Question, open topic	Rain, Question 19
Sleep, Question 36	Talking, Question 25
Unusual Facts, Any Question, open topic	Very Pretty, Question 21
Wings, Questions 7 and 8	Year, Question 32
X Marks the Spot: Favorite Flowers, Access the Butterfly Garden Web site.	Zipping Around, Questions 22 and 26

- Bookmark these Web sites: <www.uky.edu/Agriculture/Entomology/entfacts/misc/ef006.htm> (how to make butterfly gardens); <www.mesc.usgs.gov/butterfly/butterfly-faq.html> (frequently asked questions about butterflies and moths).
- Arrange for the class to work with reading buddies for the research and writing, i.e., older students who can read the information and help the students understand the facts, take notes, and write the information for the alphabet page. Research can be scheduled as a whole-class project if you have access to a computer lab. Student partners (primary-age student and his or her reading buddy from an upper grade) would work together at a computer accessing the information, reading it, and deciding what notes to record. Research also can be facilitated in small groups. Work with the reading buddy partners to identify a block of time each day where groups of students could come to the classroom or the media center and complete the research. Schedule a second collaboration time where students and their reading buddy partners can work together to turn the notes into sentences for the alphabet pages. Reading partners also can help students identify and plan the pictures they will draw to illustrate their facts.

Assignment Descriptions:

Introducing Butterflies: Share *The Very Hungry Caterpillar*. Identify the foods eaten by the caterpillar in the story. List these foods on a chart, and save the information for later in the lesson.

Construct the habitat for the caterpillars and release them into the habitat. Students will be eager to observe the habitat. Schedule center time after this lesson so that one center can be an opportunity to observe the caterpillars in their habitat. Encourage students to draw as they observe.

More About Butterflies: Play music and have students float like butterflies; then have them use their bodies to dramatize the life cycle of the butterfly.

Egg: Remain on your feet, crouch, and curl into a tight ball.

Larva: Uncurl, become a caterpillar, and begin to crawl.

Pupa: Lie on your side, draw your legs close, and pretend to sleep, wrapped tightly in your chrysalis.

Adult: Stretch, unfurl, slowly fan your wings, then fly.

Focus again on the foods caterpillars eat and review the list of foods from the story. Create a second column on the chart and have students decide if a caterpillar would really eat this food. Speculate about foods butterflies eat. A suggestion from the University of Kentucky Department of Entomology says that butterflies will form puddle clubs when tempted with small pools of sugary or salty water. Bury a bucket to the rim and fill it with gravel. Then sweet and salty liquids can be a permanent puddle for them to use.

Introduce the A to Z butterfly book. Show students the Web site of frequently asked questions and review the list of questions. Show the alphabet pages and talk about the requirements. Have students choose assignments by drawing slips from a basket. Staple or glue the strips to a blank piece of paper. Set goals for researching.

When students and their reading buddy partners have taken notes, have them work together to prepare a rough draft of the alphabet page, i.e., the facts and the picture. Conference with the students, then have them prepare final drafts for the butterfly book. Gather the pages and bind the book. Share it with students and invite the author of each page to comment, if interested.

■ Activity Focus: Structures

Technology Connection: Teacher delivery of lessons (ISTE-teacher II-III)

Collaboration: Insect parts: Teacher

Resources:
- Drawing paper, folded into thirds, enough for one piece per student
- Illustrating materials, e.g., markers or crayons
- Projection system

Preparation Tasks: Bookmark the Web site <www.bijlmakers.com/> and connect the computer to the projection system.

Assignment Description:
Play "Simon Says" to name human body parts and make them work: head (nod, turn, shake), chest (breathe in and out), legs (What can my legs do? jump, run, skip, hop, walk, bicycle), arms (How do I use my arms? lift, reach, tug).

Focus on the body parts of insects. Show the first page of the Internet site and allow speculation. (Teacher's note: Don't click yet!) Click on the body parts, share some of the information, then create movements or comparisons to the human body to help students remember the insect's body parts: head, thorax, stomach, six legs (three pairs), and two antennae.

Have students use the drawing paper and illustrating materials to make their own imaginary insects. Circulate as students work, encouraging them to include the required body parts. Create a chant to help students remember the insect's body parts. Show pictures of a variety of creatures and ask students if the creature is an insect.

■ Activity Focus: Ladybugs

Technology Connection: Communication and Collaboration (ISTE-students 4), Teacher Delivery of Lessons (ISTE-teacher II-III)

Collaboration:
- Gathering resources: Media specialist
- Introducing and observing ladybugs: Teacher

Resources:
- A book about ladybugs:
  The Grouchy Ladybug, by Eric Carle (New York: Harper Collins, 1977)
  A Ladybug's Life (Nature Upclose), by John Himmelman (New York: Children's Press, 1998)
  Ladybug: Portable Pets (Portable Pets), by Lorella Rizzatti (Illustrator), Rossana Papagni (New York: Henry Abrams, 1998)
- Ladybugs, available in spring from most garden centers (Check the telephone book.)
- Leaves with aphids, also available from garden centers
- Large aquarium with a tight mesh cover
- Variety of seedlings (flowers and weeds)
- Magnifying glasses or cardboard tubes, one per student

Preparation Tasks:
Bookmark these Web sites:
- <www.enchantedlearning.com/subjects/insects/Ladybug.shtml>. Read through the information and decide how you wish to share it with the students. Select one of the craft activities and gather the needed supplies.
- <http://www.eric-carle.com/> (official Web site for the children's author, Eric Carle)

Assignment Description:
Share a book about ladybugs. Create a web of information learned from the book; add information learned from the ladybug Web site. Create a habitat for the ladybugs.

Have students imagine that they are the size of ladybugs. What would the world look like? Go to an outdoor grassy area, use magnifying glasses or cardboard tubes (everything seems bigger when you look through these objects), crawl around and look very closely at the magic world of insects. How does it feel? What do you imagine?

Brainstorm a list of insects and create a chart identifying them as helpful or harmful. (See Figure 3.10.)

Releasing the Ladybugs: Observe the plants in the terrarium and ask students to identify which plants the ladybugs will choose. Record the selections. (A quick sketch with circles around the selected plants will help students see at a glance the chosen plants.) Before introducing the ladybugs, place the aphid-filled leaves in various spots in the terrarium. Release the ladybugs, replace

Insect	Helpful	Harmful
Honeybee	Gives us honey	
Mosquito		Stings, spreads disease
Butterfly	Makes more flowers (pollinates)	
Moth		Eats clothes
Caterpillar	Provides food for birds	Eats plant leaves

Figure 3.10 Helpful and Harmful Insects

the lid, and watch what happens. Continue to observe until students lose interest. Check the terrarium the next day to identify where the ladybugs have settled. Discuss: Do ladybugs like some plants better than others? Why? If you want ladybugs to live in your garden to eat insect pests, which plants would you grow to attract them?

Communicating with Eric Carle: As a class, compose a letter to Mr. Carle, sharing what students have learned in their study of ladybugs and what they enjoyed about his book. Access his official Web site, click on the guest book, and type and send the letter. Check the mail each day to watch for a response.

Ladybug Fun: Use one of the craft suggestions from the ladybug Web site. Have students work together to create original puppet shows with their craft projects.

■ Activity Focus: A Celebration of Learning

Technology Connection: Classroom Management (ISTE-teacher IV-V)

Collaboration: Celebrating the unit: Teacher and media specialist together

Resources:
- The various products of the unit, i.e., slide show, A to Z Book of Butterflies, letter to Mr. Carle, and imaginary insect pictures
- Insect stations: crickets, ladybugs, and caterpillars
- Insect stickers: available at office supply stores, discount stores, or teacher supply stores

Preparation Tasks:
- Work with students to prepare an invitation to families for the celebration of learning. (See Figure 3.11.) Use a word processing program to print the information. Give students time to add personal touches, i.e., illustrations and salutations. When students are finished, fold the invitations, seal with insect stickers and send them home with the students.
- Plan the schedule of events, e.g., slide show viewing, puppet show, a student reading the letter to Mr. Carle, another puppet show, showing the A to Z book, browsing the insect stations, the imaginary insect pictures, and a closer look at the A to Z book. Rehearse so that things go smoothly.
- Set up the room so that there is easy movement and room for the insect stations and the whole-class presentations.

> Please come to our celebration of learning!
>
> We want to share what we have learned about insects!
>
> Tuesday
> 4/25/2001
> 10:00–10:45 a.m.

Figure 3.11 Invitation

Wetlands Exploration

Information Retrieval	Student Productivity	Problem Solving and Decision Making
Electronic encyclopedias, e.g., *World Book*, *Grolier's* Internet sites: **Wet and Wild:** <http://library.thinkquest.org/J003192F/definiti.htm> **Wetland Kids:** <www.wetland.org/kids/kids.htm>	Digital camera pictures on the walking tour/field trip Multimedia presentation: Wild and Wonderful Wetlands Slide Show: Welcome to a Wetlands	**Lost in the Wetland: An Interactive Game:** <http://library.thinkquest.org/J003192F/definiti.htm>
		Communication and Collaboration
		E-mail Collaboration: J003192F@thinkquest.org

Teacher Delivery of Lessons	Classroom Management
Internet sites: **Wetland Kids:** <www.wetland.org/kids/kids/htm> **Wetlands Reading List from the EPA:** <www.epa.gov/owow/wetlands/science/readlist.html>	Assessment rubrics for evaluating the multimedia presentations, the slide show contributions, and the science journals Record-keeping sheet for the digital camera shots

Figure 3.12 Wetlands Exploration Unit: Technology Connections

Unit 3: Wetlands Exploration

Unit Objectives:
1. Practice science process skills: observation, prediction, data gathering, analysis, and interpretation.
2. Understand the value of wetlands habitats.

Audience: Grades 1–3

Length of the Unit: 3 weeks

The Unit Activities at a Glance

A Walking Tour	Discovering More	Wild and Wonderful Wetlands
Students visit a wetlands, make observations in their journals, and take soil and water samples.	Students learn more about different kinds of wetlands and meet in teams to decide the type of wetlands they visited.	Students learn more about the benefits/importance of wetlands and work in teams to develop multimedia presentations.
Wetlands Couplets	**Exploring Wetlands**	**Describing Our Wetlands**
Students write couplets to accompany digital camera images taken on the walking tour and construct a class slide show of the tour.	Students complete the "Lost in the Wetlands" challenge.	Students communicate electronically, sharing information about their school and the wetlands projects.

Figure 3.12a Wetlands Exploration, The Unit Activities at a Glance

■ Activity Focus: A Walking Tour

Technology Connection: Teacher Delivery of Lessons (ISTE-teacher II-III)

Collaboration:
- Gathering resources for reading: Media specialist
- Introducing the project: Teacher

Resources:
- Digital camera
- Clipboards
- Small plastic containers, enough for two per small group of five students (Teacher's note: Students will use the containers to scoop water samples; containers should be clean.)
- Aquarium
- Five sieve containers for soil samples (Teacher's note: Two-liter soda bottles can be used; cut the bottle in half, invert the top into the bottom and tape it in place. The soil will rest in the top portion, and the water will drip through the top of the bottle into the bottom.)

- Shovel or digging trowel for gathering the soil samples
- Plastic wrap to cover the soil samples so that they don't dry out

Preparation Tasks:
- For background information about wetlands, access this Web site <www.wetland.org/kids/Kids.htm> or check out a book from the library. *Wetlands*, by Lynn M. Stone (Vero Beach, Florida: Rourke Enterprises, 1989), is a quick and easy read and is filled with great information. According to scientists, wetlands habitats are hard to define because there are different kinds and they can be found in many locations. Most sources describe these types: bog, swamp (saltwater and freshwater), and marsh (saltwater and freshwater). If you can, locate a wetlands area within walking distance of your school. Otherwise, plan a field trip to a wetlands area in your region.

Wetlands Journal	Date

Figure 3.13 Journal

- The Environmental Protection Agency has prepared a wetlands reading list. Access the Web site <www.epa.gov/owow/wetlands/science/readlist.html> and gather some of the titles for students to use for independent reading/browsing.
- Use a word processing program to create a journal for the students. (See Figure 3.13.) Make multiple copies of the form, preferably on three-hole paper; students will use the journal forms in their walking tours to the wetlands area, then they will insert them into loose-leaf notebooks or folders on their return to the classroom.
- Use a program such as Microsoft Excel to create a form like the example in Figure 3.14 so that students

View	Photographer	Direction	Notes
1	Tanisha	Looking west	Red-winged blackbird in the cattails
2	Jimmy	North side	Prints in the mud
3	Shawna	Looking west	Cattails
4	Daniel	Looking east	Frogs on the log
5	Meri Sue	East side	Close-up: Hundreds of snails
6			
7			
8			

Figure 3.14 Record-keeping Sheet for Camera Shots

82 Integrating Technology: Effective Tools for Collaboration

can record their camera shots from the walking tour. Print a copy and have students record information about their camera shots.
- Create a Venn diagram comparison sheet. (See Figure 3.15.) Students will use the form to compare a wetlands soil sample and a non-wetlands soil sample.

Assignment Description:

Create a KWHL (Know, Want to Know, How to Find Out, Learned) chart on the board or a large sheet of butcher paper. (See Figure 3.16.) Pose this question: What do you know about wetlands? Give thinking time, then record responses on the chart. Don't worry about inaccurate responses at this time; students will periodically revisit the chart to confirm what is known. Responses you might receive from students include the following: animals live there, snails and fish, stumps of trees, swampy-looking, a pond, ducks and geese, cattails, or it's wet all the time.

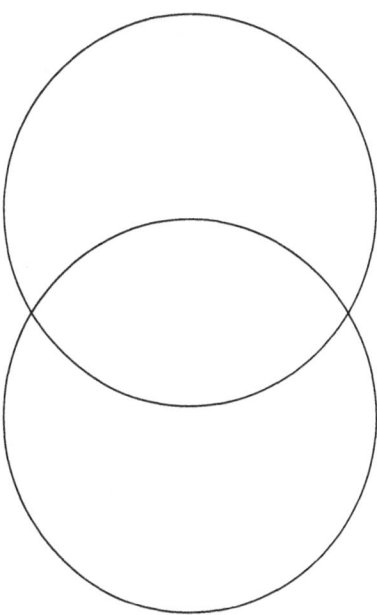

Figure 3.15 Venn Comparison

Divide the class into groups of five, distribute copies of the wetlands journal pages (at least two per student) and the clipboards, and set goals for the walking tour. Have students use notebook paper to record the goals and add these notes to their clipboards so that they have reminders for the walking tour/field trip.

Here's an example of goal setting:
Aim: Explore the Wetlands
Goal #1: Work carefully. The only things that should get wet or muddy are our hands.
Goal #2: When we arrive, find a spot to sit and observe for a while. Draw a picture and make notes about my observations.
Goal #3: Use the digital camera to take a picture of some angle of the wetlands area. Record notes about the picture on the camera sheet.
Goal #4: Work with my group to gather a soil sample. Be sure to record the location where the sample was taken and cover it with the plastic wrap (so it will not dry out) as soon as it is placed in the two-liter sieve.
Goal #5: Work with my group to gather two water samples. Use my wetlands journal to record observations and notes about the samples.

Wetlands

What We Know	What We Want To Know	How We Will Find Out	What We Learned

Take the walking tour/field trip and complete the assignments. (Teacher's note: The walking tour/field trip is a discovery experience. In the second lesson, "Discovering More," students will learn more about the types of wetlands, then meet in their small groups to classify the wetlands they visited. Classification will be based on the information shared in the "Discovering More" lesson and students' observations and experiences in the walking tour/field trip.)

Figure 3.16 KWHL Chart

Bring the soil and water samples back to the classroom. Pour the water samples into the aquarium. Use a marker to mark the water line of each soil sample (water that has dripped into the bottom of the container). Discuss the experience. What did students discover? What have they learned about wetlands? What questions do they want to explore? (Add the questions to the KWHL chart.)

Preparation Tasks for Later Lessons:

Download the camera images to the computer and save for a later lesson.

Set up two centers so that students can work with partners to make water observations and soil observations. Place the aquarium in the water observation center and place two soil samples in the soil observation center—one sample from the wetlands and one sample from a non-wetlands area. Add hand magnifiers to the centers. Magnifiers can be ordered from Delta Education (P. O. Box 3000, Nashua, New Hampshire 03061-3000; telephone: 1-800-442-5444) in a variety of diameters, from 2½ inches to 4 inches. The cost ranges from $11.95 for the smaller diameter to $18.95 for the larger diameter. Place some of the small plastic containers that students used during the walking tour in the water observation center so that students can scoop samples from the aquarium for observation under the hand lens. Place small paper plates and craft sticks/bamboo skewers (available from most grocery stores) in the soil observation center. Use a word processing program to prepare direction cards for the centers.

The water observation directions might include the following:

Water Observations

Use a page in your wetlands journal to draw a picture of the aquarium water sample, and record changes you observe in the water in the aquarium. Scoop a small amount of water from the aquarium and observe this sample under the hand lens. Discuss your observations with your partner and draw a picture on the back of your journal page to record your observations and discussion.

Soil Observations

Use the Venn comparison sheet to record your investigations of the soil samples. Label one circle "wetlands soil" and the other circle "non-wetlands soil." Use the probes (craft sticks/bamboo skewers) to closely examine the soil samples on the paper plates. Describe your observations about each soil sample, then work with your partner to compare the soil samples. The overlapping part of the circles should list the ideas that are the same about both soil samples.

■ Activity Focus: Discovering More

Technology Connection: Teacher Delivery of Lessons (ISTE-teacher II-III)

Collaboration: Lesson delivery: Teacher

Resources:
- Wetland Kids Internet site <www.wetland.org/kids/Kids.htm>
- Projection system
- Journal pages, multiple copies for the students
- Notebook paper

Preparation Tasks: Bookmark the Web site <www.wetland.org/kids/Kids.htm> and connect the projection system.

Assignment Description:
Refer to the questions column of the KWHL chart and review some of the questions that might be answered by today's lesson on characteristics and types of wetlands. Display the Web site, click on the icon "What Is a Wetland?" and discuss and review the "Common Wetlands Habitats" information. Have students use notebook paper (be sure they date the page, just like real scientists) to record notes listing key characteristics of each type of wetlands habitat. For younger students, use chart paper and create class lists.

Have students meet in their groups to discuss and decide the type of wetlands they visited in their walking tour/field trip. Have the groups choose reporters, discussion facilitators, and timekeepers, and encourage thoughtful discussion and decision making. Reporters report the decisions of the groups and the reasoning behind the decisions. Timekeepers keep the groups aware of the time limits. Discussion facilitators lead the discussion. Invite sharing and draw conclusions about the type of wetlands that the class visited.

■ Activity Focus: Wild and Wonderful Wetlands

Technology Connection: Information Retrieval (ISTE-students 5), Student Productivity (ISTE-students 3), Teacher Delivery of Lessons (ISTE-teacher II-III)

Collaboration:
- Preparing forms: Media specialist and teacher together
- Introducing the activity and research: Media specialist with teacher assisting
- Planning the storyboards: Media specialist and teacher as co-facilitators
- Developing multimedia presentations: Media specialist and teacher as co-facilitators
- Presentations: Media specialist and teacher as members of the audience
- Evaluations: Media specialist and teacher together

Resources:
- Wetland Kids Internet site: <www.wetland.org/kids/Kids.htm>
- Multimedia software, e.g., *HyperStudio, Kid Pix, PowerPoint*
- Projection system
- Notebook paper, one sheet per student

Preparation Tasks:
- Schedule a planning meeting where the teacher and media specialist can set a time line for completion of the project, i.e., research time, storyboard preparation, and development of the multimedia presentations. Also arrange a library and computer lab schedule.
- Create a note-taking graphic organizer. (See Figure 3.17.) Make a transparency of the form and multiple copies for the students. To facilitate collaborative group work and reduce the

chance of lost research notes, create a storage space for each group's research findings, i.e., file folders in a stand-up file, and baskets or boxes labeled with each habitat type.

- Create a storyboard planning sheet. (See Figure 3.18.) Make a transparency and multiple copies for the students.

Assignment Description:

Display the Web site, click on "What Wetlands Do for You," and review and discuss the information. Encourage students to take notes about the benefits and importance of wetlands habitats. For first-grade students, use chart paper to make a class list of benefits and importance.

List the wetlands habitats—bog, freshwater swamp, saltwater swamp, freshwater marsh, and saltwater marsh—and begin brainstorming for the Wild and Wonderful Wetlands project. Divide the class into teams; each team will select a wetlands habitat and prepare a multimedia presentation on that habitat. Brainstorm and decide on topics to include in the presentations about the wetlands habitats; keep it simple for younger students. (Students will have lots of ideas, but if they are stumped, here are some possibilities: a catchy slogan, location information or a map, pictures and descriptions of the characteristics of the habitat, pictures and reasons why this type of wetlands is important, animals and plants that live here, foods from the wetlands, links to more information, and facts at a glance.)

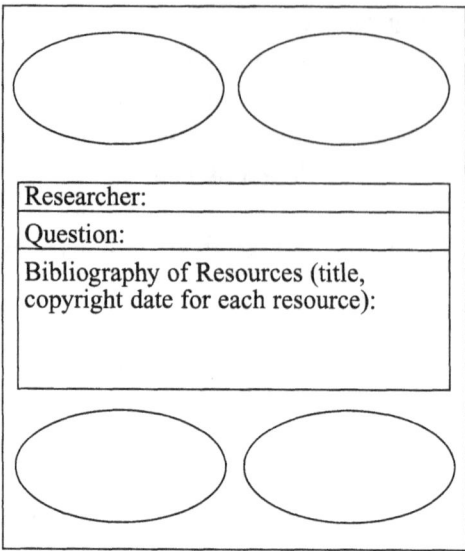

Figure 3.17 Note-taking Graphic Organizer

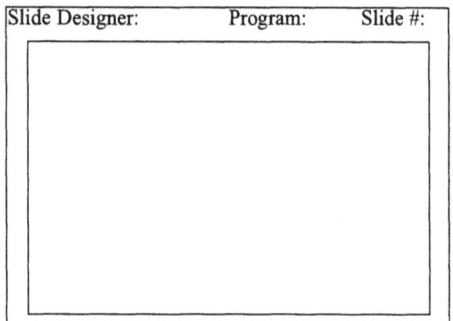

Figure 3.18 Storyboard Planning Sheet

Review the time line for the project so that students are clear about deadlines. Display the note-taking graphic organizer, and show students how to use it and where to store it when it is completed. Remind students to be thorough and careful in completing their research notes/pictures because other members of the group are relying on their input and will be using the findings. Give students practice in writing simple bibliography citations: title of the resource and copyright date. (Teacher's note: Younger students can draw pictures to show information they have gathered, e.g., animals, plants, and foods, and can use reading buddies to assist them in recording simple facts.)

Create a rubric for evaluating the finished presentations. (See Figure 3.19.) When students have completed information gathering, review the rubric to remind students of the requirements for their presentations and introduce the storyboard planning form. Have students discuss and plan their presentations and divide storyboard preparation assignments so that each member of the group makes a contribution. Use the scheduled computer time to create the multimedia shows. To share the finished projects, connect a presentation system to the computer and have each team present to the class.

■ Activity Focus: Wetlands Couplets

Technology Connection: Student Productivity (ISTE-students 3)

Collaboration:
- Delivering the lesson: Teacher and media specialist working collaboratively
- Developing the slide show: Media specialist and teacher working together

Resources:
- Slide show program, e.g., *Appleworks, PowerPoint*
- Digital camera images from the wetlands walking tour/field trip (See the first lesson, A Walking Tour, where students took the pictures)
- Picture/poster showing an interesting landscape

Preparation Tasks:
- Decide if the couplet writing will be a center activity or a small group-, teacher-, or media specialist-directed activity.
- Create a brainstorming sheet for the students. (See Figure 3.20.) This will help them be systematic in creating their couplets. Make multiple copies and a transparency of the form.

Assignment Description:
Give students practice in writing couplets. Show the landscape poster/picture you have selected so that students have time to carefully examine it. Brainstorm a list of words and phrases that describe the key elements of the picture, e.g., misty sky, craggy rocks, pine trees reaching into the clouds, soft grays and purples, and eagles soar and float.

Introduce the requirements for couplet writing:
1. End words rhyme.
2. The two lines express one thought.
3. The poem is limited to two lines.
4. You should focus on rhythm.

Use the students' ideas to write a first line for the couplet, e.g., Eagles soar into the soft, gray, misty sky. Identify the possible rhyming words for sky, by going down the letters of the alphabet and recording any words that rhyme, e.g., aye, bye, die, dye, eye, fly, guy, hi, I, lie,

Student	Outstanding	Strong	Acceptable
Research			
Used a variety of sources			
Had notes, with sources documented			
Restated notes in own words			
Organization of information			
Showed a logical sequence of information			
Included an introduction and a conclusion			
Used graphics to explain the information			
Supported the facts			
Content and Accuracy			
Included up-to-date facts			
Demonstrated depth of knowledge			
Shared Labor			
Contributed research information to the project			
Contributed ideas to the design of the show			
Showed willingness to compromise			
Dependability			
Met deadlines			
Program and Screen Design			
Included a title page with credits			
Used a pleasing type style and contrast			
Included two to four pictures of the habitat			
Sized pictures appropriately			
Provided clear navigation instructions			
Comments:			

Figure 3.19 Wetlands Habitat Rubric

Technology for Science Units 87

my, nigh, pie, rye, sigh, tie, vie, why. Have students work with partners to write a second line for the couplet, e.g., high above the towering pine trees they fly.

Display the transparency of the couplets brainstorming sheet and explain its use. Show students how to access their digital picture images (taken on the Walking Tour and downloaded into the computer), and use the brainstorming sheet to write couplets about the images. Share the center rotation schedule (if couplet writing is a center activity) or the small group rotation schedule (if the writing will be directed by the teacher or the media specialist). (Teacher's note: If couplet writing is too challenging for younger students, have them write simple captions for the pictures.) When all the couplets are written, work with the media specialist to construct the slide show. Work with the students to brainstorm a title for the show.

Student:
Words that describe the scene in my picture:
The first line of my couplet:
Words that rhyme with the last word in Line 1:
The second line of the couplet:
Conference with a partner to share your couplet. Here are some questions to discuss: 1. Does the couplet describe the picture? 2. Do my end words rhyme?

Figure 3.20 Couplets Brainstorming

■ Activity Focus: Exploring Wetlands

Technology Connection: Problem Solving and Decision Making (ISTE-students 6)

Collaboration:
- Preparing support materials: Teacher and media specialist
- Delivering the lesson: Teacher

Resources: Lost in the Wetlands: <http://library.thinkquest.org/J003192F/game.htm>

Preparation Tasks:
- Set up a center in the classroom and bookmark the Web site. (Teacher's note: If you have trouble accessing the site, try the alternate path <http://library.thinkquest.org/>. Type in "wetlands" and select the Wet and Wild site. Browse the site for the game.)
- Work with the media specialist to create a poster showing these animal footprints: dog, deer, muskrat, turtle, otter, beaver, fox, bullfrog, goose, heron, and raccoon. Label each footprint and display the poster in the center.

Activity Description:
Access the Web site and share the opening information: "You and your friends have lost your way in the swamp! If you can follow the animal tracks, you can find your way out. To get out of the swamp, identify each animal track that you come to. But you must hurry! It will be dark soon!" Encourage students to work thoughtfully and keep track of their choices.

When all the students have completed the activity, discuss the skills that helped students make effective choices, e.g., carefully reading the clues, closely examining and comparing the footprints on the screen with the footprints on the poster.

■ Activity Focus: Describing Our Wetlands

Technology Connection: Communication and Collaboration (ISTE-students 4)

Collaboration: Delivering the lesson: Media specialist with teacher assisting

Resources:
- Projection system
- Guest book: <http://library.thinkquest.org/J003192F/visitors.htm>
- Chart paper

Preparation Tasks:
- Bookmark the Web site <http://library.thinkquest.org/J003192F/visitors.htm> and set up the projection system. (Teacher's note: If you have trouble accessing the site, try the alternate path <http://library.thinkquest.org/>. Type in "wetlands" and select the Wet and Wild site. Browse the site for the guest book.)
- Set up a schedule for students to work in small groups in the library to compose the e-mail letter.

Activity Description:

Access the guest book e-mail page and work with the students to compose an introductory letter. The goal of the letter is to describe your state, town/city, school, landscape, and climate features, and to introduce the class. Some questions to ask the students as they think about what to share in the opening letter include the following:

1. How is your state unique?
2. Is your community urban, suburban, or rural?
3. Do most students in the class live in apartments or in houses? Are there yards or gardens around the houses? Do the yards have fences?
3. Describe the school. How many students are in school? How many grade levels are there?
4. How many boys and girls are in the class?
5. What would you like visitors to see and do if they came to your school?
6. How do most students get to school?
7. What are the geographical features of your community, e.g., hills, valleys, other landforms, waterways?
8. What is the climate? What are the summers and winters like?

Compose and send the introductory letter.

Have students work in their original teams (from the walking tour) to continue communication via e-mail. Brainstorm information (words and pictures) students would like to share about the wetlands, and identify questions they have. Encourage students to brainstorm a team name and sign their letters with their team names. Share the schedule for typing and sending the team letters. (Teacher's note: The letters can be typed by a volunteer and sent by the children.) Once the letters are sent, have students select representatives who will check the mail each day. Provide opportunities during the unit for students to share and discuss responses they receive.

	Civil War	
Information Retrieval	**Student Productivity**	**Problem Solving and Decision Making**
Electronic encyclopedias, e.g., *Grolier's*, *World Book* Internet sites: **Letters from an Iowa Soldier During the Civil War** <www.civilwarletters.com/home.html>	Slide Show: Important Leaders of the Civil War	*American History Inspirer: The Civil War* (Tom Snyder Productions)
		Communication and Collaboration

Teacher Delivery of Lessons	**Classroom Management**
Harriet Tubman information packet Abolitionists' Newspaper Note-taking Graphic Organizer	Assessment rubric for evaluating the slide show Record-keeping sheet for the artwork students gather for the slide shows Newsletter to families

Figure 4.1 Civil War Unit: Technology Connections

Chapter 4

Technology for Social Studies Units

Unit 1: Civil War Investigations

Unit Objectives:
1. Understand the causes and effects of the Civil War.
2. Develop awareness of important events and identify the contributions of important leaders of the period.
3. Experience the life of a soldier during the war.

Audience: Grades 6–8

Length of the Unit: 6 weeks

The Unit Activities at a Glance

People of the Civil War	Letters Home	Causes of the Civil War
Students research key figures of the Civil War period and prepare slide show presentations.	Students use the "Letters Home" site to map a soldier's travels, develop understanding of the life of a soldier, and write letters pretending to be soldiers.	Students use a computer simulation to learn about the causes of the Civil War.
Harriet Tubman	**The Abolitionists**	**Newsletters to Families**
Students learn about Harriet Tubman and write a class acrostic poem.	Students learn about the abolitionists and create skits based on information gathered from a teacher-prepared newspaper.	Students participate in developing monthly newsletters to families.

Figure 4.1a Civil War, The Unit Activities at a Glance

■ Activity Focus: People of the Civil War

Technology Connection: Information Retrieval (ISTE-students 5), Student Productivity (ISTE-students 3)

Collaboration:
- Introducing the project and selecting topics: Teacher
- Information searching, note taking, and bibliography preparation: Media specialist with teacher assisting
- Preparing storyboards: Teacher
- Gathering artwork: Media specialist
- Preparing the slide shows: Teacher and media specialist co-facilitating
- Hearing the presentations: Teacher and media specialist as audience members
- Assessment: Shared between the teacher and media specialist

Resources:
- Print and electronic resources for researching, e.g., books, encyclopedias, Internet, other databases
- Slide show program, e.g., *AppleWorks, PowerPoint*
- Scanner/digital camera

Preparation Tasks:
- Create a storyboard planner. (See Figure 4.2.) Make multiple copies of the form; students will use the storyboard sheets to plan their slide shows—one sheet for each frame of the show.
- Create a portfolio template similar to the one in Figure 4.3. Save it as a "stationery" document on your computer, i.e., each time you open the file it will open as an "untitled" document, allow you to make changes for the new project, and save as a new portfolio file. See Figure 4.4 for an example of a revised template for an actual assignment.
- Use a spreadsheet program (e.g., *AppleWorks, Microsoft Excel*) to create an assessment rubric for the slide shows. (See Figure 4.6 on page 94.) Print multiple copies and have them available for the presentations. The students use one column to self-assess, and the teacher or media specialist uses the other column. The final grade is an average of the totals of the two columns.

Figure 4.2 Slide Show Storyboard Planner

Figure 4.3 Portfolio Template

92 *Integrating Technology: Effective Tools for Collaboration*

- Set up an artwork record file on the computer or create it as a form. The file or the form is a good way to keep up with the accomplishments of the students as they gather the artwork for the slide shows. Use a spreadsheet like *Microsoft Excel* to create the file/form like the example in Figure 4.5. Print a copy if you use it as a form, and have students record information about their accomplishments, or leave it on the computer and train students to access the file and record their accomplishments. Students list dates of completion and keywords that identify the types of graphics they are gathering. Check the file periodically and communicate with the teacher.
- As soon as students identify potential artwork for their slide shows, they should arrange time with the media specialist to scan, clip, import, or bookmark their selections. These can be stored in a zip drive file or on a network server.

Assignment Description:

Have students research people involved in the Civil War and prepare slide shows sharing what they have learned. Their presentations should include answers to these key questions: Why is this person remembered? What information can you find about this person's early life (birth, childhood, parents, education, hobbies, and experiences)? What career facts can you find? How did these experiences prepare this person for a role during the Civil War? Why was this person an important figure during the Civil War period?

Other requirements:

- Research sources: at least one electronic source and one print source
- Artwork: at least two historical illustrations/photographs (They may be scanned or imported from an electronic resource. Be sure to cite the sources of the artwork.) As soon as you identify graphics, arrange with the media specialist to scan or import the images.
- Slide show: should include a title frame, a credits (bibliography) frame, and at least three information frames
- Presentation to the class

My Portfolio

Name _____ Date _____

Project Description: Research a person from the Civil War time period and create a slide show sharing his/her contributions to the period.

Project Standards:
Effectively gather and use information from research.
Develop oral presentation skills.
Identify and develop awareness of the contributions of historical figures in the United States.
Gain skill in the use of technology.
Use technology to locate, evaluate, and collect information.
Use productivity tools to effectively communicate information and ideas.

Project Requirements/Comments:
1. I researched: (Civil War figure)
2. I used a time line format to organize my notes. It's attached.
3. I used these resources in my research:
Electronic resource:

Print resource:

Reflection on creating the slide show:
_____
_____
_____
_____
_____

Product Evidence: My slide show is stored in my file on the network.

Figure 4.4 Portfolio Cover Sheet: Civil War People Project

Student	Artwork 1	Artwork 2	Artwork 3
Apple, S.	2/20 Portrait	2/20 Birthplace	2/20 General
Bosk, A.	2/17 Parents		
Cruk, N.			
Crandall, M.	2/20 Childhood	2/21 Gettysburg	
Crist, J.	2/18 Portrait	2/18 Legislature	2/29 Birthplace

Figure 4.5 Artwork Record File

Technology for Social Studies Units

Assessment Rubric: People of the Civil War Slide Show

Name _____ Date _____

Use this rating scale to help you evaluate your work:
0 - Student did not attempt the assignment.
1 - Student attempted assignment but didn't meet minimal competency level requirements.
2 - Student met minimal competency level requirements.
3 - Student did commendable work.
4 - Student demonstrated exceptional work.

Preparation

Student	Teacher
_____	_____ Used at least two resources, one print and one electronic.
_____	_____ Used a time line graphic organizer to record my notes.
_____	_____ Cited my sources.
_____	_____ Gathered at least two graphics for the slikde show.
_____	_____ Developed storyboard sheets that...
_____	_____ •Showed a logical progression of information.
_____	_____ •Presented a clear thesis.
_____	_____ •Answered the key questions in my own words.
_____	_____ •Included accurate facts.
_____	_____ •Used graphics to explain, illustrate, or clarify information.
_____	_____ Met the deadline for preparation.

Slide Show

Student	Teacher
_____	_____ Selected appropriate type style.
_____	_____ Used a pleasing type contrast.
_____	_____ Included navigation buttons or directions.
_____	_____ Included title frame, credit frame, and at least three information frames.
_____	_____ Placed graphics in an appropriate size and so they showed a connection to the frame and text.
_____	_____ Showed skill in screen design.
_____	_____ Met the deadline for development.

Oral Presentation

Student	Teacher
_____	_____ Used eye contact.
_____	_____ Spoke clearly using appropriate volume.
_____	_____ Spoke with expression.
_____	_____ Included a creative beginning and ending.
_____	_____ Totals

Comments:

Figure 4.6 Assessment Rubric: People of the Civil War Slide Show

- When students have completed their research, display the transparency of the storyboard sheet and show students how to complete the forms:

  Storyboard Screen Number: the sequence of the slides

  Program: the name of the Civil War figure

  Title: the focus of the slide, e.g., introduction, early childhood, career, and reason for fame

  Producer: the student's name. Students should use the box to design the layout of the frame and should use the "facts" lines at the bottom of the screen to record the information that will be included in the frame. (See the example in Figure 4.7.)

■ Activity Focus: Letters Home

Technology Connection:
Information Retrieval (ISTE-students 5)

Collaboration:
- Introducing the project: Teacher
- Information searching and mapping: Media specialist
- Letter writing/preparation of the daily schedule: Teacher
- Assessment of the letters/daily schedule: Teacher
- Assessment of the maps: Media specialist

Resources: Internet sites:
- <www.civilwarletters.com/home.html> (letters from an Iowa Soldier during the Civil War)
- <http://geography.miningco.com/science/geography/msub37.htm> (outline maps)

Preparation Tasks:
- Bookmark the "Letters from an Iowa Soldier" site on several computers so that students can easily access it. Set up a schedule with the teacher so that students can come throughout the day in small groups. (Teacher's note: If you have difficulty accessing the site, try the keywords "Civil War letters.")

Figure 4.7 Storyboard Planning Example

- Access the outline maps site to print a map of the southeast portion of the United States. At the site, select Blank Base Maps. When the page loads, scroll to the two southeastern United States map choices. You can print a map in a vertical format or a horizontal format. Print the map and make one copy for each student.
- Create a graphic organizer for the students. (See Figure 4.8.) Because the letters project is ongoing throughout the unit and has multiple tasks, this is a wonderful way to help students gain organizational skills and become systematic in preparing for the tasks.

Assignment Description:

Letter writing was a popular pastime for Civil War soldiers. Soldiers were homesick, often away from home for the first time, in unfamiliar surroundings, and eager to hear news of loved ones and share news of their experiences. Even with time spent preparing for battles, marching, and fighting, soldiers found time to send letters home. The Internet site, "Letters from an Iowa Soldier during the Civil War," shares 15 letters written by Newton Scott. Have students complete three tasks based on the letters site:

Task 1: Use the historical map and the information from the letters to plot the soldier's movements in the war from the first letter (October 24, 1862) to the last letter (August 18-19, 1865).
Task 2: Based on the information in the letters, prepare a daily schedule that shows the routine of a soldier's day during the Civil War.
Task 3: Pretend you are a soldier (either from the North or from the South) and write your own letter home. Be sure to use language appropriate for the time.

Introduce the site and model using the graphic organizer (Figure 4.8) to list information that will help map Mr. Scott's travel, prepare a daily schedule, and write an original letter.

Concept Question:
What was life like for a soldier in the Civil War?

Generalization:
Interview someone who fought in a present-day war, and compare a soldier's life today with a soldier's life during the Civil War.

Name			Project: Letters Home
Letter	Date Read	Location Information	Other Interesting Information

Figure 4.8 Graphic Organizer: Notes from Letters Home

Technology for Social Studies Units 95

■ Activity Focus: Causes of the Civil War

Technology Connection: Problem Solving and Decision Making (ISTE-students 6)

Collaboration: Introduction to the activity: Teacher

Resources:
- *American History Inspirer: The Civil War (*Tom Snyder Productions, 80 Coolidge Hill Road, Watertown, Massachusetts 02472. Telephone: 1-800-342-0236. Web site: <www.tomsnyder.com>. Price information: $79.95 (for one computer); multiple computers, network, and site license options also are available.
- Projection system

Preparation Tasks:
- Hook up the computer to a presentation system and model using the program.

Activity Description:
Discover the causes of the Civil War as you travel back in time to this era. Students plan routes across the country and use historical maps to learn about the developments leading up to the Civil War.

■ Activity Focus: Harriet Tubman

Technology Connection: Teacher Delivery of Lessons (ISTE-teacher II-III)

Collaboration:
Developing the resource packet on Harriet Tubman: Teacher and media specialist working together
Delivering the lesson: Teacher

Resources:
- Video resource about Harriet Tubman
- *The Quest for Freedom* (1992) is a really good video. (Grace Products Corporation, 1771 International Parkway, Suite 111, Richardson, Texas 75081-1831. Telephone: 1-800-527-4014. Web site: <www.graceproducts.com/>)
- Word-processing program, i.e., *AppleWorks, Microsoft Word*
- Scanner

Preparation Tasks:
- Create a portrait of Harriet Tubman. Choose one that is large enough for the whole class to view and one that can be displayed with the finished acrostic poem students will be writing during the lesson. A book jacket portrait scanned into the computer and printed on a color printer is one possible solution.
- Find a poem about Harriet Tubman and make a transparency. The one from *Followers of the North Star* by Susan Altman (Childrens Press, 1993) is effective. Enlarge it on the copy machine and make a transparency from the enlarged copy.
- Use a word-processing program to develop a student information packet about Harriet Tubman. The information packet gives all students quick access to information about Tubman and allows the teacher to combine information from a variety of sources (biographies and

encyclopedias), focus the information, and present it in a format that facilitates a classroom lesson. Print multiple copies so that each student has a copy. See Figure 4.9 for a sample first page. The rest of the packet can include information about her birth, her life as a child and a teen, her marriage, her hopes for freedom, her trip North, her experiences in the North (freedom), the bounty on her head, and her roles during and after the war.

- Use chart paper to prepare an acrostic poem poster. (See Figure 4.10.) Make a copy of acrostic poem line choices and cut the lines into strips so that students can select assignments from a basket.

Harriet Tubman, the "Moses" of Her People

What was she like?

Appearance
She was short and had a small frame that often fooled people because it hid her incredible physical strength. She rarely smiled, and she would look people directly in the eye.

Determination
She was willing to do whatever it took to bring fugitive (runaway) slaves to freedom and help them establish themselves. Even when she was a slave, she had a reputation for defiance and rebellion.

Sleep
When she was a child, she received a severe head wound, and this caused her to fall asleep, often at the worst times.

Soldier
She was courageous and brave and worked for the North as a spy and a scout during the war years. She made 19 trips back to the South to bring out slaves, and in the summer of 1863 she led a major raid into enemy territory to destroy enemy supplies and bring out more slaves.

Caregiver
She served as a nurse in several field hospitals during the war.

Figure 4.9 Harriet Tubman Information Packet

Assignment Description:

Show the portrait of Harriet Tubman, display the transparency of the poem, and choral read the poem. Discuss what students have learned about Tubman from the words of the poem. List ideas on the board. Why was she called the "Moses" of her people?

Harriet Ross.
At the Cooks.
Rawhide fears.
Runaway.
Illegal.
Escaping.
The Trip North, Starting.

The Trip North, Success.
Underground Railroad: Bowleys.
Bounty Hunters.
Military Leader.
Auburn Years.
Now at Rest.

Figure 4.10 Acrostic Poem

Refocus: How was her leadership similar to the leadership of Moses in the Bible? Review the description information in the student packet. Watch the video and have students look for examples in the video. Then add information to the brainstorming on the board: What additional information was learned about Tubman?

Have student partners use the information packet to create a class acrostic poem about Tubman. Each partnership is responsible for one letter in the poem, and students should use the clues listed for each letter to compose lines that explain the connections to Tubman's life. The clues are listed in chronological order and follow the events of Tubman's life. Students should fully understand the meanings of the clues they complete.

Connect: Share the finished poem; invite each partnership to read their line. Discuss.
Concept Question: What was the relationship between Tubman and the abolitionists?
Generalization: How did her efforts help shape the time period of the late 1880s? How would this time period be viewed differently without her involvement?

■ Activity Focus: The Abolitionists

Technology Connection: Teacher Delivery of Lessons (ISTE-teacher II-III)

Collaboration:
- Developing the newspaper resource on the abolitionists: Teacher and media specialist working together
- Delivering the lesson: Teacher

Resources:
- Word-processing program
- Scanner

Preparation Tasks:

Use a word processing program to develop a newspaper about the abolitionists. (See Figure 4.11.) Make multiple copies so that each student has a copy. The newspaper allows you to combine information from a variety of sources, focus the information on the people required in the objectives, provide information at appropriate reading levels, and present it in a format that facilitates a classroom lesson. To add authenticity to the resource, base it on *The Liberator*, William Lloyd Garrison's abolitionist newspaper of the time, and use historical artwork from books, encyclopedias (both print and electronic), and the Internet. Figure 4.11 shows a sample first page. Subsequent pages could include information based on these headlines:

Figure 4.11 Front Page: Abolitionists' Newspaper

Suggested Headlines for Articles on the Other Pages of the Newspaper

1. Free Lecture: Sarah and Angelina Grimke Speak
2. Dred Scott Loses Trial
3. Women in the News: Lucretia Mott Pleads the Cause of the Slaves
4. William Lloyd Garrison Jailed
5. Sojourner Truth Publishes Her Story
6. "A Nation's Strength," a Poem from Ralph Waldo Emerson
7. Hot on the Trail (an advertisement for Pinkerton's Detective Agency)
8. A Conversation with Frederick Douglass
9. $100 Reward (an advertisement for the return of a slave)
10. A Time Line of Our Successes and Challenges (compiled by the editors of *The Liberator* to chart our progress)

Assignment Description:

Enter the classroom carrying a stack of *The Liberator* newspapers, calling, "Extra, extra, John Brown raids federal arsenal in his effort to stop slavery. Extra, extra, read all about it. Abolitionists stage raid." Read the story of John Brown's raid to identify a definition for the word "abolitionist." (An abolitionist is any person who spoke out against slavery and worked to have it made illegal.)

Review the time line of the history of the movement.

Have students work individually, in small groups, and with partners to create skits that share information about important abolitionist figures of the time. Skit assignment topics could include the following:

Ralph Waldo Emerson (poet)
Frederick Douglass (former slave)
Sojourner Truth (slave/author)
Harriet Beecher Stowe (author)
Lucretia Mott (Quaker mother and stationmaster on the Underground Railroad)
Alan Pinkerton (detective)
William Lloyd Garrison (newspaper editor)
Dred Scott (slave)

Concept Question: Abolitionists met with lots of antagonism from others because of their beliefs. What issues of today might create that same kind of animosity?

Generalization: How did the beliefs shared by the abolitionists shape the time period of the early and mid 1800s?

■ Activity Focus: Newsletter to Families About the Unit

Technology Connection: Classroom Management (ISTE-teacher IV-V)

Collaboration: Preparing the newsletter: Teacher and students

Preparation Tasks: Design a newsletter template like the one in Figure 4.12. Select and create a distinctive heading that you will use all year; when parents see this heading, they will know it contains news from the class.

Activity Description:

Involve students in preparing a newsletter to families on a regular basis. The template in Figure 4.12 is an example from a fifth-grade classroom. The teacher created the headline logo and set up the newsletter format. Page 1 included a letter from the teacher about upcoming units of study, events in the classroom, and notes about important dates, e.g., school pictures, field trips, conferences, and due dates for projects. Page 2 became the responsibility of the students; they worked in teams and signed up for one of the monthly newsletters. The teacher used the computer lab to lead students in guided practice in writing, revising, and editing a newsletter page, and trained them to use the digital camera and download pictures. When it was their turn, they took pictures and reported highlights of events in the classroom. They scheduled an editorial meeting with the teacher over a lunch hour and brainstormed ideas for the page; then they divided responsibilities and used class time and lunchtime to develop the page.

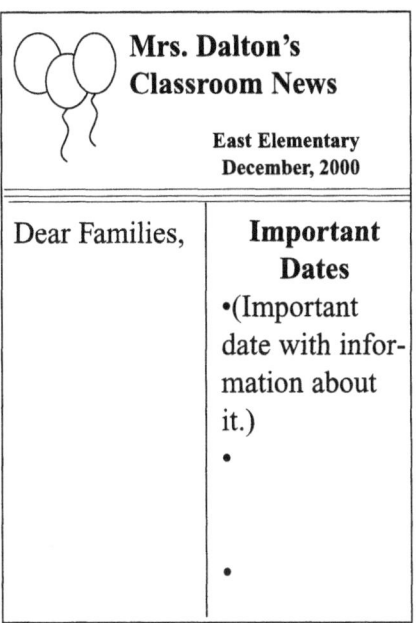

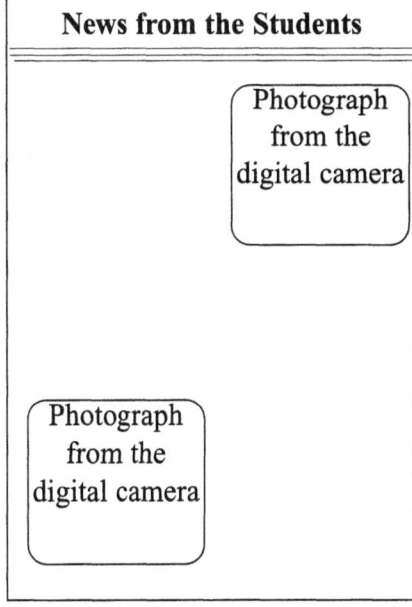

Figure 4.12 Newspaper Template

Technology for Social Studies Units

I Packed My Bag: Stories from Around the World

Information Retrieval	Student Productivity	Problem Solving and Decision Making
Electronic encyclopedias, e.g., *World Book, Grolier's*. Internet sites: **Chinese Zodiac Calendar:** <www.new-year.co.uk/chinese/calendar.htm> **Kids Web Japan:** <http://jin.jcic.or.jp/kidsweb> **Pasta Information:** <www.ilovepasta.org>	Slide Show: Stories from Around the World Slide Show: Ice Cream Facts Personal narratives Poems Fantasy stories Riddles	Internet site: **Mileage Calculations:** <www.tripadvice.com/airport_calculator.htm> Graphing
		Communication and Collaboration
		E-mail Pen Pals: <www.epals.com/> <http://teaching.com/keypals/> **Author Correspondence (Jan Brett):** <www.janbrett.com/>

Teacher Delivery of Lessons	Classroom Management
Internet site: **Origami Directions (Cranes):** <www.jwindow.net/OLD/KIDS/SCHOOL/ART/origami/kids_origami_crane1.html> Mileage chart Travel and continent signs Note from the Gingerbread Man Coat of Arms template Science Investigation Sheet Heroes Chart Extra Mile Awards	Invitation to families for the Thanksgiving feast Portfolio Pictures: Fantasy lands

Figure 4.13 I Packed My Bag Unit: Technology Connections

Unit 2: I Packed My Bag: Stories from Around the World

Unit Objectives:
1. Develop geography skills
2. Enjoy and appreciate stories from around the world.
3. Discuss and become aware of customs and traditions around the world.

Audience: Grades 1–3

Length of the Unit: Ongoing throughout the year

The Unit Activities at a Glance

Getting Started	Continuing the Travels	*Tikki Tikki Tembo*
Students search for the gingerbread man in a tour of the school and begin the year's long travel with stories from around the world.	The lesson description shares the process for working with the stories.	Extension activities include graphing, developing a coat of arms, and investigating materials that float and sink.
One Grain of Rice	***The Cock, the Mouse, and the Little Red Hen***	***The Paper Crane***
Extension activities include problem solving, pattern making, and counting by twos and fives.	Extension activities focus on experiences that build an effective classroom learning environment.	Students create a photo display of life in Japan and discuss how family life is similar and different.
Strega Nona	***Stone Soup***	***The Mitten***
Students communicate electronically with key-pals in Italy.	Students learn about the Thanksgiving story, and plan and host a "stone soup" Thanksgiving feast.	Extension activities include learning about the author, making handprint mittens, exploring foreshadowing, dramatizing the story, creating winter paintings, and researching the sizes of animals in the story.
The Lion's Whiskers	***Why Mosquitoes Buzz in People's Ears***	***Bring the Rain to Kapiti Plain***
Students focus on describing characteristics of heroes and identifying heroes in real life and literature.	Students observe animal behaviors and write riddles about animals.	Students write rainy day poems, create rainy day watercolor pictures, and explore features of weather.
James and the Vine Puller* and *Panda and the Bunyips		
Students create maps of imaginary lands and write a class story based on one of the imaginary land settings.		

Figure 4.13a I Packed My Bag, The Unit Activities at a Glance

■ Activity Focus: Getting Started

Technology Connection: Student Productivity (ISTE-students 3), Teacher Delivery of Lesson (ISTE-teacher II-III)

Collaboration:
- Gathering the stories: Media specialist
- Developing the resources: Teacher
- Sharing the story: Teacher

Resources:
- World map (Teacher's note: Use a simple world map that shows and names the continents and the countries of the world. Nystrom and CRAM offer world maps. Access their sites to identify the map you wish to order: <www.nystromnet.com/products.html> or <www.georgefcram.com/>.)
- A map of the school
- An old, well-worn suitcase (Teacher's note: If you don't have one, look at flea markets or garage sales.)
- *The Gingerbread Man*, retold by Eric A. Kimmel, illustrated by Megan Lloyd (New York: Holiday House, 1993)
- Gingerbread cookies in the shape of the gingerbread man, enough for one per student
- A mixing bowl, measuring spoons, and a large mixing spoon
- A measuring cup with a small amount of flour in the measuring cup
- Frosting and candy decorations for the cookies
- Plastic knives for spreading the frosting
- Small paper cups
- Digital camera
- Slide show program, e.g., *AppleWorks*, *PowerPoint*
- Stories from around the world (Teacher's note: See the suggested list on pages 102–104.)

Preparation Tasks:
- Create a wall display with the world map; hang it low enough so children can easily reach points on the map.
- Enlarge the school map so that it is floor size and identifies key places in the school where children will be traveling during the school year, i.e., office, nurse's clinic, art room, music room, physical education space, computer lab, media center, cafeteria, and playground. Place it on the floor for the first day of school, ready for the arrival of the students. When students ask questions, be mysterious and say that you found it on the floor this morning when you arrived and you don't know where the map came from.
- Use a spreadsheet to create a mileage chart for the "book" travels you will be making during the school year. Make a poster of the chart and display it next to the world map. (See Figure 4.14.)
- Identify the books you will be using throughout the year; the following titles work well.
  Africa
  The Lion's Whiskers, an Ethiopian folktale by Nancy Raines Day, illustrated by Ann Grifalconi (New York: Scholastic, 1995)
  Why Mosquitoes Buzz in People's Ears, a West African tale retold by Verna Aardema, pictures by Leo and Diane Dillon (New York: Dial Books, 1975)

Bringing the Rain to Kapiti Plain, a Nandi tale retold by Verna Aardema, pictures by Beatriz Vidal (New York: Dian Books, 1981)

Asia

The Paper Crane, by Molly Bang (New York: Greenwillow Books, 1985)

Tikki Tikki Tembo, retold by Arlene Mosel, illustrated by Blair Lent (New York: Henry Holt, 1968)

One Grain of Rice, by Demi (New York: Scholastic Press, 1997)

Mileage Graph

Number of Miles

10,000						
9,000						
8,500						
8,000						
7,500						
7,000						
6,500						
6,000						
5,500						
5,000						
4,500						
4,000						
3,500						
3,000						
2,500						
2,000						
1,500						
1,000						
950						
900						
850						
800						
750						
700						
650						
600						
550						
500						
450						
400						
350						
300						
250						
200						
150						
100						

Places

Figure 4.14 Mileage Chart

Australia
Panda and the Bunyips, by Michael Foreman (New York: Schocken Books, 1987)
Europe
The Cock, the Mouse, and the Little Red Hen, a traditional tale illustrated by Graham Percy (Cambridge, Massachusetts: Candlewick Press, 1992)
Strega Nona, an original tale written and illustrated by Tomie dePaola (New York: Simon and Schuster, 1975)
Stone Soup, told and pictured by Marcia Brown (New York: Atheneum Books, 1975)
The Mitten, a Ukrainian folktale adapted and illustrated by Jan Brett (New York: G. P. Putnam's Sons, 1989)
South America
James the Vine Puller, retelling of a Brazilian version of an African folktale by Martha Bennett
Stiles (Minneapolis: Carolrhoda, 1992)

- Make travel signs for the books you will be sharing. Use the Internet to locate one or two pictures from the countries you are visiting, and copy and paste them on the signs. To find the pictures, use any search engine (*Google, Yahoo*), type in the name of the country, and browse some of the Web sites to locate pictures you want to use.
- Make continent signs, and place them in a basket/container for later in the lesson. (See Figure 4.15.)
- Set up a slide show template so that students can make one or two original drawings per book to record the book travels. (Teacher's note: Be sure that all of the students have an opportunity to contribute at least one slide.) (See Figure 4.16.)
- Develop a note from the gingerbread man, and write it on colorful stationery. (See Figure 4.17.)

Assignment Description:

Prepare for your tour of the school by informing the helpers in each area you will be visiting that you will be searching for the gingerbread man, who has run away. Schedule the tour for the first day of school right after lunch. While students are at lunch on the first day of school, place the mixing bowl, measuring spoons, mixing spoon, and cup of flour on the floor map. Spill a little of the flour on the map and trail some out the door of the classroom; display the book and the note from the gingerbread man.

As you enter the classroom after lunch, comment on the flour mess and act puzzled. Pick up the note and read it to the class. Share the story, but stop on the page before the gingerbread man meets the fox. Close the book and make comments connecting the note from the gingerbread man to the book, "So that's what the note meant. Where do you suppose the gingerbread man has gone?" Invite responses.

Figure 4.15 Continent Signs

Go on a tour of the school in search of the gingerbread man. Use the digital camera and take pictures of the helpers in each area of the school you visit. Ask the helpers if they have seen the gingerbread man. (Teacher's note: Arrange for an adult in the school to set out the gingerbread cookies, plastic knives, frosting in small paper cups, and candy pieces in small paper cups at the students' work spaces, ready for your return to the classroom.) On your return to the classroom, give students time to frost, decorate, and eat the cookies. While the students are engaged in this activity, print the digital camera pictures.

After they are finished with the cookies, gather the students in a large circle around the map. Have the students find the classroom and mark it with a large colorful star. Show a picture of one of the helpers you visited, and ask students to name the helper and identify where the helper works e.g., Ms. Jones, the principal, who works in the office. Find the area on the map; cut out the picture and paste/tape it on the map. Ask a student volunteer to show how he or she would walk to the office on the map. Ask questions about the location, e.g., Is it near or far from our classroom? Do you turn right or left? What is it next to? Repeat the process with the other helpers. When you are finished, display the map at students' eye level.

Display the suitcase, introduce the world map, and share with students that they will be traveling around the world through books during the school year. Ask for a volunteer to locate and mark where you are on the map. Identify the continent you live on. Have other student volunteers pull continent signs from the basket/container. Locate the continents on the map and attach the signs to the map. Invite discussion and sharing about where students have traveled/lived or what they imagine about various places in the world.

Invite two students to contribute drawings to the slide show. Save their drawings in the show, and also print and display them on the world map in the place where you live. (Teacher's note: Mount the drawings on colorful construction paper.)

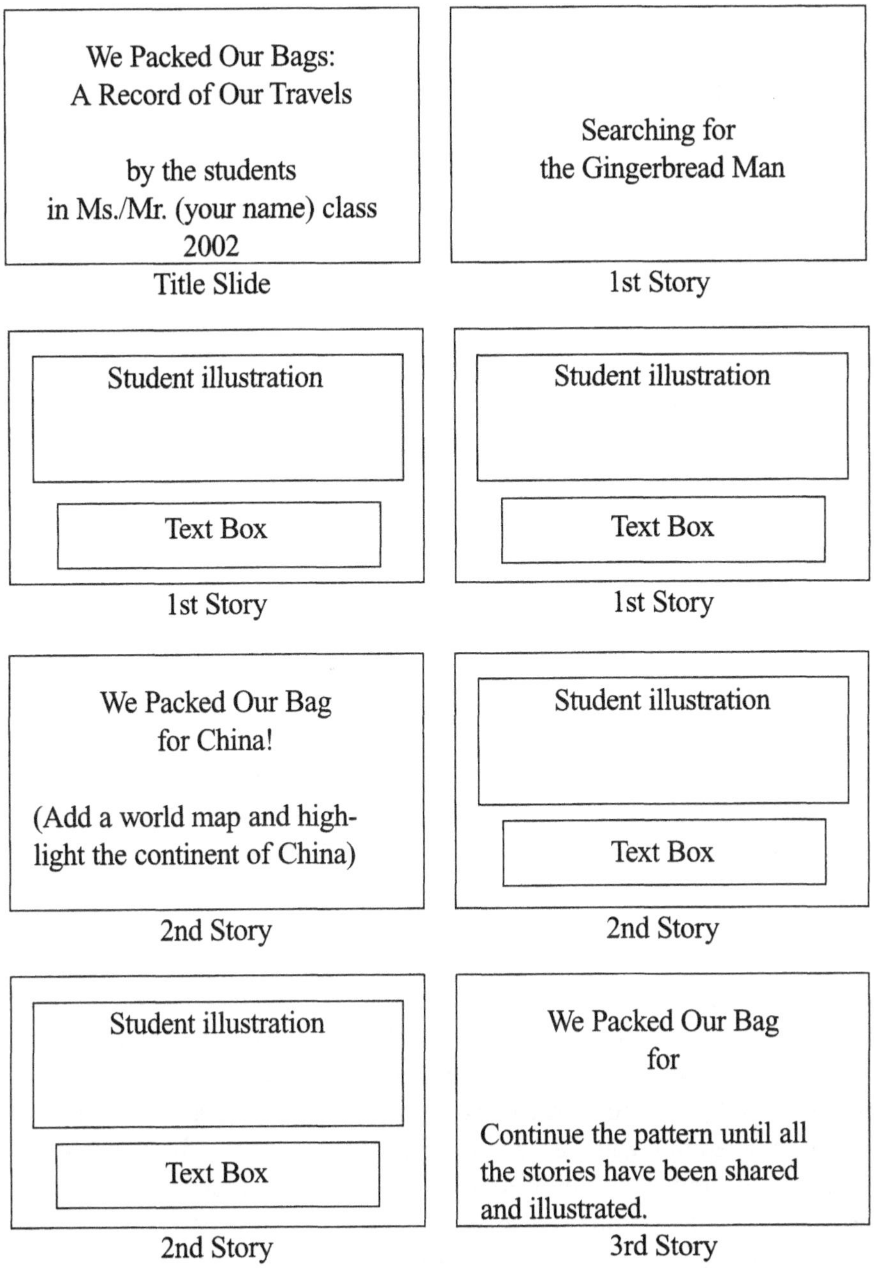

Figure 4.16 Slide Show Template

■ Activity Focus: Continuing the Travels

Technology Connection: Student Productivity (ISTE-students 3), Problem Solving and Decision Making (ISTE-students 6), Teacher Delivery of Lesson (ISTE-teacher II-III)

Collaboration:
- Sharing the stories: Teacher
- Extension activities: Teacher and media specialist as co-facilitators

Resources:
- World map
- An old, well-worn suitcase
- The travel signs
- Slide show program, e.g., *AppleWorks, PowerPoint*
- Stories from around the world
- Mileage calculator from Internet site: <www.tripadvice.com/airport_calculator.htm>

Preparation Tasks:
- Bookmark the mileage calculator Web site; it will help calculate mileage for the mileage chart. Unless you live in a major city on either coast, there will be two steps:

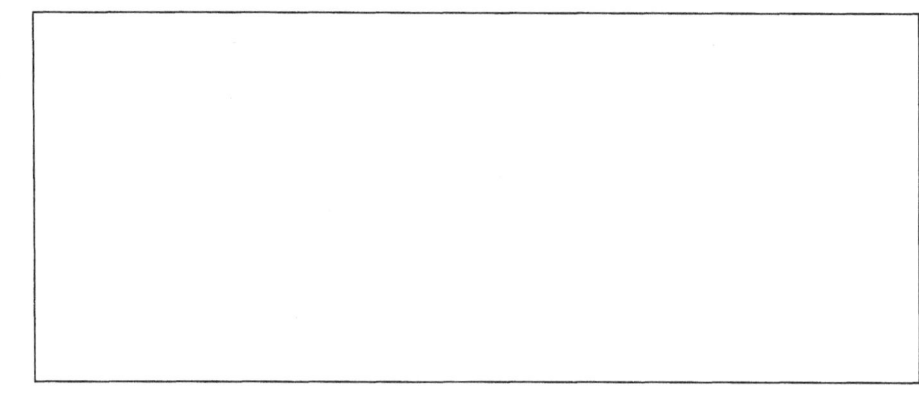

Figure 4.17 Note from the Gingerbread Man

  1. Within the United States, calculate the mileage from your location to a city on the coast.
  2. International: calculate the mileage from the coastal city to the country of the story.

- Total the numbers and have students complete the mileage chart for this destination.
- Plan a sequence for sharing the books, and identify curriculum connections to ongoing units of study and curriculum objectives you must meet. (See the suggestions listed on pages 106–107.)

Working with the Stories:

Place supplies for the journey in the suitcase, i.e., travel sign, a copy of the book, and supplies for the extension activities. Display the suitcase in the classroom so that students anticipate that this is the day for traveling. (Teacher's note: Vary the days for traveling—introducing a story—and put the suitcase in the closet when not traveling to keep engagement peaked. Students will not need encouragement to browse the map to try to figure out the new destination. After the first few travels, many of the students will look for clues around the classroom (center activities, books in the reading corner, or a new bulletin board display).

When you are ready to share the story, gather the students near the world map, open the suitcase, and remove the travel sign.

1. Use the sign to locate the continent and country/area where the story takes place. Attach the sign to the world map.
2. Introduce the story. Make predictions about the story based on the title and cover illustrations; then share the story.
3. Extend the story through discussions and introduction of the center/follow-up activities. (See suggestions in Item 5.)
4. Identify two students who will make drawings for the slide show and the map.
5. Celebrate the close of the journey. (Some journeys can last three days; some journeys are longer, depending on the curriculum connections.) Celebrations also follow a pattern:

sharing a food from the country/area of the world, calculating the mileage and filling in the mileage chart, presenting the students' illustrations from the slide show, framing them and attaching them to the map, and sharing any products developed during the extension activities. Geography questions focus on cardinal directions: north, south, east, and west, and a discussion of place, the second theme of geography. In describing place, students answer the question "What's it like there?" and focus on describing the physical and human characteristics of the place based on their observations from the stories and their experiences following the stories.

■ Story: *Tikki Tikki Tembo*, retold by Arlene Mosel

Location: China

Curriculum Connections: Math and Science

Collaboration: Classroom

Technology Connection: Information Retrieval (ISTE-students 5), Problem Solving and Decision Making (spreadsheet) (ISTE-students 6), Teacher Delivery of Lessons (ISTE-teacher II-III)
Spreadsheet #1: Print Tikki Tikki Tembo's full name on a long sheet of paper and have students use unifix cubes to count the letters in his name. Create a unifix line yourself for Tikki's name and leave it in a row on the floor. Have students write their first names, then use unifix cubes to count the letters in their names. Compare their names to Tikki's name. Create a graph showing the results. Discuss the results: shortest name? longest name? longest to shortest names in sequence? number of names of children in the class to equal the length of Tikki's name?
Spreadsheet #2: Getting to know each other. Create a database listing information about the students in the classroom, e.g., favorite colors, desserts, toys, seasons, best sport, most enjoyable hobby, pets, and siblings. Create a variety of graphs of the information.

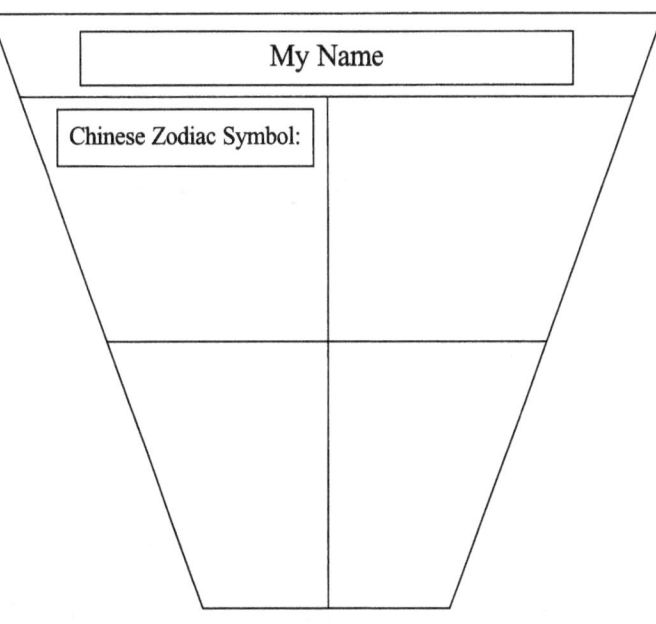

Figure 4.18 Coat of Arms

Food: Fortune cookies (They can be purchased or donated by a local restaurant.)

Art: Create a coat of arms template, print multiple copies, and have students use pictures and words to make personal coats of arms to hang at their work spaces. (See Figure 4.18.) The Chinese believe that the year of a person's birth determines what the person will be like. Each year is named after an animal to give character to the year. Use the Chinese calendar Web site <www.new-year.co.uk/chinese/calendar.htm> and have students find their birth years, symbols, and information about the symbols to add to the coats of arms. (To assist younger students with this task, connect the computer to a presentation system, access the site, choose the relevant years for the students in

Name		Date	
Objects	Predictions	Results Plain Water	Salt Water
1	Plain Water: Salt Water:		
2	Plain Water: Salt Water:		
3	Plain Water: Salt Water:		
4	Plain Water: Salt Water:		
5	Plain Water: Salt Water:		
6	Plain Water: Salt Water:		

F=Float   S=Sink

Figure 4.19 Sinking and Floating Investigation Log

your classroom, and create posters in the classroom sharing the information.

Science Investigation: Create a center to investigate materials that float and sink. Gather a variety of objects for students to test, e.g., washer, nail, golf tee, pipe cleaner, plastic spoon, sponge, cork, small rubber ball, paper clip, rock, and aluminum foil in various shapes. Set up two containers of water, one that is filled with plain water and one that is filled with salt water. Introduce the investigation sheet (See Figure 4.19) and test one of the objects, showing the students how to make predictions for the plain water and for the salt water and how to record their results.

■ Story: *One Grain of Rice,* by Demi

Location: India

Curriculum Connections: Math

Collaboration: Classroom

Technology Connection: Problem Solving and Decision Making (ISTE-students 6)
Select math software that gives students practice in math skills for the grade level. Companies that offer a variety of programs include: Sunburst Technology, 101 Castleton Street, Pleasantville, New York 10570, Telephone: 1-800-321-7511, Web site: <www.sunburst.com>; Scholastic, 555 Broadway, New York, New York 10012, Telephone: 1-800-Scholastic, Web site: <www.scholastic.com/>; and The Learning Company, 500 Redwood Boulevard, Novato, California 94947, Telephone: 1-800-825-4420, Web site: <www.learningcompanyschool.com/>.

Food: Neruppu Vazhai (banana dessert). Peel and halve lengthwise six firm bananas. Place them in a single layer in a buttered baking dish and sprinkle them with ¼ cup of orange juice, ½ cup of brown sugar, 1 cup of grated coconut, ½ cup of chopped almonds, 1 teaspoon of ground cardamom, and ¼ cup of melted butter. Bake the bananas in a 400° oven for 25 minutes. Serve warm.

Art: Have students look at the illustrations in the book to examine the patterns; then use a geometric shape (circle, square, triangle, or rectangle) and markers to create a mathematical pattern.

Math: Focus on math objectives and activities from your textbook that help students count by twos and fives.

■ Story: *The Cock, the Mouse, and the Little Red Hen*, a traditional tale illustrated by Graham Percy

Location: England

Curriculum Connections: The Classroom Learning Environment

Collaboration:
- Strategies for the classroom (mission statement, small circle discussions, conflict management): Teacher
- Collaborative learning projects: Teacher, with media specialist assisting

Technology Connection: Student Productivity (ISTE-students 3), Classroom Management (ISTE-teacher IV-V)

Food: Scones. Sift into a mixing bowl 2 cups of flour, 2 teaspoons of baking powder, and a dash of salt. Add 4 tablespoons of butter and mix quickly with your fingers until the dough is crumbly. Mix in ¼ cup of sugar and ½ cup of currants. Add ¼ cup of buttermilk and make a stiff dough. Form the dough into a ball, then pat or roll it out until it is less than an inch thick. Cut the dough into small circles, place the circles on a cookie sheet, and bake them in a 425° oven for about 10 minutes or until golden brown on top. Serve with butter and jam.

Mission Statement (Defining the classroom environment):

Begin by creating a jobs chart: student, teacher, and family members. Brainstorm and discuss answers to these questions: Why are we here? What do we need to do? What do we need to have a great year? What does a good student look like and sound like? What are your responsibilities? What are my responsibilities? (Teacher) Make a jobs chart display like the one in Figure 4.20. List the student responsibilities and the teacher responsibilities. Create the family members' responsibilities list with input from families, e.g.,

Whose Job Is It?		
Student Responsibilities	Teacher Responsibilities	Parent Responsibilities
•attend school	•provide a safe environment	•communicate with the teacher
•follow class rules	•communicate with families	•read with you
•be respectful	•create opportunities for independence	•help you get a good night's rest
•listen	•treat student fairly	•help you have a good start to the day (on time, breakfast, materials you need)
•ask questions	•make exciting lessons	
•do quality work	•meet individual needs	
•be prepared		•participate in school activities
•follow directions		
•stay on task		
•read at home		
•complete my homework		

Figure 4.20 Job Charts

brainstorming at a "Back to School" night session, gathering the information on enrollment day, sending a note to families, and having students interview family members. When the jobs chart is complete, display it in the classroom; it's a great responsibility check when there are difficulties.

Work with students to create a mission statement for the year. Review what it is and why it is important. (**What?** A mission statement is a clearly written statement that identifies a group, describes the tasks it is responsible for, and lists the reasons for its existence. **Why?** A mission statement sets clear goals for the group and guides class activities and expectations.)

Break down the mission statement into three parts:

Who? A statement that describes the class or gives the class a label.
What? A statement that describes what the class is going to do.
Why? A statement that explains why the class is going to do the "what."

Develop a mission statement, create a poster, and have students sign their names to the poster. (See Figure 4.21.)

Our Mission

We, the students in Ms. Jones's third grade class, want to learn and grow this year and be the best third grade ever. We want to become better writers, readers, problem solvers, researchers, and scientists.

We will do this by using the writing process, writing every day, and faithfully studying and learning our spelling words. We will also practice our math skills and have fun solving the weekly story problems. We will always have a book to read and will read each evening at home. In our science units, we will get along on our teams and keep good science journals.

We will follow class rules, listen and ask lots of questions, and be prepared for each day. We will be nice to each other because that's how we want to be treated.

Figure 4.21 Mission Statement

Small Circle (Building opportunities for communication):

Sit in a large circle and play a round of the "gossip" game, i.e., one student whispers a phrase or word into the ear of the next student, and the phrase/word continues to be passed around the circle until it reaches the last student in the circle who announces the phrase/word. Rarely is the phrase/word at the end of the circle the same as at the beginning of the circle. Discuss what is involved in effective communication (speaking truthfully and respectfully, listening attentively, and being empathetic).

Introduce the techniques of small circle—an opportunity to celebrate successes or recognize positive qualities in students, identify and reflect on expectations, or share and brainstorm solutions to classroom challenges and difficulties. In small circle, everyone must join the circle, and the leader (can be a student) introduces the subject or theme for the discussion, e.g., feeling overwhelmed, playground conflicts, recognitions, or behavior expectations for the field trip to the ballet. Begin at the left or right of the leader and have students share ideas, comments, and concerns about the theme. If a student does not wish to speak, he or she passes. Students cannot interrupt, but they may raise their hands to ask questions for clarification. Students should avoid using other students' names when talking about personal experiences. After one trip around the circle, the leader summarizes and mirrors back to the group key points of the discussion. In a second trip around the circle, students who passed may wish to comment. Sometimes small circle has closure in one session; other times it carries over to the next session. Students may be ready to offer solutions to the problem, or students may need to still discuss the issue.

For the first small circle discussions, focus on a beginning-of-the-school-year classroom environment need, e.g., reviewing rules we will use to guide our behavior for the year or defining respectful and responsible behaviors or the meaning of fairness and helpfulness. After the small circle discussion, have students work in small groups to develop "rules" for classroom behavior. Display each group's contributions and build a classroom "rules" list from the contributions of the groups. Keep the list small and manageable.

Identify a way for students to submit topics for small circle discussions (a box with a slit in the top, a poster), and share how often small circle discussions will occur (daily at the close of the day, twice daily at the open and close of the day, three times a week, once a week, or as needed).

Conflict Management: Model a simple strategy that students can use to resolve conflicts. Here is one example: Say the person's name (Jeremy). Tell how you feel (I feel angry). Tell what they did to make you feel that way (when you push in front of me when we are lining up for recess). Say what you want them to do (I want you to go back in line).

Ask for student volunteers to role play the strategy with other situations, e.g., taking another person's seat in the lunchroom, excluding a person from a game or the pretend center, making a mark on someone else's paper, or not sharing the art supplies. Introduce the conflict resolution poster and review the strategies. (See Figure 4.22.)

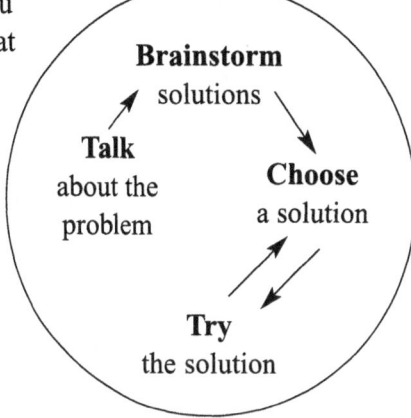

Figure 4.22 Conflict Resolution Poster

Art: At the end of the story, the cock and the mouse have had a change in behavior because of the encounter with the fox. Have students work with a partner and design a picture that shows other examples of how they have changed, e.g., preparing dinner, going to the grocery store, ironing or doing the laundry. Have them use *Kid Pix* or another drawing program to create their illustration.

Math: Have students work with a partner and use manipulatives or real objects from the classroom to show all the ways to make the sum of four, e.g., two pencils and two erasers equal four desk items, one bear plus three bears equals four bears. Have them choose one equation they and their partner feel is most unusual and show that equation using numbers and correct signs.

■ Story: *The Paper Crane,* by Molly Bang

Location: Japan

Curriculum Connections: Social Studies

Collaboration:
- Sharing the Story: Classroom
- Research on Japan: Media Center

Technology Connection: Information Retrieval (ISTE-students 5), Teacher Delivery of Lesson (ISTE-teacher II-III)

Have students develop a photo essay display about living in Japan. Bookmark the Web site <http://jin.jcic.or.jp/kidsweb/> (Kids Web Japan), and have students work with partners and reading buddies (older students who can help with reading the information and navigating the site) to explore life in Japan. The site is easy to navigate and offers these topics: nature and climate, sports, regions of Japan, politics and constitution, daily life, schools, economy and industry, tradition and culture, protecting the environment, international relations, outside the classroom, and history. Students should read about their topics, select pictures, print them, and write a sentence or two describing the pictures and their topics. Assemble the display.

Food: Rice and green tea

Art: Have the students make origami cranes. Access the Web site <www.jwindow.net/OLD/KIDS/SCHOOL/ART/origami/kids_origami_crane1.html> and print the directions for making folded cranes. Depending on their age, students may need assistance with the folding tasks; invite reading buddies to join you for this activity.

Social Studies: Use the study of Japan to discuss how families in other areas are similar and different.

■ Story: *Strega Nona*, by Tomie dePaola

Location: Italy

Curriculum Connections: Social Studies, Art

Collaboration:
- Communicating with e-pals in Italy: Teacher
- Researching pasta: Media specialist
- Art project: Art teacher

Technology Connection: Information Retrieval (ISTE-students 5), Problem Solving and Decision Making (ISTE-students 6), Communication and Collaboration (ISTE-students 4), Teacher Delivery of Lesson (ISTE-teacher II-III)

Use the Web sites <www.epals.com/> and <http://teaching.com/keypals/> to locate a classroom in Italy for ongoing communication. Help the students compose an e-mail letter telling about themselves. Use the e-mail collaboration to gain understanding of daily life in Italy for school-age children.

Bookmark this pasta site: <www.ilovepasta.org/>.

Assignment Description:

Introduce the research project. Make a KWHL chart and brainstorm the facts students already know about pasta (first column). (See Figure 4.23.) Brainstorm questions they have about pasta (second column). Access the Web site and show students how to click on "frequently asked questions." If needed, arrange research buddies to help students read the information. Distribute the note-taking sheet, and have students write their names on the sheets and list the questions they are researching. (See Figure 4.24.) When research is complete, return to the KWHL chart, gather students in a circle on the floor, and invite sharing. Record the information students have learned in the final column.

Brainstorm ideas for a book or a slide show (audience, title, dedication, format), and record students' names next to the jobs/facts they will complete for the book or the slide show.

Book pages: Cover, Title, Dedication, Bibliography, Fact Pages (one per student)

Slide show pages: Opening slide (title), dedication, fact slides (one per student), bibliography

K	W	H	L
Know	Want To Know	How We Find Out	Learned

Figure 4.23 KWHL Chart

Food: Pasta

Figure 4.24 Note-taking Sheet

Art: Connect with the art teacher, and focus on line and how line can be used to create movement in art. Browse the illustrations in the book to find examples, e.g., the steam from the pasta kettle, the pasta as it bubbles out of the pot and into the town, the sense of movement in the figures through the lines of the body stances and the angle of legs, the pattern of the five birds on the page illustrating Strega Nona's return to town. Have students sketch and paint a picture using different kinds of line to show movement.

Social Studies: Use the e-mail collaboration and the focus on foods of Italy to discuss how families in other areas are similar and different. Pasta is certainly one food we associate with Italian customs and traditions. Have students interview family members to identify all the ways they have eaten pasta. Makes lists and graph the information. Pizza is another food we attribute to Italy. Take a second survey of students to create a graph showing favorite pizza combinations.

■ Story: *Stone Soup*, by Marcia Brown

Location: France

Curriculum Connections: Social Studies: The Thanksgiving Story

Collaboration:
- Gathering resources about Thanksgiving: Media specialist
- Personal narrative writing: Teacher
- Exploring the Thanksgiving story: Teacher

Technology Connection: Student Productivity (word processing) (ISTE-students 3), Communication and Collaboration (ISTE-students 4), Classroom Management (ISTE-teacher IV-V)

Create an invitation to families, requesting their participation in a Thanksgiving feast. Make your own version of "stone soup" and ask families to donate one item for the soup. Make or purchase bread, and serve soup and bread at the feast.

Begin a focus on personal narrative writing about family customs at Thanksgiving.

1. Use the brainstorming prewrite to help students identify memorable parts of family Thanksgiving celebrations; then narrow to one idea for a narrative paragraph about the celebration. (See Figure 4.25.)
2. Collect details using the cluster web graphic organizer. (See Figure 4.26.)
3. Begin the rough draft and focus on using the "who" and "where" details to write a topic sentence for the paragraph, e.g., Grandma's house smells like cinnamon at Thanksgiving time.
4. Once topic sentences are written, have students add supporting detail sentences using the "what" and "what else happened" information from their webs. For example, I can smell it as soon as we walk in the door, and Grandma and Grandpa give us big "scruncher hugs." We run to the kitchen to see the row of pumpkin pies fresh from the oven. There's always enough for dinner and one for each guest to take home too. They are made from scratch from pumpkins Grandma grew herself, and each one is filled with tiny bits of cinnamon stick.
5. Finish the rough drafts by helping students compose closing sentences, e.g., Grandma hasn't washed the mixing bowl, so we each get a taste! I can hardly wait for dessert.
6. Conference with students to make revisions in their paragraphs, e.g., adding details, using more powerful verbs or more colorful adjectives.
7. Help students edit their paragraphs for punctuation, capitalization, and spelling errors.
8. Publish the stories by having students type them on the computer. Create Thanksgiving cards using folded construction paper sheets. Decorate the covers with illustrations that relate to the stories the students wrote. Attach the stories to the inside of the cards. Place the cards on the feast table where the student and his or her family will sit.

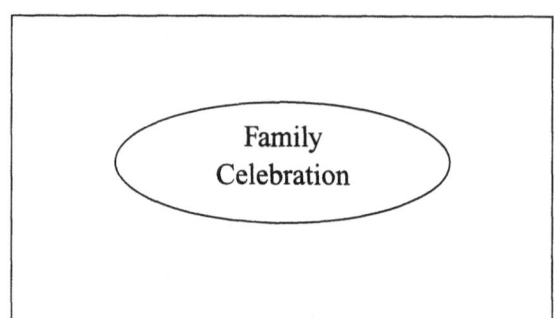

Figure 4.25 Prewrite Brainstorming Sheet

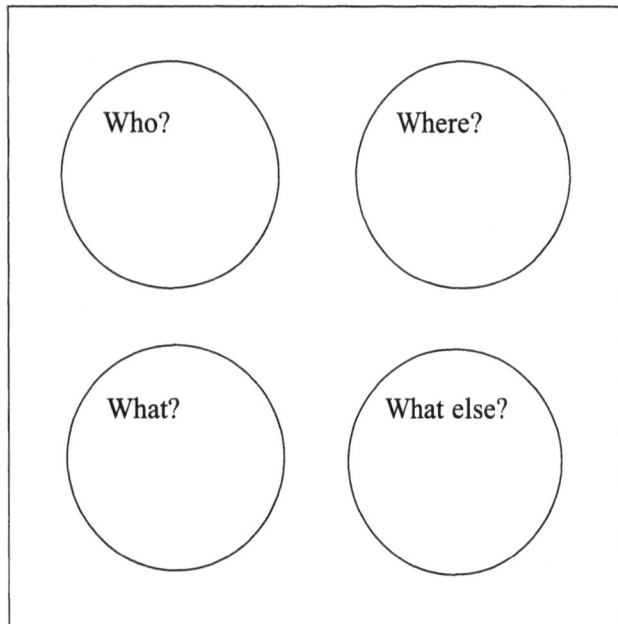

Figure 4.26 Cluster Web

Food: "Stone Soup." Brainstorm with the students the ingredients they would like to include in their own version of "stone soup" for the Thanksgiving feast. Assign one ingredient to each student, and have students write the ingredients they will bring in the invitations to family members.

Art: Have students prepare place mats and centerpieces for the Thanksgiving "stone soup" feast. Place mats can be made from large sheets of construction paper; centerpieces can be turkey sculptures made from a ball of clay, pipe cleaners, beads, and feathers. Have students form a ball of clay and smooth one side so that it rests evenly on a table. Use a colorful pipe cleaner and bend the top portion into the shape of a turkey's head; poke the other end into the clay on one side. Poke feathers, additional pipe cleaners, and pipe cleaners rounded and filled with beads into the other side of the clay ball, forming the tail feathers. Let the clay harden so that the materials that are poked into it remain attached. The turkeys become delightful sculptures that the students can take home to their own family celebrations. (See Figure 4.27.)

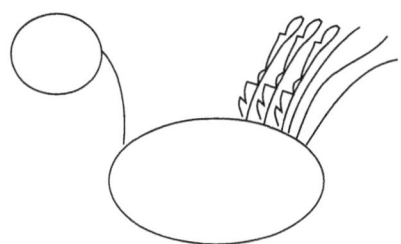

Figure 4.27 Turkey Centerpiece

Social Studies: Share books and audiovisual resources telling the Thanksgiving story.

■ Story: *The Mitten*, adapted and translated by Jan Brett

Location: Ukraine

Curriculum Connections: Science (Seasons-Winter), Reading, Math

Collaboration:
- Gathering picture books showing examples of foreshadowing and other titles by Jan Brett: Media specialist
- Research on animal sizes: Media specialist
- Science, math, and reading lessons: Teacher

Technology Connection: Information Retrieval (ISTE-students 5), Communication and Collaboration (ISTE-students 4), Teacher Delivery of Lesson (ISTE-teacher II-III)

Bookmark Jan Brett's Web site at <www.janbrett.com>. It is filled with a wealth of activities; print the animal masks for *The Mitten* for dramatizing the story. Students will be accessing the portion of the Web site that gives information "about Jan Brett," but they will have fun browsing the other choices. If you want to focus the time at the Web site, just bookmark the "About Jan Brett" page.

Set up a center that encourages students to find out about the author. Invite sharing during morning opening routines, and record interesting details about the author on chart paper.

As you continue to share books by Jan Brett, have students compose a class letter telling about their experiences and thoughts after reading her books. Access the e-mail opportunity at her Web site and send the letter.

Food: Borsch (beet soup). The Ukraine is known for this soup, and although students may not love it, encourage them to try a small sip. To make the soup, saute 1 diced carrot and 1 diced onion in oil until soft, then add 2 tablespoons of tomato puree. Heat 1½ quarts of beef stock, add a peeled and diced potato, and let simmer for about 10 minutes; add 3–4 cups of shredded cabbage and sliced beets (from an 8-ounce can or if fresh, a small bunch; steam the fresh beets until they are tender before adding them to the stock). Cover the pot and let simmer for a few minutes. Add the carrot/onion/tomato mixture and seasonings (1 bay leaf, a few peppercorns, two or three sprigs of snipped parsley, a crushed garlic glove, 1 tablespoon of cider vinegar, and salt to taste). Cover the pot and let the soup cook on low heat for about 20 minutes. Serve in small bowls with a dollop of sour cream and pass a basket of black rye bread.

Art: Revisit the illustrations in the picture and identify details that show that this story takes place in another culture, e.g., clothing, Baba's hair, wall decorations, the house, and the fence.

Have students make their own handprint mittens. Use a variety of colors of tempera paint poured into flat containers. (Disposable aluminum pans, available at most discount stores, are great.) Have students coat the bottoms of their hands with paint, and then make handprints on background papers. Remind them to be sure that they hold their fingers together, with thumbs slightly separated as they print their "mittens." Let the mittens dry, cut them out, attach yarn strings, and use markers to add colorful details, e.g., stripes or polka dots. Display the mittens.

Reading: As you read *The Mitten* for the first time, help students notice the side pictures on each page. What hints do they give for the development of the story? Pause on the page that shows all of the animals in the mitten and describes the arrival of the meadow mouse. Examine the side pictures and pose this prediction question: How will Nicki recover his lost mitten? Refocus question: What will happen next? Invite comments and discussion; then read the rest of the book. Linger on the last page and imagine the thoughts and conversation between Nicki and Baba. If you were Nicki, what would you say? How would you explain the difference in sizes in the mittens?

Introduce the concept of foreshadowing (clues left by the author to hint at events that will happen later), and revisit and browse the pictures in *The Mitten* to reinforce understanding of this concept. Share another title and look for examples of foreshadowing. Continue to search for examples of foreshadowing in other books by Jan Brett and in the following titles. Discuss with students how foreshadowing by an author helps them predict the direction of stories and helps them understand stories more effectively.

Other picture books that include examples of foreshadowing:
Miss Nelson Has a Field Day, by Harry Allard (Boston: Houghton Mifflin, 1985)
No Jumping on the Bed, by Tedd Arnold (New York: Dial, 1987)
Hattie and the Fox, by Mem Fox (New York: Bradbury, 1987)
Knots on a Counting Rope, by Bill Martin and John Archambault (New York: Henry Holt, 1987)
Do Not Open, by Brinton Turkle (New York: Dutton, 1981)
The Stranger, by Chris Van Allsburg (Boston: Houghton Mifflin, 1986)

Focus on the language in the stories by Jan Brett and add words to your word wall that are particularly descriptive. There are some great verbs in *The Mitten*, e.g., burrowed, wiggled, snuffled, bumped, jostled, swooped, grumbled, climbed, trotted, poked, lumbered, spied, bulged and swelled, wriggled, tickled, and scattered.

Use the animal masks from Brett's Web site to dramatize the story. Place the masks in a center and encourage students to have fun with the masks during center time. They might imagine the conversations of the animals as they snuggled together in the mitten.

Science: Focus on the season of winter, and have students make observation paintings of signs of the season. Gather the paintings into a book for the class. Use the book *The Stranger*, by Chris Van Allsburg, to make comparisons between the two seasons of fall and winter.

Math: Pose this question to students: Could that many animals really fit inside the mitten? How big would the mitten really have to be to hold the animals it held? Investigate the sizes of the animals and measure out a mitten that is more realistic. Draw its outline on the floor using masking tape. Have students work with partners or in small groups as they investigate the animals' sizes: mole, rabbit, hedgehog, owl, badger, fox, a great bear, and a meadow mouse who rested on the bear's nose.

Story: *The Lion's Whiskers*, by Nancy Raines Day

Location: Ethiopia

Curriculum Connections: Social Studies: Heroes

Collaboration:
- Gathering books about heroes (For younger students, select simple biographies that could be read aloud; for students who are reading, select biographies that the students can read.): Media specialist
- Learning about heroes: Teacher

Technology Connection: Teacher Delivery of Lesson (ISTE-teacher II-III)

Use the computer to create headings for a large chart on heroes. (See Figure 4.28.) Assemble the chart and create spaces for recording information on the people you will be reading about.

Use the computer to create an "Extra Mile" award. Print multiple copies to use as you pique students' interest in the heroes unit. (See Figure 4.29.)

Hero	Birth Facts (Where/When)	Accomplishments	Obstacles/ Challenges	Age (Most Important Accomplishments)	Hero Characteristics

Figure 4.28 Heroes Chart

Food: Alleecha (vegetable stew). Cut cabbage into small chunks and steam it until it is tender. Dice and saute 1 onion in oil in a large saucepan or electric skillet until soft. Sprinkle in 1 tablespoon of curry powder; stir and cook for one minute. Add ¼ cup of water and cook for 5 more minutes. Add carrots, potatoes, and cauliflower (cut into small pieces) to the mixture, and cook for 15 minutes. Add the cabbage and cook for another 15 minutes. Serve warm.

Art: The illustrations in the book are a wonderful example of collage. Revisit the illustrations and discuss the materials used by the illustrator. Have students plan their own collage pictures, gather materials, and create.

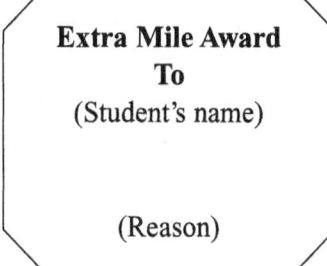

Figure 4.29 Extra Mile Award

Social Studies: Use this lesson plan series to build awareness of heroes:

Week 1: The "Extra Mile" Award

Use the "Extra Mile" awards to recognize students' "hero" behaviors during the week before starting the unit. Quietly give students the awards, and when they question you, tell them that you are recognizing their extra mile in (name the behavior). Be sure to find a way to recognize each student during the week.

Week 2: Recognizing Heroes

Share and discuss the story. As students identify characteristics of heroes, begin a brainstorming web. What are the characteristics of a hero? How is Fanaye a hero to Abebe? Who are people who are heroes in your life? Why? (See Figure 4.30 for a sample web.) Narrow the characteristics of a hero to three or four characteristics and create a second chart entitled, "A Hero Is..." (See Figure 4.31.)

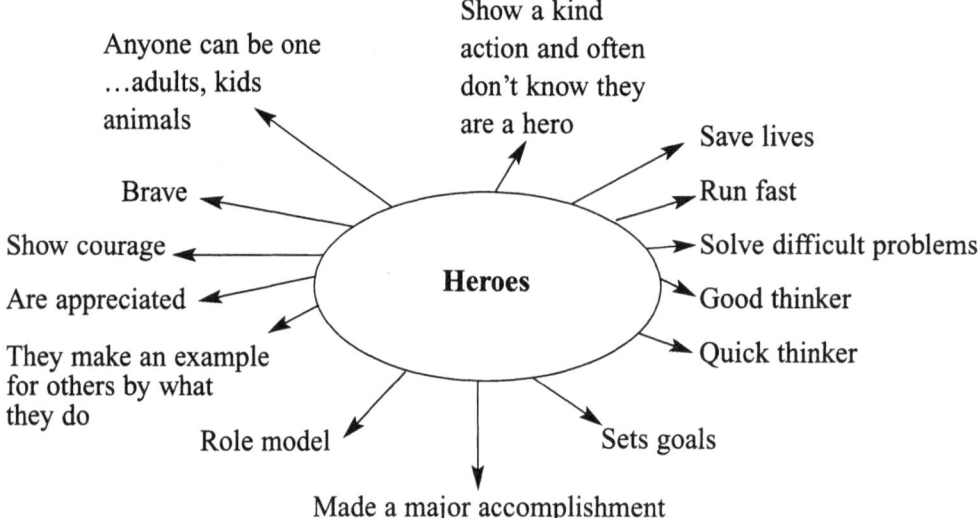

Figure 4.30 Hero Characteristics

Use the large Heroes Chart and fill in information showing how Fanaye is a hero:

Hero: Fanaye; Birth facts: Ethiopia; Accomplishment: Taught Abebe to love through her patience and courage; Challenges/Obstacles: Suffered through Abebe rejection and unhappiness, braved the lion day after day; Age: Older woman; Hero Characteristics: Set goals, thought, solved a difficult problem, showed courage.

Continue to share stories about heroes, e.g., the biographies of the presidents, inventors, and discoverers. As students read or listen to the stories, encourage them to think about the hero's life in terms of the categories on the Heroes Chart. Complete information on the chart for each of the heroes, either those shared as read-alouds or those read independently by the students.

> A hero is someone who…
>
> 1. Sets goals and is a thinker.
> 2. Solves a difficult problem.
> 3. Shows courage.
> 4. Has accomplished something BIG!

Figure 4.31 A Hero Is…

Week 3: The Heroes In My Life

Have students conduct interviews with family members to discover the heroes in their eyes. Brainstorm some interview questions, e.g. Who is your hero? Why is he or she a hero in your eyes? What did he or she accomplish or do to be your hero? Also, have students work with family members to identify heroes in the community, e.g., through the newspaper, through television or radio news broadcasts. Give time during morning opening routines for students to share their heroes.

■ Story: *Why Mosquitoes Buzz in People's Ears,* retold by Verna Aardema

Location: West Africa (Locate this area on the map and identify some of the countries of West Africa, e.g., Senegal, Gambia, Guinea, Sierra Leone, Togo, Nigeria, and the Ivory Coast.)

Curriculum Connections: Science

Collaboration:
- Sharing the story: Classroom
- Research on animals: Media center

Technology Connection: Information Retrieval (ISTE-students 5), Student Productivity (ISTE-students 3)

Once you have shared the story and students have had opportunities to observe live animals, have students choose animals from the story and investigate their behaviors; then write riddles describing their animals. Use a variety of electronic resources, e.g., encyclopedias or databases focusing exclusively on animals. Show students how to access the resources and take notes that focus on animal behaviors. Invite older students to be research buddies for younger students to help them in reading the information.

When students are ready to write the riddles, show them how to organize their clues so that they sequence from hard to give-away clues. Set guidelines for the number of lines in the riddle, i.e., two to three lines for younger students and three to five lines for older students. Here's an example from a first grader: The treetops are my home; I swing and sway from one branch to another. What am I? Here's an example from a third grader: I listen carefully to hunt for prey; I'm awake at night and sleep through the day; I have huge eyes, and some people say that makes me wise; I have a special call that you definitely will recognize...Whooooooo! What am I?

In creating the riddle display, have students type their riddles using a word processing program, then create habitat pictures of their animals on half-sheets of paper. Fold sheets of construction paper in half, paste the riddle on the outside, and paste the habitat picture on the inside. (See Figure 4.32.)

Food: Yam balls. Peel 1½ pounds of yams and cook until soft; mash the yams. Finely chop 1 medium onion and 2 tomatoes and cook them in oil until soft. Combine the yams, the onion/tomato mixture, ½ pound of chopped corned beef, salt and cayenne pepper to taste, and two eggs. Mix well. Sprinkle flour on your working surface and dust your hands with flour; then form the mixture into small golf-ball-size shapes. Saute the yam balls in hot oil until golden brown. Drain on paper towels and serve hot.

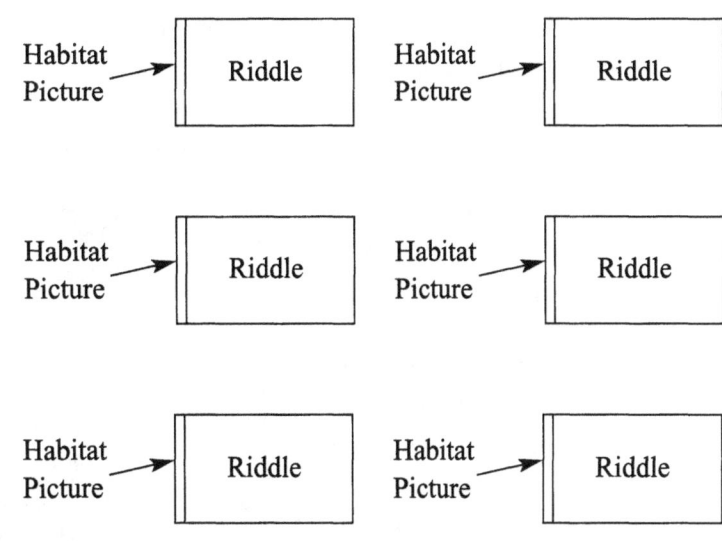

Figure 4.32 Riddle Display

Art: Revisit the illustrations in the book and notice how the animals are designed, e.g., contrasting outlines that define and emphasize the various features of the animal. Look at the birds on the page where the snake slithers into a rabbit's hole and the rabbit scurries out the back way. The sections of the bird's features almost look like small bits of construction paper cut to shape and placed on the paper so a white border shows between all the shapes. Giraffe is another example; look at the page where King Lion first calls the meeting of the animals. Giraffe also has the distinctive white outline and a variety of yellow shapes to indicate skin texture. The yellow shapes appear as though they were layered on top of the brown background.

Show students how to create an animal by cutting and pasting bits and pieces of construction paper, leaving the distinctive white outline from the background paper.

Science: Create opportunities for students to observe live animals, e.g., classroom pets or aquaria or terraria, a trip to the zoo, or a nature walk.

■ Story: *Bringing the Rain to Kapiti Plain*, retold by Verna Aardema

Location: Kenya

Curriculum Connections: Language Arts and Science

Technology Connection: Student Productivity (word processing) (ISTE-students 3)

Have students write "rainy day" cinquain poems. In preparation for writing the poems, create four brainstorming lists with the students: describing words (misty, gray, foggy, windy, quiet, stormy), action words (thundering, pouring, drizzling, dripping, drumming on my window), rainy day activity phrases (watching lightning streaks, protected under my red umbrella, splashing through the puddles in my yellow boots, floating boats, curled in the window watching the storm, hiding in a tent in the house, watching for a rainbow), and feeling phrases about rainy days (happy, lazy day, imagining, family fun). Display the word lists.

Give the guidelines for writing cinquain poems. They are five lines in length, and each line uses different kinds of words.

Line 1: Rainy Days
Line 2: Two describing words, e.g., misty, gray
Line 3: Three action words, e.g., drizzling, dripping, sloshing
Line 4: Short phrase describing a rainy day activity, e.g., splashing through puddles in my bright yellow boots
Line 5: Feeling word or phrase about rainy days, e.g., happy

Roles for the Drama	
Role	**Description**
Clouds	Three-four students standing in a circle on chairs
Grass	Three-four students lying on the floor
Cows	Six-eight students; encourage them to bellow and moo as though they are really hungry
Ki-pat	One student; give the student a small piece of string
Eagle	One student; make a paper feather to drop at the appropriate time
Arrow	Find a stick and put it on the floor
Bow	Have Ki-pat pretend this motion
Wife	One student
Little Ki-pat	Another student

Figure 4.33 Roles for the Drama

Once the poems are written, have students use a word-processing program to type their poems. Show them how to center each line. Print the poems, cut them into unusual shapes, and paste them into the rainy day watercolor pictures.

Food: Fruit Smoothies. Place fruit (banana, peach, or strawberries), honey, orange juice, plain yogurt in a blender and mix until smooth. Add crushed ice if you want to chill them. Pour into small paper cups.

Art: Use watercolor paints and make a "rainy day" picture.

Drama: This is a fun story to dramatize. (See Figure 4.33 for the roles.) Assign/choose roles, read the story, and have the students add actions as you read.

Science: Focus on weather unit objectives.

■ Story: James and the Vine Puller, a Brazilian folktale retold by Martha Bennett Stiles
Panda and the Bunyips, by Michael Foreman

Location: Brazil and Australia

Curriculum Connections: Language Arts (Story writing)

Collaboration: Story writing: Teacher

Technology Connection: Classroom management (Portfolios) (ISTE-teacher IV-V)

Food: Pavlova (a dessert named after the Russian ballerina, Anna Pavlova, after she performed in Australia). Beat 4 egg whites until very stiff and slowly add 1 cup of fine white sugar, beating until the mixture is even stiffer. Fold in 1 tablespoon of cornstarch, 2 teaspoons of vinegar, and 1 teaspoon of vanilla. Mound the mixture on a cookie sheet that has been buttered and sprinkled with powdered sugar and cornstarch. Bake in 250° oven for 90 minutes or until firm; do not allow the top to brown. When it is cool, spread the meringue with whipped cream and sprinkle with sliced bananas and strawberries.

Art: Have students create imaginary lands, e.g., Sugar Plum Island (in the shape of a lollipop, with cities and geographic features named after candies, inhabited by the plum people), Nikiland (in the shape of a shoe, inhabited by shoe people), Sunflower Plain (in the shape of a large sunflower, with cities and geographic features named after flowers and plants, inhabited by flower children). Set requirements for the imaginary lands based on the geographic features of the area where you live so that students have a visual image of the features. (Teacher's note: This also could be a whole-class or small-groups project. As a class project, brainstorm lots of ideas, select one of the ideas, then brainstorm the cities, features, and people. Have students contribute one piece to the land. As a small-groups project, divide students into teams (three to five students per team), meet with two or three teams to brainstorm ideas for imaginary lands, and have the teams select their ideas and begin to create. Repeat the process with the other teams.)

Language Arts: Use one of the imaginary lands, and write a class story based on this setting (or have students write individual stories based on these settings).

1. Identify characters for the story. Think about the inhabitants of the imaginary land. What are their characteristics and abilities? What are their names? (Plum people: round, purple, able to pull in their arms and legs and roll wherever they want to go; the shoe people: short, like clothing that laces, make their homes out of shoes; the flower children: tall and thin, long green arms, slurp juices through their root-feet)
2. Identify a problem to solve, e.g., the plum people could be lost at sea and must find a way home, the shoe people could be searching for treasure in an abandoned shoe house, and the flower children could be puzzling over the disappearance of a flower friend.
3. Create the story. Use a digital camera to record pictures of the imaginary lands; take additional pictures of the students and develop portfolio entries for the project.

If I Ran for President

Information Retrieval	Student Productivity	Problem Solving and Decision Making
Electronic encyclopedias, e.g., *World Book, Grolier's*. Internet sites: **Comparison Facts-Ages:** <www.fujisan.demon.co.uk/USPresidents/plist2b.htm> <http://memory.loc.gov/ammem/pihtml/pioaths.html> **Quick Facts:** <http://memory.loc.gov/ammem/pihtml/piotable.html> **Biographical Information:** <www.ipl.org/ref/POTUS/> **Inauguration Speeches:** <www.bartleby.com/124/>	Slide Show: What's It Like to Be President? Time Line Narrative poem Photo essay captions Letter from a President	Internet site: **Smithsonian: The American President:** <http://americanhistory.si.edu/presidency/home.html>
		Communication and Collaboration

Teacher Delivery of Lessons	Classroom Management
Internet site: **United States Constitution:** <www.nara.gov/exhall/charters/constitution/conmain.html> **United States Map:** <http://geography.about.com/msub37.htm?once=true&> Leadership definitions Preamble to the Constitution Election committee assignments	Assessment rubric for evaluating the letter from a president Contract Activity Packet Leadership Chart

Figure 4.34 If I Ran for President Unit: Technology Connections

Unit 3: If I Ran for President

Unit Objectives:
1. Identify qualities of effective leaders.
2. Work as a leader.
3. Identify the current president and vice president and develop an understanding of the role of the president and the qualifications for becoming president.
4. Explore government at the national level, i.e., organization (executive, legislative, and judicial), purposes and responsibilities of the three branches, and sources of revenue.
5. Develop understanding of the process of choosing leaders (election, appointment).

Audience: Grades 4–8

Length of the Unit: 3 weeks

The Contract Activities Packet Objectives at a Glance

Objective 1: The Presidency	Objective 2: Leadership	Objective 3: The National Government
Activity: Investigating the President Activity: A Letter from the President	Activity: Definitions of Leadership Activity: I Am a Leader	Activity: Separation of Powers and Checks and Balances

Objective 4: Elections	Objective 5: Culminating Assessment
Activity: Getting Elected Activity: Seeking an Appointment	Activity: What Have We Learned?

The Focus Lessons at a Glance

The President's Job	The President's Job II	The President's Job III
Introduction to the contract	Introduction to the letter writing project	Presentation of projects and culminating discussion
Leadership	**The Organization of the National Government**	**The Election Process**
Culminating discussion	Culminating discussion	Culminating discussion and activity

Figure 4.34a If I Ran for President, The Unit Activities at a Glance

■ Activity Focus: The Contract Activity Packet

Technology Connection: Teacher Delivery of Lesson, Classroom Management (ISTE-teacher II-V)

Collaboration:
- Developing the Contract Activity Packet: Teacher and media specialist working together
- Mentoring students as they work in the packet: Teacher and media specialist as co-facilitators
- Focus lessons during the period of the Contract Activity Packet: Teacher and media specialist working together

Resources:
- Internet Web sites:
  <www.fujisan.demon.co.uk/USPresidents/plist2b.htm> (Comparison facts: ages when presidents took office, left office, and their fathers died)
  <http://memory.loc.gov/ammem/pihtml/pioaths.html> (Comparison facts: Oaths of Office and their dates, presidents, locations, people administering the oaths)
  <http://memory.loc.gov/ammem/pihtml/pinotable.html> (quick facts: precedents and notable events associated with inaugurations)
  <http://memory.loc.gov/ammem/pihtml/pibible.html> (Quick facts: biblical/scripture passages at the inaugurations)
  <www.bartleby.com/124/> (inauguration speeches from George Washington to George W. Bush)
  <www.ipl.org/ref/POTUS/> (biographical information about the presidents)
  <http://gi.grolier.com/presidents/ea/bios/> (biographical information about the presidents)
  <http://americanhistory.si.edu/presidency/home.html> (Smithsonian site on the United States presidency)
- *TimeLiner* 5.0 (Tom Snyder Productions, 80 Coolidge Hill Road, Watertown, Massachusetts 02472. Telephone: 1-800-342-0236. Web site: <www.tomsnyder.com>)
- Slide show program, e.g., *AppleWorks, Microsoft PowerPoint*
- Word-processing and spreadsheet software, e.g., *AppleWorks, Microsoft Word, Microsoft Excel*

Preparation Tasks:
- The teacher and media specialist work together to develop the Contract Activity Packet for the unit. The Contract Activity Packet (see Figure 4.35 for an outline of the format) identifies key objectives—what students should know (facts), understand (concepts), and be able to do (skills)—provides activities and experiences to build knowledge, understanding, and skills; facilitates ownership of learning by students (pacing managed by students); and establishes criteria for success.
- The first packet is the most challenging to create, but once you have the format and the activities developed, subsequent contracts are relatively easy to develop. Create a folder on the computer and save the first packet (like a template); when you are ready to develop another contract, open the original file, choose "Save As," and rename the file with the new contract name. Work through the "template," substituting new objectives and activity descriptions.

Assignment Description:
The "If I Ran for President" contract can be implemented during October in a presidential election year and can culminate in school-wide voting in early November, or it can be introduced and completed during the month of February when President's Day is celebrated. Students use spiral notebooks as their journals during the contract and record their notes, discussion reflections, rough drafts, and activity experiences in them. After introducing the contract, reviewing its

requirements, and setting deadlines, have students staple the contract into the inside front cover of the spiral notebook so that they have a constant reminder of its requirements and what they have accomplished. A calendar of days for the unit (recording deadlines, activities, and dates for whole-class focus lessons) also is a helpful tool and can be pasted on the opening page of the notebook. Focus lessons provide opportunities for culminating discussions on particular objectives, for introductory lessons, and for sharing products with the class.

The "If I Ran for President" Contract

■ Activity: Investigate the Presidency

Objective 1: Identify the current president and vice president and develop an understanding of the role of the president and the qualifications for becoming president.

Learn about the job of the president and the qualifications for becoming president. Report your findings through one of these products:

1. A narrative poem, set to music
2. A photo essay — A Week in the Life of a President
3. A slide show — What's It Like to Be a President?

In addition to other resources in the media center, here is an Internet site that has been bookmarked for your use: <http://americanhistory.si.edu/presidency/home.html>. When you access the site, go to Foundations and gather information from these pages.

Page 1

Contract Activity Packet:
If I Ran For President

Student's Name:
Starting Date:
Ending Date:
Culminating Assessment Score:
Student's Signature:
Teacher's Signature:

Objectives:
1
2
3

Page 2

Objective:

Activity:

Activity:

Criteria for Success:

Completion Date:

Pages 3-5

Objective:

Activity:

Activity:

Criteria for Success:

Team Members:
Completion Date:

Page 6

Objective: Culminating Assessment

Activity:

Activity:

Criteria for Success:

Completion Date:

Figure 4.35 Contract Activity Packet

Technology for Social Studies Units

■ Activity: A Letter from the President

Choose a president who interests you and review the question sheet for the president. Research answers to the question, then write your letter. Your letter will be four paragraphs in length. The first paragraph will show your knowledge of the person you are writing to. The second, third, and fourth paragraphs will show your understanding and interpretation of the events in the president's administration.

Be sure to include a bibliography page listing the sources of your information. In addition to other resources in the media center, here are some Internet Web sites that have been bookmarked for your use:

<www.bartleby.com/124/> (inauguration speeches from George Washington to George W. Bush)
<www.ipl.org/ref/POTUS/> (biographical information about the presidents)
<http://gi.grolier.com/presidents/ea/bios/> (biographical information about the presidents)
<www.fujisan.demon.co.uk/USPresidents/plist2b.htm> (comparison facts: ages when presidents took office, left office, and their fathers died)
<http://memory.loc.gov/ammem/pihtml/pioaths.html> (comparison facts: oaths of office and their dates, presidents, locations, and people administering the oaths)
<http://memory.loc.gov/ammem/pihtml/pinotable.html> (quick facts: precedents and notable events associated with inaugurations)
<http://memory.loc.gov/ammem/pihtml/pibible.html> (quick facts: biblical/scripture passages at the inaugurations).

Criteria for Success:

1. Thorough research notes restated in your own words
2. Detailed bibliography of resources
3. Careful development of final product, i.e., attention to effective writing, meeting the information guidelines for the assignment, and making the product easy to understand and follow
4. Evidence of creativity and originality
5. Meeting deadline

Completion Date:

■ Activity: Definitions of Leadership

Objective 2: Identify qualities of effective leaders and work as a leader.

Work with a team of four to six students and brainstorm and record qualities of leadership. Use the dictionary and encyclopedia to add to your information about leadership. Use a priority matrix (5-most important quality, 3-an important quality, 1-not needed in the definition) to narrow the list to the most important qualities for leadership; then use your narrowed list to construct a definition of leadership.

■ Activity: I Am a Leader

Now that you have defined qualities of leadership, work with your team to develop an action plan for working as leaders in the school, in the community, and in your home. Interview school leaders (principal, teachers, and specialists), community leaders, and family members to create a list of leadership opportunities in those three settings. Identify the opportunities you will be responsible for and plan a way to share your successes with the class.

Team Members:

Criteria for Success:
1. Thoroughness of brainstorming and researching
2. Demonstration of respect for the ideas, suggestions, and priorities of the group
3. Thoughtfulness of the leadership definition
4. Practicality of the goals for working as a leader

Completion Date:

■ Activity: Separation of Power and Checks and Balances

Objective 3: Explore government at the national level, i.e., organization (executive, legislative, and judicial), purposes and responsibilities of the three branches, and sources of revenue.

Work on a team of three and research the three branches of government. Report your findings through one of these products:

1. A dramatization, with each member of your team taking on a role from one of the branches
2. A Venn diagram comparison of the three branches of government
3. A mural, with contributions from each team member

Work with your team to develop an explanation of your understanding of these key phrases: "separation of power" and "checks and balances." Find a way to show your understanding in your product.

Team Members:

Criteria for Success:
1. Respectful cooperation and collaboration with team members
2. Thorough research on the branches of government
3. Thoughtful preparation of the final product
4. Evidence of rehearsal in the presentation of the product

Completion Date:

■ Activity: Getting Elected

Objective 4: Develop understanding of the process of choosing leaders (election and appointment).

Work with a small team (three to four students) to create a time line of the election process. Begin your work by defining these key terms: political parties, Republican, Democrat, Independent, donkey, elephant, primary (open and closed), caucus, convention, campaign, issues, polls, booth, ballot, favorite son, image, dark horse, elector, conservative, liberal, right wing, alternates, bandwagon, demonstration, nominate, roll call of states, delegates, keynote speech, platform, electoral college, brokered convention, and coattails. Use *TimeLiner* to create your time line showing the sequence of events in a presidential election year. Be sure to use the key terms in your time line descriptions. This Web site also may be helpful: <http://americanhistory.si.edu/presidency/home.html>. After accessing the site, select "The Campaign Trail" and browse these pages for pertinent information.

■ **Activity: Seeking an Appointment**

Objective 4: Develop understanding of the process of choosing leaders (election and appointment).

Work with your team to identify government jobs that are filled by appointments. Create posters that describe the responsibilities of the jobs and identify the process for receiving an appointment.

Team Members:

Criteria for Success:
1. Quality of the definitions
2. Inclusion of the election terms in the time line
3. Accuracy in the time line of election events
4. Thoroughness in the explanation of the appointment process

Completion Date:

Objective 5: Culminating Assessment

■ **Activity: What Have We Learned?**

Working with a partner, access the Smithsonian Web site <http://americanhistory.si.edu/presidency/home.html> and go to the "activities" page. Review the four choices (The President Has Many Roles, All the President's Children, Children Write to the President, Polling: Your Opinion Counts), and select two that you and your partner will complete. Select your first choice, and complete the activity directions and assignments. Select your second choice and complete those assignments.

Criteria for Success:
1. Thoughtfulness of your responses
2. Care in following the requirements of the activity

Completion Date:

■ Focus Lesson 1: The President's Job
(introducing the Contract and the first objective)

Technology Connection: Teacher Delivery of Lesson (ISTE-teacher II-III)

Collaboration:
Gathering resources: Media specialist
Implementing the lesson: Teacher

Resources:
- *Shhh! We're Writing the Constitution,* by Jean Fritz (New York: G. P. Putnam, 1987) or *If You Were There When They Signed the Constitution,* by Elizabeth Levy (New York: Scholastic, 1987)
- Narrative poem, e.g., "The Midnight Ride of Paul Revere"
- Chart paper

Preparation Tasks:
- Gather resources/copies of the United States Constitution and the amendments to the Constitution.
- Access the Web site <www.nara.gov/exhall/charters/constitution/conmain.html>, and then click on transcription for information on the Constitution, Bill of Rights, and amendments. (Teacher's note: If you have trouble accessing the site, try this keyword search: "U. S. Constitution.")

Assignment Description:
Introduce the Constitution and its amendments, and have students work with partners to gather information about the job of the presidency. What guidelines/requirements are listed in the Constitution (look at Article II) and the amendments that refer to the president's role/job? Invite sharing, and record the information on chart paper, i.e., The Constitution Says... The Amendments Say...

Read and discuss one of the books. Establish a visual time line of the sequence of events leading to the development of the Constitution and the sequence of its ratification.

Introduce the Contract Activity Packet and review its requirements. Fill in the calendar with deadline dates and focus lesson dates. Review the guidelines for the first activity under Objective 1, and talk about and show examples of the product choices.

■ Focus Lesson 2: The President's Job II
(introducing the letter-writing activity)

Technology Connection: Information Retrieval (ISTE-students 5), Student Productivity (word processing) (ISTE-students 3)

Collaboration:
- Research: Media specialist and teacher as co-facilitators
- Letter writing: Teacher

Resources: A list of the presidents

Preparation Tasks:
- Print copies of the assignment topic lists.
- Make transparencies of the sample letter, the topic list for Lyndon Johnson, and the list of the presidents.

Assignment Description:
Students pretend to be a president and write friendly letters from the president. Letters share research information about the president.

A Sample Letter: Lyndon B. Johnson writing to his wife, Lady Bird

January 5, 1966

Dear Lady Bird,

How are you, Lynda, and Luci? I'm glad we could be together at the ranch over the holidays. This has been one of our most enjoyable Christmases since that tragic day in Dallas in 1963. I sure do wish I could still be in Texas with you and the girls. Oh, has Luci gotten over the flu yet? Please tell her I hope she gets well soon, and I look forward to your return to Washington.

Since I've been back at the White House, I have been really busy working on my speech to Congress for the State of the Union address. I think I will review my major programs in the speech. Do you think this is a good idea? Of course, I must describe the new programs I'm adding to the big one, The Great Society. They will include the war on poverty, improving the educational system, providing for elder citizens, and aiding urban areas. Since I started the war on poverty with the Economic Opportunity Act in 1964, we have set up the Job Corps, Volunteers in Service to America (VISTA), a work-study program, and community action programs like Head Start for preschoolers. I must add in this area Medicare and Medicaid for elder citizens; I'm confident of the support of both houses in Congress because of my early leadership in the Senate and the Democratic majority we hold. I also want to emphasize the success of these programs and how they have benefited many of our poor and disadvantaged Americans.

The second big area I need to report on in the State of the Union speech is the Vietnam War—the news is very troubling. I keep on thinking about our best young men who are fighting over there. But, as you know, when the Viet Cong soldiers attacked the base at Pleiku, we had to strike back. I ordered air strikes against several North Vietnamese military bases, but I stated, "We still seek no wider war." Once we passed the Gulf of Tonkin Resolution, we had a legal basis on which the United States could conduct the war. I hope we can end this war soon.

Finally, I must tell Congress about our successes in the Civil Rights Movement. Since Martin Luther King, Jr. led more than 200,000 demonstrators in the march on Washington back in 1963, we have made some changes. The Civil Rights Act in 1964 helped end discrimination in employment and public facilities. As you know, my proudest achievement was the Voting Rights Act of 1965. This outlawed the ridiculous literacy tests. Nevertheless, we are still having major racial problems. Riots in neighborhoods, like the ones in Watts last year, have cost us lots and lots of money and deaths. Groups like the Black Panthers in California are encouraging armed rebellion against the white establishment. Hopefully, some of our achievements will stop these acts of violence.

Well, I must go now because I have a cabinet meeting where Dean Rusk and Robert McNamara are presenting Pentagon recommendations on Vietnam. I hope to see you soon. Give the girls my love.

Love,
Lyndon

George Washington writing to Thomas Jefferson in 1794
1. Thomas Jefferson, Washington's inauguration
2. Jay's Treaty
3. Whiskey Rebellion
4. 11th Amendment

John Adams writing to George Washington in 1798
1. Washington's retirement years, Adams' inauguration
2. The XYZ Affair
3. Alien and Sedition Acts
4. The Department of the Navy

Thomas Jefferson writing to Martha Jefferson Randolph in 1804
1. Martha Jefferson Randolph, the first child born in the White House, Jefferson's inauguration
2. Hamilton/Burr duel
3. Jefferson's five-part policy on government
4. Louisiana Purchase, Lewis and Clark expedition

James Madison writing to Eleanor Conway Madison in 1815
1. Eleanor Conway Madison, Madison's inauguration
2. War of 1812, the burning of Washington, DC
3. Peace Treaty of Ghent
4. Hartford Convention of 1814

James Monroe writing to Elizabeth Kortright Monroe in 1823
1. Elizabeth Kortright Monroe, Monroe's inauguration
2. Monroe Doctrine
3. Seminole wars
4. Missouri Compromise

John Quincy Adams writing to John Adams in 1825
1. The relationship between John Quincy Adams and John Adams, John Quincy Adams' inauguration
2. Lafayette's visit to the United States in 1825
3. Democrat-Republican party in 1825
4. Tariff of Abominations

Andrew Jackson writing to his adopted son in 1835
1. Andrew Jackson's adopted son, Jackson's inauguration
2. The Spoils System, Kitchen Cabinet
3. Jackson's fight with the Second Bank of the United States and Nicholas Biddle
4. Gun invented in 1835

Martin Van Buren writing to William H. Harrison in 1840
1. William H. Harrison, Van Buren's inauguration
2. The Underground Railroad, Harriet Tubman
3. Independent Treasury Act
4. Panic of 1837

Technology for Social Studies Units

William H. Harrison writing to Anna Symmes Harrison in 1840
  1. Anna Symmes Harrison, Harrison's nickname, Harrison's inauguration
  2. Whig political party
  3. John Tyler
  4. Photography, Louis Daguerre, William Henry Fox Talbot

John Tyler writing to Julia Gardiner Tyler in 1845
  1. Julia Gardiner Tyler, Tyler's inauguration
  2. Texas statehood
  3. Webster-Ashburton Treaty
  4. Invention of the pneumatic, state was admitted to the Union during Tyler's presidency

James K. Polk writing to Sarah Childress Polk in 1848
  1. Sarah Childress Polk, Polk's nickname, Polk's inauguration
  2. California acquired 1848, Battle of Buena Vista
  3. The Oregon question
  4. The invention of the sewing machine

Zachary Taylor writing to Margaret Smith Taylor in 1850
  1. Margaret Smith Taylor, Taylor's nickname, Taylor's inauguration
  2. Fugitive Slave Laws
  3. Clayton Bulwer Treaty
  4. California Gold Rush

Millard Fillmore writing to Abigail Powers Fillmore in 1852
  1. Abigail Powers Fillmore, Fillmore's inauguration
  2. Compromise of 1850
  3. Fugitive Slave Law
  4. Harriet Beecher Stowe, Uncle Tom's Cabin

Franklin Pierce writing to Jean Appleton Pierce in 1854
  1. Jean Appleton Pierce, Pierce's inauguration
  2. Ostend Manifesto
  3. Kansas-Nebraska Act
  4. The founding of the Republican Party

James Buchanan writing to John C. Breckinridge in 1859
  1. John C. Breckinridge, Buchanan's inauguration
  2. Dred Scott case
  3. The raid at Harper's Ferry by John Brown
  4. Pony Express Mail Service

Abraham Lincoln writing to Mary Todd Lincoln in 1863
  1. Mary Todd Lincoln, Lincoln's inauguration
  2. Emancipation Proclamation
  3. Gettysburg Address
  4. National holiday declared in 1863

Andrew Johnson writing to Mary Todd Lincoln in 1868
   1. Mary Todd Lincoln, Johnson's inauguration
   2. Johnson's impeachment
   3. Reconstruction
   4. William Seward's purchase of Alaska, "Seward's Folly" or "Seward's Ice Box"

Ulysses S. Grant writing to Jesse Root Grant in 1871
   1. Jesse Root Grant, Grant's career before he became president, Grant's inauguration
   2. Ku Klux Klan
   3. Whiskey Ring
   4. The transcontinental

Rutherford B. Hayes writing to Birchard Hayes in 1877
   1. Birchard Hayes, Hayes' inauguration
   2. Reconstruction
   3. Thomas Edison
   4. The Spoils System

James Garfield writing to Lucretia Rudolph Garfield in 1881, shortly before he was assassinated
   1. Lucretia Rudolph Garfield, Garfield's inauguration
   2. Garfield's assassination
   3. Clara Barton
   4. Chester A. Arthur

Chester A. Arthur writing to Chester Alan Arthur, Jr. in 1883
   1. Chester Alan Arthur, Jr., First Lady for President Arthur, Arthur's inauguration
   2. Chester A. Arthur's rise to the presidency
   3. Protective tariffs
   4. Pendleton Act

Benjamin Harrison writing to Caroline Lavinia Scott in 1890
   1. Caroline Lavinia Scott, Harrison's nicknames, Harrison's inauguration
   2. The Pan American Union
   3. Sherman Anti-Trust Act, The Sherman Silver Purchase Act, The McKinley Tariff Act
   4. Oklahoma Land Rush, its effect on the Indians, states admitted to the Union at this time

Grover Cleveland writing to Frances Cleveland in 1886
   1. Frances Cleveland, Cleveland's inauguration
   2. Presidential Succession Act
   3. American Federation of Labor, Samuel Gompers
   4. Statue of Liberty

William McKinley writing to Garret Hobart in 1899
   1. Garret Hobart, McKinley's inauguration
   2. Spanish-American War, Treaty of Paris
   3. Open Door Policy
   4. Territory acquired in 1898

Theodore Roosevelt writing to Edith Carow Roosevelt in 1906
1. Edith Roosevelt, Nobel Peace Prize, Roosevelt's inauguration
2. Hepburn Act, Pure Food and Drug Act
3. Roosevelt's corollary to the Monroe Doctrine
4. San Francisco disaster in 1906

William H. Taft writing to Helen Herron Taft in 1909
1. Helen Herron Taft, Taft's inauguration
2. Payne-Aldrich Tariff, "dollar diplomacy"
3. Robert E. Peary
4. The invention of the helicopter

Woodrow Wilson writing to Jessie Woodrow Wilson in 1917
1. Jessie Woodrow Wilson, Wilson's inauguration
2. War with Germany, Wilson's 14-point plan, League of Nations
3. Wilson's New Freedom program of reform for tariffs, banking, and control of the trusts
4. Virgin Islands purchase

Warren G. Harding writing to George Harding in 1923
1. George Harding, Harding's inauguration
2. Teapot Dome scandals
3. Prohibition
4. Washington Conference of 1921–22

Calvin Coolidge writing to Grace Anna Coolidge in 1926
1. Grace Anna Coolidge, Coolidge's nickname, Coolidge's inauguration
2. Scopes trial
3. Citizenship for Native Americans
4. Richard Byrd's explorations of the North Pole

Herbert Hoover writing to Lou Henry Hoover in 1930
1. Lou Henry Hoover, Hoover's inauguration
2. Great Depression, Stock Market in 1929, "run on banks"
3. Hoover Relief Policy
4. Establishment of the Veterans Administration

Franklin D. Roosevelt writing to Anna Eleanor Roosevelt in 1941
1. Anna Eleanor Roosevelt, Roosevelt's health problems, Roosevelt's inauguration
2. FDR's Four Freedoms
3. State of national emergency declared in 1941, Pearl Harbor
4. Atlantic Charter
5. FDR running for a third presidential term

Harry S. Truman writing to Elizabeth Wallace Truman in 1949
1. Elizabeth Wallace Truman, Truman's inauguration
2. Marshall Plan
3. Cold War, the Berlin Blockade and Airlift
4. Alger Hiss

Dwight D. Eisenhower writing to Richard Nixon in 1959
  1. Richard Nixon's position in 1959, Eisenhower's health at this time, Eisenhower's inauguration
  2. The launch of *Sputnik*
  3. Black civil rights movement in the 1950s, Supreme Court, Little Rock, Arkansas, in 1957
  4. States admitted to the Union in 1959

John F. Kennedy writing to Rose Fitzgerald Kennedy in 1962
  1. Rose Kennedy, Kennedy's nickname, Kennedy's inauguration
  2. Bay of Pigs invasion, Cuban missile crisis
  3. Establishment of the Peace Corps
  4. Lieutenant Colonel John Glenn's accomplishment in 1962, space program

Lyndon Baines Johnson writing to Claudia Taylor Johnson in 1966
  1. Claudia Taylor Johnson, Johnson's inauguration
  2. The Great Society program
  3. Vietnam War during Johnson's administration
  4. Racial problems occurring at this time

Richard M. Nixon writing to Tricia Nixon in 1972 from Peking
  1. Tricia Nixon, Nixon's inauguration
  2. Nixon's visit to Peking
  3. Civil rights controversy concerning school busing
  4. SALT Talks

Gerald Ford writing to Richard Nixon in 1975
  1. Richard Nixon, Ford's inauguration
  2. Amnesty Program
  3. Two assassination attempts on Ford's life
  4. Economy problems: "inflation"

James E. Carter writing to Rosalyn Carter in 1980
  1. Rosalyn Carter, Carter's inauguration
  2. Carter's human rights policy
  3. Iranian hostage crisis
  4. Three Mile Island nuclear plant

Ronald Reagan writing to Nancy Reagan in 1987 at the Western White House
  1. Nancy Reagan, Reagan's career, Reagan's inauguration
  2. "Reaganomics"
  3. Iran-contra affair
  4. The assassination attempt on Reagan's life, gun control

George H. W. Bush writing to Ronald Reagan in 1992
  1. Ronald Reagan, Bush's inauguration
  2. The environment: oil spills, cleaning up the air
  3. Persian Gulf War
  4. The launch of the Hubble space telescope

William Clinton writing to Hillary Rodham Clinton in New York in 2000
1. Hillary Rodham Clinton, Clinton's inauguration
2. The economy of the United States during Clinton's administration
3. Foreign policy accomplishments, i.e., with China, Northern Ireland, Iraq, Israel, and Bosnia
4. Scandals, Whitewater, impeachment

■ Focus Lesson 3: The President's Job III
(culminating discussion)

Technology Connection: Teacher Delivery of Lesson (ISTE-teacher II-III)

Collaboration: Presentations and discussions: Teacher and media specialist as co-facilitators

Resources: Students' products from the first objective

Preparation Tasks:
- Create a figure showing the roles of the president and make a transparency of it. (See Figure 4.36.)
- Create an assessment rubric for the letter-writing assignment. (See Figure 4.37.)

Assignment Description:
Display the roles-of-the-president transparency and review each role to gauge students' understanding of the responsibilities of the roles. Have students present one of their products from Objective 1, then their journals to reflect on the roles in terms of the letter from the president that they wrote. As they look at the paragraphs in their letters, which roles are in evidence and why?

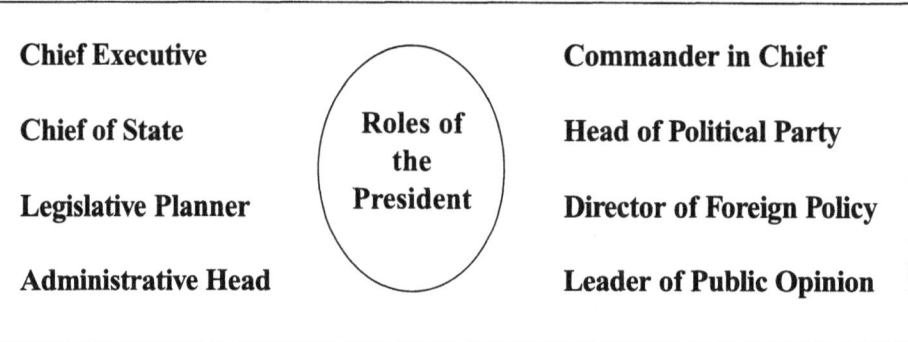

Figure 4.36 Roles of the President

■ Focus Lesson 4: Leadership
(culminating discussion)

Technology Connection: Teacher Delivery of Lesson (ISTE-teacher II-III)

Collaboration: Discussion: Teacher and media specialist as co-facilitators

Resources: Students' definition of leadership

Preparation Tasks:

- Prepare a poster-size leadership graph. (See Figure 4.38.)
- Gather each team's leadership definition and list them together on a page. Print multiple copies for each student and make a transparency. (See Figure 4.39.)
- Identify four or five figures in history/current news; choose figures that are familiar to the class and are a mix of men and women, e.g., sports figure, celebrity, president/world leader, rights activist, and writer/artist. List the names on a transparency.

Assignment Description:

Display the leadership definitions and invite each team to share. Circle the qualities that are repeated. Apply the leadership qualities to the presidents and pose these questions for discussion:

Assessment Rubric: Presidents Letters			
Student:			
Topic:			
	3	2	1
Demonstrated understanding of friendly letter format.			
Research was thorough and restated in own words.			
Research was incorporated into the letter.			
Demonstrated appropriate conventions in writing: complete thoughts and sentences			
Wrote in a conversational tone.			
Used descriptive language.			
Demonstrated appropriate conventions in punctuation, capitalization, spelling.			
Included a bibliography.			
Used the correct format for the bibliography.			
Met the deadline for completion.			
Comments:			

Scale:
3 = Exceptional work
2 = Commendable work
1 = Minimal competency

Figure 4.37 Assessment Rubric: Presidents' Letters

What are examples of these qualities in the presidents we have been studying? We sometimes use the expression "She was a great leader." How is a "great" leader different from a leader? What does that expression mean? Which presidents would students identify as "great presidents"? Why?

Introduce the leadership graph and explain how it will work. The class will keep a weekly running chart on their leadership examples. At the end of each week, the class will tally the opportunities for leadership each student acted upon and will mark that number on the graph. For example, if there are 25 students in the class and 4 students engaged in leadership twice during the previous week while 15 students performed one act of leadership during the week and 6 students did not perform any acts of leadership, the tally mark on the graph would be 23.

Display the list of names and have students evaluate the figures for their leadership qualities based on the circled terms on the definitions list. Invite sharing and discussion.

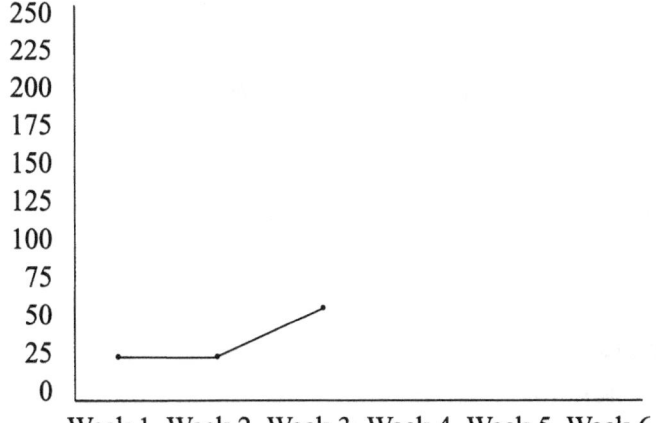

Figure 4.38 Leadership Graph

Technology for Social Studies Units 139

```
Leadership Definitions
Leadership is...


              Team 1


Leadership is...


              Team 2
```

Figure 4.39 Leadership Definitions

■ Focus Lesson 5: The Organization of the National Government
(culminating discussion)

Technology Connection: Teacher Delivery of Lesson (ISTE-teacher II-III)

Collaboration: Discussion: Teacher and media specialist as co-facilitators

Resources:
- Students' branches-of-government products
- Visual time line of the sequence of events leading to the Constitutional conventions and the ratification process (from the focus lesson at the beginning of the unit)
- Dictionaries, enough for one per partnership or small group

Preparation Tasks: Prepare small strips of paper presenting the preamble to the Constitution, enough copies for one per student.

Lesson Plan:
Review the time line for the ratification of the Constitution created in the first focus lesson. Have students imagine themselves as delegates to the conventions. Their task is to review the preamble to the Constitution written by a small group at the convention and to analyze and interpret its meaning. Distribute the slips of paper, read the preamble, and assign words and phrases to students in the class working in partnerships and small groups. Students will use the dictionaries and their discussions to interpret their phrases and present brief explanations to the class.

Have students present their branches-of-government products. Discuss how the goals of the preamble are accomplished through the roles of the branches of government and the concepts of separation of power and checks and balances.

■ Focus Lesson 6: The Election Process
(culminating discussion/activity)

Technology Connection: Student Productivity (ISTE-students 3), Teacher Delivery of Lessons (ISTE-teacher II-III)

Collaboration: Mentoring the election committees: Teacher and media specialist working together

Resources:
- Time lines developed by the students
- Word-processing software, e.g., *AppleWorks, Microsoft Word*
- Slide show software, e.g., *AppleWorks, PowerPoint, HyperStudio*
- Outline map of the United States, enough copies for one per student

Preparation Tasks:
- The teacher and media specialist work together to identify the election committees, i.e., voter registration, election day, and committees for the candidates.
- Develop assignment descriptions for each of the committees. (See Figure 4.40.)
- Access the map Web site <http://geography.about.com/msub37.htm?once=true&> and print an outline map of the United States. Make one copy for each student.

Assignment Description:

Have students share (briefly) from their time line products.

Introduce the election day voting project and divide students into committees. Review and discuss the committee responsibilities. Have students work in their committees to plan and complete their responsibilities. Schedule a school-wide election the day before the actual election.

At Home Connection: Have students use the outline maps, listen to election returns, and color the map to show how the states voted for the candidates.

Voter Registration Committee

Develop a plan for registering students as voters for the school-wide election.

1. What will be your process?
2. Why is it necessary to register to vote?
3. Will party affiliation be an important consideration?

Election Committee

Plan and implement a school-wide election.

1. How will you run the election?
2. What will be the hours for the voting booths?
3. Where will the polls be located?

Campaign Committee

Organize a campaign for (candidate's name from the national election).

1. What is your candidate's platform?
2. How will you inform students about your candidate?
3. What kind of publicity materials will you develop?

Create copies of the "Campaign Committee" descriptions, depending on the number of candidates running for president.

Figure 4.40 Election Committee Responsibilities

Technology for Social Studies Units

Neighborhood Walk		
Information Retrieval	**Student Productivity**	**Problem Solving and Decision Making**
Internet site: **Roxaboxen revisited:** <www.alicemclerran.com/thepark.html>	Three-dimensional Buildings: *Community Construction Kit* (Tom Snyder Productions)	
		Communication and Collaboration
		Letter to the Author: <www.alicemclerran.com/>
Teacher Delivery of Lessons		**Classroom Management**
Internet site: **Roxaboxen revisited:** <www.alicemclerran.com/thepark.html>		Neighborhood Workshop journal

Figure 4.41 Neighborhood Walk Unit: Technology Connections

Unit 4: Neighborhood Walk

Unit Objectives:
1. Develop a beginning understanding of land use purposes and how city planners develop neighborhood communities.
2. Identify features of neighborhoods.

Audience: Grades 1–3

Length of the Unit: 3 weeks

The Unit Activities at a Glance

Introduction	Neighborhood Planning
Students explore *Roxaboxen*, write an acrostic poem, research facts about the author, and write a letter to the author.	Students read more about neighborhoods and how they change, conduct a survey and discuss different kinds of land uses, and plan and construct a three-dimensional neighborhood.

Figure 4.41a Neighborhood Walk, The Unit Activities at a Glance

Technology Connection: Information Retrieval (ISTE-students 5), Communication and Collaboration (ISTE-students 4), Teacher Delivery of Lesson (ISTE-teacher II-III)

Collaboration:
- Sharing the story: Teacher
- Researching the author: Media specialist
- Communicating with the author: Teacher

Resources:
- *Roxaboxen,* by Alice McLerran, four or five copies
- Drawing paper
- Illustrating materials, e.g., crayons, colored pencils, markers
- Projection system
- *Roxaboxen* floor model (Teacher's note: Use a large sheet of cardboard, and use beans or small stones or aquarium gravel to outline roads for the new town that the students will create. Cut construction paper pieces [like a jigsaw puzzle] and fit them on the model. These pieces will become the stores/houses/services of the new Roxaboxen.)
- Construction materials, e.g., beads, beach glass, shells, feathers, twigs, cotton balls, paper, scissors, glue (Teacher's note: Don't purchase anything; just use found materials and recycled materials.)
- Tagboard

Preparation Tasks:
- Bookmark these Web sites:
  <www.alicemclerran.com/thepark.html> (*Roxaboxen* revisited)
  <www.alicemclerran.com/> (Author's Web site)
- Use chart paper and set up an acrostic poem format for a poem about Roxaboxen. (See Figure 4.42.)
- Create a poster of bridge words that students can use in writing the acrostic poem. (See Figure 4.43.)

Assignment Descriptions:
Visiting Roxaboxen: Distribute drawing paper, and have students picture favorite places in their neighborhoods and make drawings of the places. Have them share their pictures with a partner, describing why this is a favorite/special place.

Create a two-column chart on the board or on newsprint paper. Label the first column, "Our neighborhood places are special because…;" label the second column, "Roxaboxen is special because…" (See Figure 4.44.) Invite sharing from student partners and list their reasons in the first column. (Teacher's note: Collect the neighborhood drawings and make a bulletin board display using the ideas from the chart and the drawings.)

```
R
O
X
A
B
O
X
E
N
```

Figure 4.42 *Roxaboxen* Acrostic Poem

	Bridge Words
A	and, an, after, about, around, as
B	because, before, between, by, but, both
C	could, can
D	down, during
E	each, every, even, except, either
F	for, from
G	go, going, get
H	he, his, her
I	in, into, instead of, if, in addition to
J	just
K	key, keep
L	like
M	most, more
N	none, near, not, neither, nor, never, next, now
O	on, over
P	please, put
Q	quickly, quite
R	rarely
S	so, some, since
T	to, through
U	under, upon, unless, until
V	very
W	with, without, where, while
Y	yet

Our neighborhood places are special because…	Roxaboxen is special because…

Figure 4.44 Response Chart

Figure 4.43 Bridge Words

Read and discuss the story, *Roxaboxen*. Read the author and illustrator notes on the last page. Access the "*Roxaboxen* revisited" site and share and discuss the pictures. Show students the author's Web site, and explain that they will be gathering information from the site and creating a display about the author.

Have the students create an acrostic poem about Roxaboxen. Have them work with partners or in groups of three. Each group/partnership will have an assigned letter. Encourage them to pore over the book to reflect the descriptions and events of the story in the poem. Show students the list of bridge words. These can be used if they are stumped about how to begin a line. The letter "X" will be tough; see the example poem to help if students are struggling. Here's a sample written by a group of second-grade students:

Roxaboxen was a very special place to play. Made
Of sand and rocks and some old wooden boxes,
X could mark the spot…just ford the River Rhode
And watch the town of Roxaboxen grow.
Buried treasure, a tin box filled with round black pebbles, was found by Marian.
On Main Street, the road was edged with whitest stones, then houses were shaped, plain at first. Soon,
X marked another spot, the town hall, where Marian became mayor, but nobody really minded.
Everyone had plenty of money and plenty of places to shop, and everyone had a car because all you needed was something round. Roxaboxen was a
Neat place to play: if you had a horse (just a stick and a bridle would do), you could go as fast as the wind. Once there was a great war! with whirling swords of ocotillo.

Making Our Own Roxaboxen: Display the floor model and explain that students will be making their own town of Roxaboxen. Introduce the concept of goods and services, and brainstorm ideas for the stores/services in the town. Identify areas on the map where the houses and the stores and services will be located.

Have students trace their shapes onto pieces of tagboard, then write bottom side on the puzzle piece (so they know which side is up and which side is down). Have students plan their houses, stores, and service areas, and identify the supplies they will bring from home. Decorate the puzzle pieces and construct the town of "Roxaboxen." View the final layout.

All About the Author: Set up a schedule for small groups to use the media center and gather information about the author from her Web site. Have students work with partners to create their contributions for a display about the author. Suggested assignments include: a picture of the author, a list of the books she has written and the ones that are in the media center collection, a time line showing events in her life, pictures of the awards and honors she has received, a map of the places she has lived with captions about her homes, personal facts about the author, a description of her hobbies, a review of one of her books, pictures of special house guests, information about Roxaboxen, and The Park.

A Letter to the Author: Work together as a class to compose an e-mail letter to the author. Use a digital camera to take pictures of the new town and describe the activities of the class. Access her Web site, and send the letter and the attached pictures. Show students how to check for responses.

■ Activity Focus: Neighborhood Planning

Technology Connection: Student Productivity (ISTE-students 3), Teacher Delivery of Lesson (ISTE-teacher II-III)

Collaboration:
- Sharing *The Little House* (Planning session 1): Media specialist with teacher participating
- Understanding land use (Planning sessions 2 and 3): Teacher
- A walking tour: Teacher and media specialist as co-facilitators

- Getting started with construction: Teacher
- Developing the buildings: Media specialist
- Finishing details: Teacher and media specialist as co-facilitators

Resources:

- *The Little House*, story and pictures by Virginia Burton (Boston: Houghton Mifflin, 1942)
- "Neighborhood Workshop" journals, enough copies for one per student
- *Me on the Map*, by Joan Sweeney (New York: Crown, 1996)
- Chart paper
- *Community Construction Kit* (Tom Snyder Productions, <www.teachtsp.com>, 1998). This is an easy-to-use computer program for designing and printing three-dimensional buildings. (We had six copies of the program.)
- Large sheet of butcher paper to form the background for the neighborhood. (Teacher's note: We used a six-foot length of paper for a class of 22 students. The paper was long enough so that students could make infrastructure, such as roads and undeveloped land, as well as building contributions to the neighborhood.
- Construction paper sheets (gray—roads, greens in assorted colors—grass/fields, blues in assorted colors—waterways)
- Chalk/white crayon—road lines
- Scissors
- Glue
- Road templates (Teacher's note: Use cardboard and cut a variety of lengths to form templates for tracing—straight pieces, curved pieces, short and long pieces.)

Preparation Tasks:

- Use a word-processing or spreadsheet program to create a "Neighborhood Workshop" journal for students to use as they plan and develop a model neighborhood. (See Figure 4.46.)
- Adult assistance: Recruit one or two family helpers to assist students during the actual construction of the three-dimensional buildings (the "building the three-dimensional structures" portion of Neighborhood Planning 5).

Assignment Descriptions:

Neighborhood Planning 1: Distribute the journals and begin with the brainstorming activity with the rectangles. As students share their drawings, comment on the changes made to the rectangles. Introduce *The Little House* and have students take note of all the changes experienced by the little house as you read the story. Brainstorm a list of the changes that happened to the little house (springtime, summer days, fall, winter, widening road, surrounding houses, apartments and stores, streetlights, arrival of the trolley line, addition of the elevated train and then the subway, skyscrapers, and return to the country and a new look).

Create a graph illustrating the effects of the changes on the little house. (See Figure 4.45.)

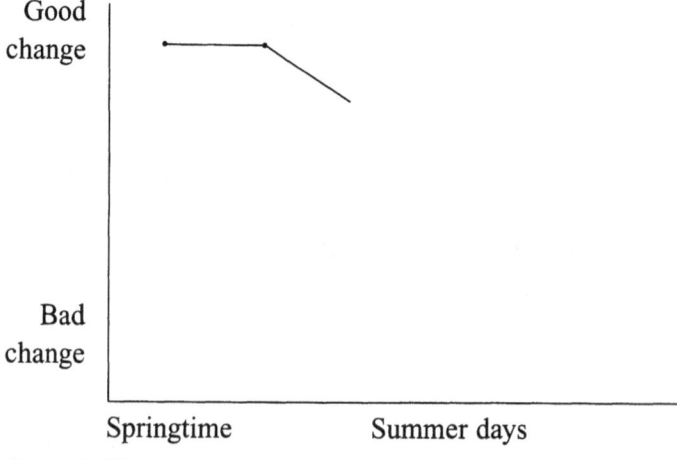

Figure 4.45 Changes Graph

146 Integrating Technology: Effective Tools for Collaboration

Cover Page

Neighborhood Workshop
Journal

Student:
Winter, 2001

It's more than a rectangle...

Land Use
Land can be used for many things: houses, schools, stores, parks, factories, churches, government offices, and lots more. Building a city is like putting together a jigsaw puzzle. Certain land uses, like puzzle pieces, will not fit well together. Only when each piece is in the right place, will you have a wonderful community with great neighborhoods.

A Survey
1. Where is the center of your neighborhood? (street, shopping place, park, school, other)

2. What landmarks are in your neighborhood? (church, school, fire station, stores, other landmarks)

3. What is your favorite place in the neighborhood?

4. Where do children play in the neighborhood?

Page 1

Land Use Definitions

Land Use: The way land is used.

Commercial: Space used for stores, offices, and services.

Residential: Spaces where people live.

Industrial: Space used for factories, machine shops, warehouses.

Recreational: Space used for amusement parks, bowling centers, miniature golf, golf courses, sports stadiums, parks, movies, and theaters.

Undeveloped Land: Open space in a neighborhood or community.

Putting together the land use pieces is an important part of what a city planner does. City planners must find the right balance among various land uses.

If we were city planners putting together a new neighborhood, here's what we should include:

_____

_____

_____

_____

_____

_____

_____

Page 2

Figure 4.46 Neighborhood Workshop Journal (continued on page 148)

Neighborhood planning

Page 3

You can learn a lot about a neighborhood by studying its buildings. Choose a building during the neighborhood walk and sketch a picture. What material is used on the outside of the building? What is the design of the windows and the door? How is the building landscaped?

Page 4

Senses observations from the neighborhood walk:

Page 5

Figure 4.46 (cont'd) Neighborhood Workshop Journal (continued on page 149)

My neighborhood commercial assignment:

Page 6

My neighborhood residential assignment:

Page 7

Reflecting on the project…

I learned…

I think it is interesting that…

Page 8

Figure 4.46 (cont'd) Neighborhood Workshop Journal

Close the activity period with a discussion of the land use information. Assign the survey as a homework connection.

Neighborhood Planning 2: Gather students in a community circle and invite them to share from the surveys: landmarks, places where children play, and favorite places. Create a list of their ideas as they share. Discuss land use definitions (page 2 of the "Neighborhood Workshop" journal), then categorize the places listed on the chart (C = Commercial; Res = Residential; Rec = Recreational; I = Industrial; and U = Undeveloped land). (Teacher's note: Land use is a challenging concept for young students, so don't worry if it seems confusing at this time. By the time students create the model neighborhood, you will hear them saying things like, "You can't have a factory near a house" or "The traffic will be bad if you put the police station right in the middle of the neighborhood.")

Share and discuss the book *Me on the Map* by Joan Sweeney. Focus on the little girl's neighborhood and map, showing where her neighborhood is in relationship to the town. Have students work with partners to identify the places they would like to include if they were planning a new neighborhood. Have them evaluate each category of land use and identify what they might include in that category. Remind them that it is okay to exclude a land use category, but they need to state a reason.

Neighborhood Planning 3: Gather students in community circle. Divide the chart paper into four sections: commercial, residential, recreational, undeveloped/industrial, and have each partnership share their land use planning ideas for a new neighborhood. List the ideas in the appropriate columns; when there are repeat responses, place tally marks next to the ideas that are repeated. Review the ideas and circle the ideas that have several tally marks. These become the "must include" buildings/land use ideas for the new neighborhood. Look again at the ideas that were not repeated, and analyze and discuss whether some of these also should be included.

Talk about infrastructure needs of a neighborhood, such as roads, rivers, ponds, and fields. Revisit the town layout in *Me on the Map* and discuss how the various land use sections complement each other. Have students work with their partners and plan a neighborhood layout using page 3 in their journals.

Neighborhood Planning 4: A Walking Tour: Plan a walking tour of a neighborhood. Have students sketch buildings they see on page 4 in their journals. The walking tour and the sketches will give them ideas for the buildings in the new neighborhood. Have students use page 5 in their journals to record impressions from their senses: sights (distinctive signs, vehicles, unusual mail boxes), sounds, smells, and textures (take a rubbing or two). When you return to the classroom, invite sharing and discuss students' observations.

Neighborhood Planning 5: Construction Time! Getting Started: Students will be eager to focus on the construction of the neighborhood, so plan several large blocks of time for students to work. Through goal setting, identify a variety of tasks that need to be accomplished during that block of time. Some of the tasks will focus on neighborhood construction, and some of the tasks will focus on regular morning or afternoon work, i.e., spelling, math, reading, and writing.

To develop partnership and individual assignments, return to the brainstorming from Neighborhood Planning 3.

Have students identify the infrastructure needs from the list and from discussions (roads, undeveloped land, waterways, and parks). List those needs on chart paper and make assignments. (See Figure 4.47.) Show students the materials for building infrastructure ideas (construction paper, road templates, glue) and have them review their neighborhood planning sketches on page 3 in their journals. Have them meet with their partners to discuss their infrastructure assignments.

Encourage them to create names for their contributions, e.g., Riverview Street, Fairview Park, Farmer Johnson's land, or Brookfield Pond. List the buildings for the neighborhood and make assignments. Students can create a living place (house, apartment, and condominium) and a commercial facility for the neighborhood. (See Figure 4.48.)

Access the computer program *Community Construction* and demonstrate its use. Encourage students to think about a complete picture of the buildings they design, i.e., front, back, left side, and right side. Show students how to add details to all four views of the building, including a name for the building if it is a commercial space, and how to save their buildings. (Teacher's note: We asked students to save the buildings they had designed and conference with an adult before printing the buildings. These are helpful steps to add to the process so that students are truly ready to print a finished building that includes appropriate details. Conferencing may take a little extra time, but it saves wasted paper and ink.)

For the first large block of working time, focus on creating the infrastructure and on students planning their building designs. Refer students to pages 6 and 7 in their journals; one page should show the front and back views of their commercial space design, and one page should show the front and back views of their residential design. Set goals so that students have several tasks to accomplish during the block of time, e.g., design my buildings, work with my partner and make my infrastructure contribution to the neighborhood map, work on my Day 2 spelling activities, choose an activity from the math center, and work on my "Flat Stanley/Stephanie" figure. Station yourself near the neighborhood road map to consult and to facilitate development of the infrastructure pieces.

```
Assignments: Infrastructure

Main road 1:     Jared, James
Main road 2:     Tanisha, Maria
Cul de sac:      Heather, Abigail
Side road 1:     Karyn, Lynn
Side road 2:     Samantha, Michelle
Side road 3:     Jeremy, Jake
Park:            Sam, Victor
Farmer's field:  Jennie, Ammie
Pond:            Stephen, Tate
Creek:           Mariah, Julie
```

Figure 4.47 Infrastructure Assignments

```
Assignments: Buildings

House, grocery store:             Jared
House, video store:               James
Apartment building, restaurant:   Tanisha
Apartment building, book store:   Maria
```

Figure 4.48 Building Assignments

Designing the Buildings: For this block of time, students design and print their buildings and continue to make additions to the neighborhood map. The software is loaded on computers in the media center, and small groups of students work with the media specialist. Again, setting goals helps students effectively use this block of time.

Finishing Details: Building and Placing the Three-Dimensional Structures: Once the buildings are printed (we printed them in black and white), have students color them and carefully cut them out. Help students fold and glue the designs into three-dimensional structures, then place them on the neighborhood map. Use double-sided tape to attach them to the map.

Create finishing details, e.g., road signs and small vehicles (cars, buses, and taxis). Leave the neighborhood set up in a space in the classroom, and give students time to revisit the neighborhood and imagine and play in small groups.

Reflecting: Have students reflect on learning using page 8 in their journals.

Who Are We? Immigration in the United States

Information Retrieval	Student Productivity	Problem Solving and Decision Making
Electronic encyclopedias, e.g., *World Book, Grolier's* Internet sites: **Oral History Scrapbook** <http://teacher.scholastic.com/immigrat/scapbk/index.htm> **Map of New York Harbor:** <www.americanpark.network.com/parkinfo/sl/aag/planning.html#map> **Immigration Statistics by County of Origin:** <www.infoplease.com/ipa/A0201398.html> **American Immigration Home Page:** <www.bergen.org/AAST/Projects/Immigration/>	Graphing Web Page	Internet site: **American Memory: Immigration:** <http://memory.loc.gov/ammem/ndlpedu/activity/port/start.html> *Decisions, Decisions: Immigration (Tom Snyder)*
		Communication and Collaboration
		Global Schoolhouse, Lightspan Company: <www.lightspan.com/corporate/pages/lsnetwork.asp?_prod=LS&_nav=nl_lsnetwork>

Teacher Delivery of Lessons	Classroom Management
Internet site: **Outline Maps:** <http://geography.miningco.com/cs/blankoutlinemaps/> **Stories from Today…Meet 5 Young People:** <http://teacher.scholastic.com/immigrat/bio/index.htm> **Seeking Citizenship in the U.S.:** <http://bensguide.gpo.gov/9-12/citizenship/examination.html> <www.washingtonpost.com/wp-srv/national/longterm/citizen/cittest.htm> Characteristics of historical fiction chart Interview sheet Reasons for emigrating chart	Reading assessment continuum

Figure 4.49 Immigration Unit: Technology Connections

Unit 5: Who Are We? Immigration in the United States

Unit Objectives:
1. Explore patterns of immigration in the United States.
2. Develop understanding of the reasons people are immigrants.
3. Become aware of symbols of America, e.g., Statue of Liberty and Ellis Island.
4. Understand the process by which immigrants become citizens.

Audience: Grades 4–8

Length of the Unit: 6 weeks

The Unit Activities at a Glance

What Is an American?	If You Were an Immigrant…
Students meet in teams to create images of Americans, then work as historians analyzing historical photographs.	Students put themselves in the shoes of recent immigrants, and discuss what they would bring and where they would settle.
Land of Hope: **Journey to America**	**Neighborhood Planning**
Students read the novel, interview family members, graph immigration statistics, explore reasons for immigration, compare "freedom" and "opportunity," research immigrants and their contributions to America, and investigate the process of becoming a citizen.	Students participate in the *Decisions, Decisions* immigration simulation.

Figure 4.49a Immigration, The Unit Activities at a Glance

■ Activity Focus: What Is an American?

Technology Connection: Problem Solving and Decision Making (ISTE-students 6)

Collaboration:
- Gathering poem resources: Media specialist
- Implementing the lesson: Teacher

Resources:
- Clear glass container
- Water, sugar, ice cubes, powdered drink mix
- A sheet of construction paper
- Small pieces of construction paper cut in geometric shapes in various colors
- Large sheets of butcher paper

Technology for Social Studies Units 153

- Decorating materials: markers, yarn, felt, glue, tape, pipe cleaners, fabric scraps, construction paper, and cotton
- Dictionaries
- Projection system

Preparation Tasks: Bookmark the Web site <http://memory.loc.gov/ammem/ndlpedu/activity/port/start.html> (American Memory: Immigration). Preview the site to develop a schedule for analyzing and interpreting the photographs and primary documents during the six weeks of the unit. The goal of the activity is to build visual literacy and to give students opportunities to work as historians.

Assignment Description:

Have students meet in small groups and discuss the terms "melting pot" and "mosaic," and decide which phrase/word students feel more accurately describes America and why. Before students decide, expand on students' understanding of the words with this demonstration.

Melting Pot: Use a clear glass container and mix a variety of materials

> I am an American kid.
> I worry about people getting along in the world.
> I wonder what I will be when I grow up.
> I love the excitement and fun of a 4th of July celebration...
> Fireworks, hamburgers on the grill,
> Remembering that I am free.
> I feel alive hanging with my friends.
> I am an American kid.

Figure 4.50 I Am an American

into a solution (water, sugar, powdered drink mix, ice cubes). The materials when mixed into the container lose their distinctive characteristics and become sweetened, iced drink.

Mosaic: Use small bits of paper cut into various geometric shapes and a larger piece of paper for the background. Create a design with the geometric shapes. The shapes retain their distinctive shapes and colors, but they now have become part of an overall design or picture.

Encourage sharing from the small groups; then introduce the products students will be creating—poems and body models representing a "typical" American child. Create a web of words and images describing a "typical" American child, then have students work in small groups (two to three students) and use the ideas in the web to write poems (see Figure 4.50) about their hopes and fears as American children and to create "butcher-paper models" of typical Americans. To make the models, have each small group trace one person's figure on butcher paper, then plan how to illustrate the model to characterize the American child. Use the construction paper and other supplies to decorate the figures. Present the poems and figures to the class.

Close the lesson by accessing the *American Memory* site, talking about how historians work (examining artifacts and piecing together the stories they tell), introducing the activity, then analyzing and interpreting the first photograph.

■ Activity Focus: If You Were an Immigrant...

Technology Connection: Communication and Collaboration (ISTE-students 4)

Collaboration:
- Project posting with *Global Schoolhouse*: Media specialist and teacher
- Analysis of the responses: Teacher and media specialist as co-facilitators

Resources: Web site software. e.g., *Navigator Composer, Claris HomePage*

Preparation Tasks:
- Several weeks before the unit, access *Global Schoolhouse* on the Lightspan Network <www.lightspan.com/corporate/pages/lsnetwork.asp?_prod=LS&_nav=n1_lsnetwork>, and register an online project for communication and collaboration with other students/classrooms across the United States. At the *Global Schoolhouse* page, click on "Project Registry," then select "add your project." Follow the online directions to register your project. Information requirements for project registry include the following details: Project Information: Author (name and e-mail address), title, beginning and ending dates, brief summary; Project Details: Level (beginning), curriculum areas (social studies), full description of the project, objectives; Project Registration Information: e-mail address, registration acceptance dates, number of classrooms, age range, target audience, additional registration information if needed. Assignment Description:
- For this unit, introduce the questions by sharing briefly from the book *Land of Hope*. Invite students to put themselves in the shoes of a recent immigrant and respond to these questions: What country would you emigrate to? Why? If you could bring only five items (besides a few items of clothing) with you, what five items would you bring? Why? Analyze and organize the responses from the participating classrooms and post the information on the Web site with the reports on immigrants and their contributions.
- Continue with the *American Memory* activity introduced in the first lesson.

■ Activity Focus: *Land of Hope:* The Journey to America

Technology Connection: Teacher Delivery of Lesson (ISTE-teacher II-III)

Collaboration: Beginning the novel: Teacher

Resources:
- *Land of Hope*, by Joan Lowery Nixon (New York: Bantam Books, 1992), enough copies for one per student
- Journals (Teacher's note: Use a spiral notebook or a folder filled with lined and unlined paper.)
- World maps, enough for one per student
- Atlases
- Colored pencils
- Dictionaries
- A large world map for a bulletin board display
- Yarn

Preparation Tasks:
- Bookmark these Web sites:
  <www.infoplease.com/ipa/A0201398.html> (immigration statistics by country of origin, from 1820)
  <http://teacher.scholastic.com/immigrat/bio/index.htm> (Meet five young people today and discover their stories.)

<www.bergen.org/AAST/Projects/Immigration/> (American Immigration home page)
<http://teacher.scholastic.com/immigrat/scrapbk/index.htm> (oral history scrapbook)
<www.americanparknetwork.com/parkinfo/sl/aag/planning.html#map> (map of New York Harbor)
<http://teacher.scholastic.com/immigrat/ellis/index.htm> (interactive tour of Ellis Island)
<http://bensguide.gpo.gov/9-12/citizenship/examination.html> (interesting resources about seeking citizenship in the United States)
<www.washingtonpost.com/wp-srv/national/longterm/citizen/cittest.htm> (citizenship test sample questions)

- Access the Web site <http://geography.miningco.com/cs/blankoutlinemaps/> and print a world map. Make copies for each student.
- Make a transparency showing the characteristics of historical fiction (See Figure 4.51.)
- Create an interview sheet for students to use as they visit with family members about their ancestors. (See Figure 4.52.)
- Begin a bulletin board display by posting the world map and making a title for the display, e.g., Family Heritage: Where Did Our Families Come From?
- Create a large chart to record reasons for immigrating to the United States. (See Figure 4.53.)
- Make two large circles (about a yard in diameter) that can be used to construct a Venn diagram; title one circle "freedom" and the other circle "opportunity." Because students will write on the circles, create a line where the circles will overlap to allow space to list ideas that are similar in both circles.
- Create a note-taking graphic organizer for students to use as they gather research notes. (See Figure 4.54.)

Historical Fiction Characteristics

1. Helps us experience and personalize the past.
   - to enter into the conflicts, despair, and joys of those who lived before us
   - to understand the private struggles behind public events in history

2. Offer opportunities to compare past and present

3. Builds recognition of universal human needs that do not change over time
   - respect
   - belonging
   - love
   - freedom
   - security

4. Provides a good story that balances fact with fiction.
   - includes authenticity of language, clothing, customs, and setting and events details
   - introduces characters who are true to the values and beliefs of the time

Figure 4.51 Historical Fiction Characteristics

Assignment Descriptions:

Beginning the novel: Introduce the novel *Land of Hope*. Look at the cover and title and make predictions, read the landing card information, and form mental pictures from the beginning paragraphs of the story. Continue reading aloud the first chapter in the story. Pause to remark on scenes, words, and events that really affect you. Some possibilities include: "lies and vain dreams" (page 2), "Mordecai, who had been gathering tidbits of information like a squirrel

Student:		
Date:		
Interview with Family Members		
	County of Birth	Customs
Dad		
Mom		
Grandparent		
Grandparent		
Grandparent		
Grandparent		
Great Grandparent		
Great Grandparent		
Great Grandparent		
Great Grandparent		
Special Celebration in Our Family:		

Figure 4.52 Interview Sheet

hoarding for winter…" (page 4 mental picture), the third paragraph on page 5, and imagining the feelings of relief, the sense of how much the family had left behind and how much they hope for a new way of life…without fear on pages 6–9.

Display the transparency of historical fiction characteristics and review the ideas. Have students write responses to this question in their journals: How does this first chapter show you that *Land of Hope* is historical fiction?

Making a Map: Distribute the world maps, and as a class, use the clues in the chapter to trace the family's journey so far.

Identify the Characters: Reread the third paragraph on page 3: "Elias sold what he could of the family's belongings, pooled his meager savings with his father's, and purchased **seven** steamship tickets." Have students make small face sketches in their journals of the members of the family. Encourage them to add names to the faces.

At-Home Connection: Distribute the interview sheet and ask students to interview a family member. Give students a day or two to gather the information. When students have completed the interview sheet, add to the bulletin board display; surround the map with index cards that share the heritages of the students in the classroom. Stretch yarn or string from the cards to the locations. (See Figure 4.55.)

Coming to America: Stand in the door to the class and simulate the experience described by Rebekah at the end of chapter 1. As students enter your classroom (or if they are already there, stand in the doorway, and ask them to leave the classroom), tell them to hurry, hurry, hurry. Poke and prod them along, telling them, "Hurry, you're going to miss it." Discuss the experience, reread the last paragraph on page 10, and have students imagine themselves in Rebekah's shoes.

Refer to the students' maps and read the opening paragraph in chapter 2. If you were Rebekah's father, what would your answer be? What difficulties/joys do you think they still face? (Have students briefly visit with partners and share with the class.) Have students read with partners and then discuss the chapter, e.g., what experiences continue to strongly affect their lives?

Reasons for Coming to America		
Country/ Person	County of Origin	Reasons

Figure 4.53 Immigration to America: Reasons

Technology for Social Studies Units 157

Research and Graphing: Have students work with partners, access the immigration statistics Web site, gather statistics for an assigned year, and create graphs showing the results of their investigations. In order to compare the graphs, discuss ways to build some consistency among the graphs, e.g., pie graphs showing immigration by continents or bar graphs showing immigration from selected countries of the world.

Reasons for Leaving: Read aloud the opening pages of chapter 3 (pages 17–19 to the last sentence at the top of page 20) and encourage students to build mental pictures of the scene facing the family. Read slowly and comment as you read to allow the images to build. If you were Rebekah, what thoughts would be running through your mind? What would your concerns be? Have students partner with peers and write some questions Rebekah would be asking herself; then have them read and respond to the chapter.

Student's Name:
Topic:
Sources
County of Origin:
Where did he/she settle?
Contributions to America:
Childhood Experience:
Graphics Citations:

Figure 4.54 Note-taking Graphic Organizer

Have students present, discuss, and compare their immigration graphs. What countries/areas of the world are consistently represented on the graphs? What countries/areas of the world are represented only one time or are not very well represented on the graphs?

Access the Web site (Meet five young people today and discover their stories), share the information with the students, and discuss why these young people have immigrated to the United States. Have students continue their investigations on immigration patterns by completing the following tasks; have them record the results of their findings on the large "reasons" chart (see Figure 4.53). Select countries/areas of the world represented on the graphs and research reasons for the immigration patterns, e.g., what events in the history/economy of the country have caused these immigration patterns? Access the oral history scrapbook Web site and the American Immigration Web site to explore reasons for immigrating.

The Journey Is So Long: Where are the immigrants in their journey to America? Read aloud the first paragraph in chapter 5 (page 33), then trace the continuing journey on the students' world maps. Conduct a lesson on context clues, using these words from the coming chapters: boundary, overstepped, customary, and offend. Set goals for reading and responding to chapters 5 through 8, e.g., customs that are changing for the immigrants and why this is necessary, and customs students observe with their families. Discuss:

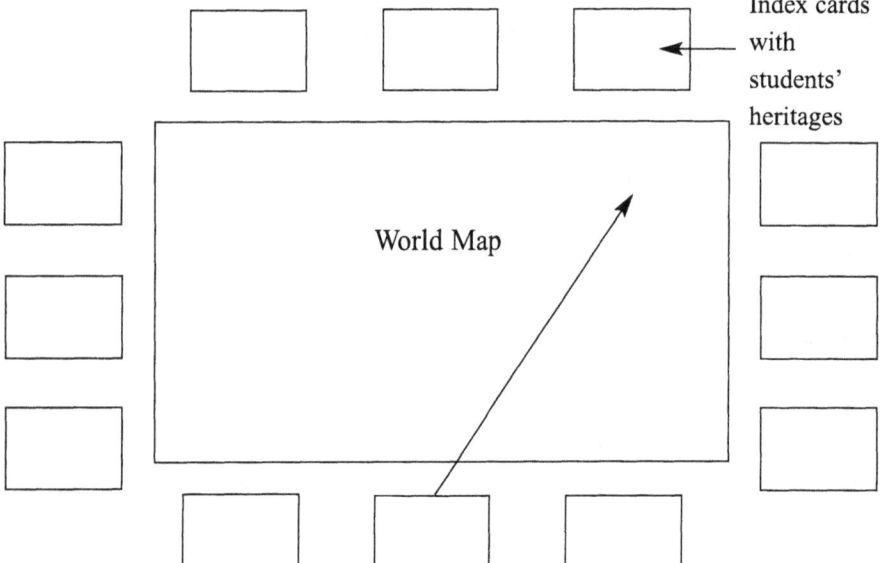

Figure 4.55 Family Heritages

How is Rebekah handling these changes? What is her reaction to the new ideas and new ways of doing things?

Have students report on their research findings and create a list showing major reasons for immigration in the countries displayed in the immigration graphs from the previous lesson.

Freedom and Opportunity: Divide the class into two sections. Assign research and investigation on the meaning of freedom to one section, and research and investigation on the meaning of opportunity to the other section. Students should record their ideas on the circles, leaving an open area for comparison. Review the two circles to identify how freedom and opportunity are similar. List those ideas in the overlap area. Which ideas of freedom and opportunity would be in Rebekah's mind?

Arrival at Ellis Island: Use self-stick notes and markers to circulate and label students (simulating the experience of the immigrants in the chapters for today). Don't reveal what the initials represent: R = red head, NWB = no water bottle, E = eyeglasses, C = cough, Sk = skin problem (cut, bruise, scrape). If you were an immigrant coming through Ellis Island and you were marked with one of these letters, what would be your reaction? What do you think the labels mean? Are they fair?

The ship is moving closer to America and will soon arrive in New York Harbor. Access the map of the New York Harbor Web site, find pictures that show New York and New York Harbor, and have students make sketches in their journals. Tour the Ellis Island Web site to prepare students for reading chapters 11–13, then set goals for reading and responding, e.g., have students create a flow chart illustrating the family's process of entry.

Making a Mark: Review the reality faced by the Levinskys. What would you do if you were in Grandfather's shoes? How would you react if you were a member of the family? What are the bright spots in their lives? Write the word "mitzvah" on the board, and ask students to discover the meaning of the word in their reading for the day and plan ways they can do "mitzvahs" during the day.

Introduce the research project. Students will research the lives of various immigrants to the United States throughout history and develop reports that share their contributions. The reports should explain how the immigrants "made their mark" in America and will be posted on a Web page. Distribute the note-taking graphic organizer (See Figure 4.54), review its requirements, and model how to gather the information. Students should list the countries where the immigrants or their families came from (country of origin), identify the area of the United States where the immigrant settled (sometimes this is not available), read and analyze the biographical information to identify contributions/accomplishments of the immigrants, and describe a childhood experience (sometimes this is not available). In planning pictures, students should identify sources for portraits or other pictures about the immigrant, or plan original drawings illustrating the immigrant's accomplishments.

Here are some suggested names for research; additional names and biographical information can be found at the Web site <http://immigration.about.com/newsissues/immigration/cs/famousimmigrants/index.htm>.

Karen Horney	David Sarnoff	Isaac Bashevis Singer
H. J. Heinz	Jacob Riis	Thomas Nast
Albert Einstein	John A. Roeblin	Leo Hendrik Baekeland
Connie Chung	Nikola Tesla	Alexander Graham Bell
Samuel Slater	Arthur Rubinstein	Nadia Comaneci
An Wang	Bela Bartok	Michael Dukakis
Isaac Asimov	Benjamin Bonneville	Henry Kissinger
Henry Morgenthau	Jascha Heifetz	Colin Powell
Louise Nevelson	Irving Berlin	Frederick Weyerhaeuser
James Wong Howe	Enrico Fermi	Andrew Carnegie
Mario Cuomo	Joseph Pulitzer	Mikhail Baryshnikov

A suggested layout for the Web page can be seen in Figure 4.56.

Becoming a Citizen: As students prepare to read the last chapter, have them think about the events of the story, particularly the last two chapters and the title. Discuss: Will the United States ever be a true "land of hope"? What needs to happen in this chapter to make this come true for each character? For Elias? For Leah? For Rebekah? For Nessin? For Jacob? For Sofia? Read chapter 19 aloud, and pause and comment as you read. Read Ms. Nixon's

Web Page Layout

Our Class	Write to Us	Famous Immigrants
Interesting Links	Reasons for coming to America	Traveling to America

Index Page

Information about the class

Link from "Our Class"

E-mail connection so that students/classrooms can correspond with your class.

Link from "Write to Us"

Famous Immigrant Reports

Link from "Famous Immigrants"

Other Web sites with links for immigration information

Link from "Interesting Links"

Chart on reasons for coming to America

Link from "Reasons for Coming to America"

Information for the collaboration opportunity...items students would bring if they were traveling to America

Figure 4.56 Web Page Planning

closing comments about Ellis Island. As students look at the graphs and chart on immigration statistics, review today's immigrants. Who are the people immigrating to America today? How do they become citizens of the United States? Access the Web site on citizenship; take students through the eligibility self-test and discuss the questions. Look at the civics test and try some of the questions.

■ Activity Focus: A New Situation

Technology Connection: Problem Solving and Decision Making (ISTE-students 6)

Collaboration: Implementing the simulation: Media specialist and teacher as co-facilitators

Resources:
- *Decisions, Decisions: Immigration* (Tom Snyder Productions. Telephone: 1-800-342-0236. Web site: <www.tomsnyder.com>)
- Advisor booklets from the software package
- Projection system

Preparation Tasks:
- Make multiple copies of the decision logs from the software package, enough for several per student.
- Create signs listing the names of the four advisor groups from the program: Counsel, USA, America, Chief. Each group will represent the advice of one of these roles and will make decisions based on the viewpoint of this role. Divide the class into four teams.

Assignment Description:
Introduce the simulation in a dramatic voice: "Good Morning, and welcome to the White House. I'm looking forward to working with you. Let me introduce myself: I'm President (your last name) and this is Vice-President (teacher's last name). We need your advice and opinions on some important decisions we are facing as a nation. We were elected three years ago, and it is time to think about re-election. Our first primary is rapidly approaching, and we face opposition from others in the party.

We also are facing a crisis! Boatloads of refugees are about to land on the shores of the country. In fact, they're headed for Fremont, the main port city of the state that will hold the first primary we face. Lots of volunteers are working to find homes for these refugees, but there are too many of them. In addition, there are a lot of people in Fremont who are not eager to welcome the newcomers. We really have a problem, and officials in Fremont want to know what we plan to do. So let me summarize our situation." (Write these facts on the board: three years in office, re-election ahead, boatloads of refugees about to land, and some say yes while others say no!)

Continue to follow the rules of the simulation. The simulation will take two to three days, and students will want opportunities to play again. After the whole class experience, set the program as a center in the classroom and give students opportunities to play again.

Chapter 5

Technology Projects for the Class

■ Portfolios

Audience: Grades 1–8

Length of Project: Ongoing throughout the year

Activity Focus: Portfolios

Technology Connection: Student Productivity (ISTE-students 3)

Collaboration:
- Storyboard and planning: Teacher
- Portfolio development: Teacher and media specialist as co-facilitators

Resources:
- *HyperStudio* or a similar multimedia presentation program
- Scanner
- Digital camera

Preparation Tasks:
- Create a continuum sheet that helps students rate their proficiency levels in each subject area. (See Figure 5.1.)
- Create a *HyperStudio* portfolio template that students can use to create an ongoing record of their successes and growth areas. (See Figure 5.2.)
- Set up a schedule that includes whole-class computer lab time and small-group follow up in the media center or the classroom.

Assignment Description:
Take students through a process of reflecting on their accomplishments in each of the subject areas. Identify and describe the levels of proficiency, i.e., acquiring skill (I usually need help and I rely on the teacher a lot), developing skill (I need some help and feedback, but usually I can get started and make some progress on my own), working independently (I need little assistance or feedback, I know and use lots of strategies and take ideas and go with them, and I often have an unusual or unique perspective). Help students mark the continua for their levels of proficiency and develop short explanations listing the reasons for their proficiency-level ratings, e.g., "I am a good writer. I use lots of description and show organization in the way I develop my pieces. I am most proud of my personal narrative because I used dialogue and spent a lot of time on editing, particularly my spelling, which is hard for me. This is a story about a fishing and hiking trip that

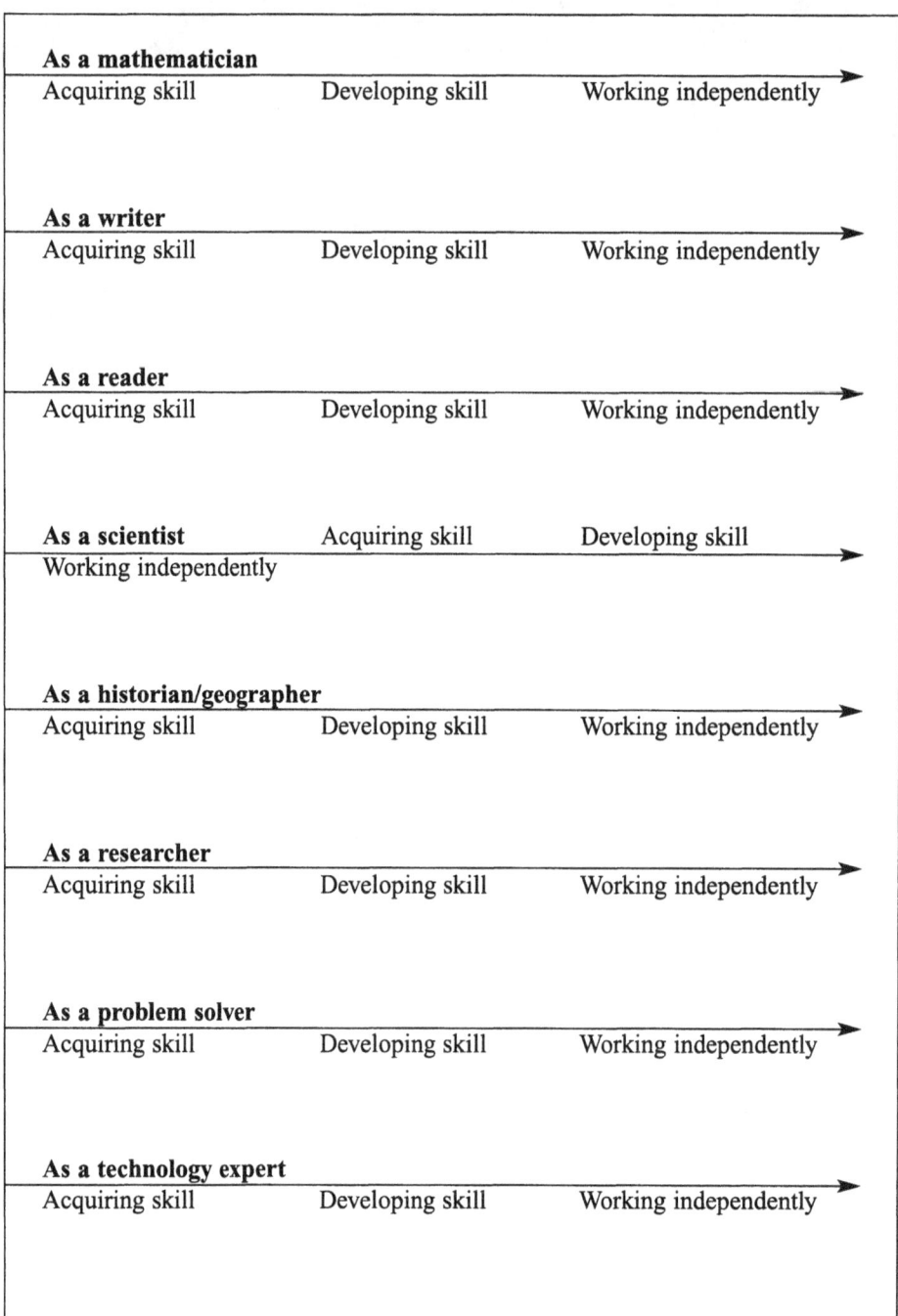

Figure 5.1 Continuum Rating Sheet

my dad and I took last summer. When I read it to the class, they really complimented me on my descriptions."

Help students identify examples of their work that they wish to include in the portfolio, e.g., a computation or problem solving example in math; a writing piece; a favorite book passage; a science, history, or geography project; an example of their research skills; or other examples that show their skills as thinkers. Have students use the digital camera to take pictures of one other. Save these pictures in a file on the computer.

Use computer lab time and small-group time to develop the portfolios. When the portfolios are ready for viewing, encourage students to invite family members for lunch, before school, or after school for private showings. They will be eager to share.

Figure 5.2 Portfolio Template

Card 1: Portfolio of (name) / Biographical Facts — Import a picture and add biographical details.

Card 2: Comments about Writing / Piece of Writing — Type reflection comments, and cut and paste the writing sample.

Card 3: Comments about reading, book jacket of a favorite book, and a recording of the student reading. — Type reflection comments and record yourself reading a favorite passage.

Card 4: Comments about math and samples of student's computation skills and problem solving skills. — Scan and import the math examples, then type reflection comments.

Card 5: Project example from history, science, or geography with comments. — Type reflection comments and scan and import, or use the digital camera to take a picture of the science, history, or geography project. If students are proficient with *HyperStudio*, they may wish to add a video clip of a project.

Card 6: Research example with comments — Add an example that reflects research skills or thinking skills or another area of proficiency.

■ Our Year in Pictures

Audience: Grades K–8

Length of Project: Ongoing throughout the year

Activity Focus: Our Year in Pictures

Technology Connection: Classroom Management (ISTE-teacher IV-V)

Collaboration: Slide show: Teacher

Technology Projects for the Class 165

Resources:
- Slide show program
- Scanner
- Digital camera

Preparation Tasks: Set up a slide show template.

Project Description:

"Our Year in Pictures" is a wonderful project for open house events in spring. During the year, get in the habit of taking pictures of classroom activities and events using the digital camera or a regular camera. Every two weeks or so, take time to select two or three pictures and import them into the slide show. (If they are taken with the digital camera, they are already on the computer; if they are taken with a regular camera, scan the pictures and add them to the show.)

Allow time the next day during your opening or closing routines to show the pictures to the students and develop captions together. Type the captions and save. Repeat the process throughout the year, and by open house, you will have a great show!

■ Mother's Day Tea

Audience: Grades 1–3

Length of Project: 1 week

Activity Focus: Mother's Day Tea

Technology Connection: Student Productivity (ISTE-students 3)

Collaboration:

Cards and preparation for the slide show: Teacher
Slide show: Media specialist

Resources:

construction paper
illustrating materials, e.g., markers, crayons, and colored pencils
slide show program
digital camera

Preparation Tasks:
- Set up a slide show template.
- Develop a graphic organizer/insert for the students to use as they prepare their Mother's Day cards and their ideas for the slide show. Use half sheets (8½" × 5½"). (See Figure 5.3.)
- Use school pictures or take pictures of the students using the digital camera. Print the pictures.
- Browse your photograph albums and select a childhood picture when you were one of the ages of the children you teach.

Project Description:

Have students select construction paper covers, fold them in half, and decorate the outsides. On the inside front cover, have them write Mother's Day wishes and sign the cards.

Work on the graphic organizer/insert packet. Attach current pictures of the students in the frame on the "Here I am" page. Have students write a sentence or two about themselves at this age. (For example, "I'm in the second grade, and I love to draw. My favorite sport is tennis.") Have students draw pictures imagining what they will look like in 20 years; then complete the "When I grow up, I might be" page. (For example, "When I was your age I wanted to be an engineer for a toy company, then I wanted to be an artist and live in a loft. I even thought about becoming a writer.") Choose one of the ideas and use the webbing page to brainstorm the activities you would enjoy in that job. (For example, "If I were an artist, I would work in a studio, take walks with my sketch pad, set up my easel and begin a new painting, order art supplies, and have a show.")

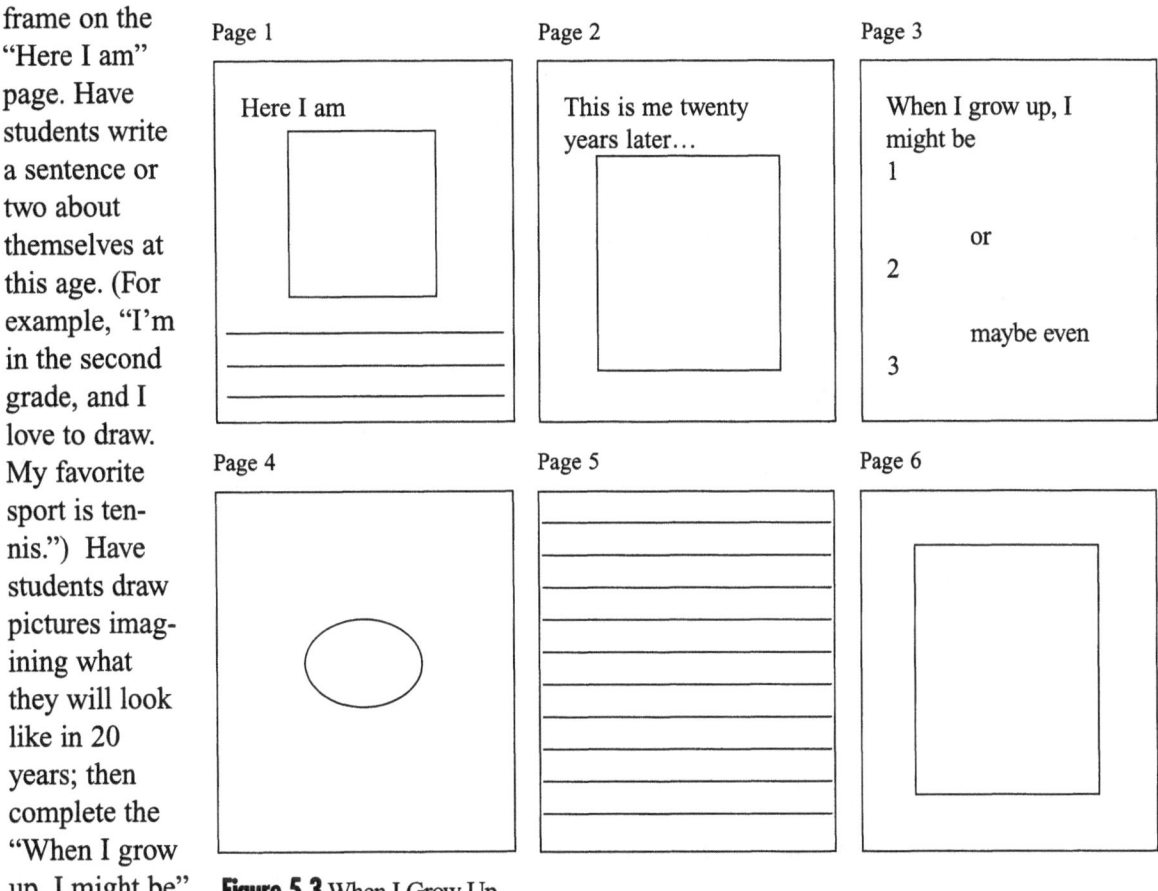

Figure 5.3 When I Grow Up

Focus on developing paragraphs and model the process for the students. The topic sentence should name the job and express a feeling or opinion about the job. (For example, "The best part about being an artist will be using my imagination.") The supporting detail sentences should describe the "where" and "what" of the job. (For example, "My studio will be filled with light, and most of the walls will be covered with sketches and ideas for paintings. Some days, I will spend time walking and sketching. When I'm ready to paint, I will set up my easel and begin to work. I will sell my work at a gallery.") The closing sentence finishes the paragraph. (For example, "An artist's job will be fun and creative.") Have students use their web ideas to write paragraphs describing the job they will have when they grow up. Record the polished paragraphs on page 5 of the packet. Use the final page of the packet to have students draw pictures showing themselves working at their "grown-up" jobs.

Set up a schedule for small groups to work in the media center creating the slide show. Each student will contribute one slide to the show; the slide will include their "grown-up" job picture and the paragraph about the job. Brainstorm a title for the show and invite one student to create this title slide.

Finish preparing the cards. Attach the graphic organizer packet to the inside of the card. Make construction paper envelopes and insert the cards into the envelopes. Address the envelopes. Prepare invitations for the tea party and send them home. Plan and prepare for the tea party, i.e., foods, songs, the slide show, and presentation of the cards.

■ Reading Log

Audience: Grades 1–8

Length of Project: Beginning of the Year Task

Activity Focus: Reading Log

Technology Connection: Classroom Management (ISTE-teacher IV-V)

Collaboration: Creating the log: Teacher

Resources:
- Clip art Web sites:
  <www.arttoday.com/PD-0031927/Main/searching/search> (This is a convenient site because you can enter search terms, e.g., history or fantasy, and the site narrows art selections to those meeting your search requirements. You still have to browse a little, but it's more purposeful and successful.)
  <www.awesomeclipartforkids.com/> (colorful and fun stuff)
  <http://webclipart.tqn.com/internet/webclipart/msub64.htm> (This is another site that can be narrowed to a selected category, then has lots of choices in the category.)

Preparation Tasks:
- Identify genres you want the students to read during the school year or during each semester.
- Bookmark the clip art sites so that they are easy to return to and use. Browse the Web sites to identify clip art that would make fun symbols for the genres. Save them in a folder or import them directly into your reading log.

Student	Independent Reading, 2001-2002
	Reading Titles
Adventure/Survival Story	
Animal Story	
Biography	
Fantasy Story	
Historical Fiction Story	
Humorous Fiction Story	
Mystery Story	
Newbery Award Fiction	
Poetry	
Realistic Fiction Story	

Figure 5.4 Reading Log

Project Description:

Create a reading log for students for the year. (See Figure 5.4.) Print multiple copies so that each student has one for the front of his or her reading journal.

For younger students, your sheet might include favorite author (with space to record several books by the author that the student reads), Caldecott Award fiction, animal stories, nonfiction, poetry, fairy tale, or folktale.

One-Page Learning Contracts

Audience: Grades 1–8

Length of Project: Off and on during the school year

Activity Focus: One-Page Learning Contracts

Technology Connection: Classroom Management (ISTE-teacher IV-V)

Collaboration: Development and implementation of the contracts: Teacher

Resources:
- Clip art Web sites:
  <www.arttoday.com/PD-0031927/Main/searching/search> (This is a convenient site because you can enter search terms, e.g., history or fantasy, and the site narrows art selections to those meeting your search requirements. You still have to browse a little, but it's more purposeful and successful.)
  <www.awesomeclipartforkids.com/> (colorful and fun stuff)
  <http://webclipart.tqn.com/internet/webclipart/msub64.htm> (This is another site that can be narrowed to a selected category, then has lots of choices in the category.)
- Spreadsheet software, e.g., *AppleWorks, Microsoft Excel*

Preparation Tasks:

Develop a variety of one-page learning contract grids like the ones in Figure 5.5—a grid with room for four activity choices, six activity choices, eight activity choices, and nine activity choices. Save them individually as stationery files, i.e., four grid, six grid, eight grid, and nine grid. As a stationery file, each time you open the file, it will open as an untitled document and allow you to save it for the particular unit or focus of activities.

Identify a selection of learning tasks (four to nine, depending on the slots in your

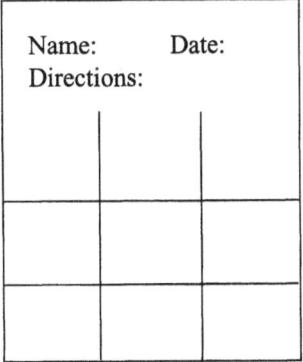

Figure 5.5 Learning Contract Grid

learning grid, the length of time for the contract, and the needs of the students) that give students opportunities to practice skills, develop skills, and extend and enrich content objectives. Organize the activities on the learning contract grid. (See Figure 5.6.) The Learning Stations example is suitable for younger students, and the Poetry Contract is one that would be used by older students.

Project Description:

One-page learning contracts give students flexibility and choice, and allow teachers to differentiate to meet the needs of students. Introduce students to a short-term, four-choice contract at the beginning of the year, and closely monitor and support their completion of the contract activities. Continue to monitor and support through several contracts to ensure that students understand the process and grow accustomed to the responsibility. Schedule weekly or periodic celebration afternoons or times during opening morning activities where students have opportunities to share products from a contract activity.

Learning Stations

| Name | | Series 1 |

Your goal is to complete all of the learning station activities. You may do them only once. Place all completed work in the learning station basket. If you have work you haven't finished, keep it in a safe place—your learning stations folder. You will need to continue with that activity when you begin work again. Be sure to record the date you complete an activity.

M A T H	**Number Facts** Work with a partner and use the addition flashcards or the game It All Adds Up to practice your addition facts. Date completed:	**My Favorite Graph** Get to know your classmates! Create a question. You might want to know what kind of pets your friends have or their favorite colors or summer trips. Collect data and make a graph of your results. Date completed:	**Number Facts** Use unifix cubes in two colors. Using both colors, show an addition fact. Write the number sentence. Show the fact family. Date completed:
R E A D I N G	**Independent Reading** Pick a Henry and Mudge book that you really want to read. Write a reading review on the computer. BE SURE TO SAVE YOUR REVIEW! Check with your teacher before printing. Date completed:	**Reading Aloud** Pick a poem from the poetry tub. Read it several times, then practice reading it aloud with lots of expression and good pauses. Finally, share it with your teacher. Date completed:	**Compound Words** Use the "Working with Compound Words" worksheet; find a partner and complete the worksheet together. Date completed:
W R I T I N G	**Writing a Description** Choose a favorite place you want to describe in a paragraph. Use the senses brainstorming web and collect details about the place. Date completed:	**Changes** Go to the mixing center. Pick two items of your choice. Place them in a cup of water. Record on the observation sheet with pictures and words what you observed. Date completed:	**Riddles** KEEP IT A SECRET! Pick an object from the bucket. Write four descriptive words or phrases about the object. If the object was a crayon, your words and phrases might be: lime green, smooth and pointed, wrapped in paper, and lives in a box with many neighbors. Put the object and your descriptive words in the completed work bucket. Date completed:

Figure 5.6 Learning Contract Example

Poetry Contract

Name _____

Use the contract activities to create your own poetry journal. Your journal should include a decorative cover and a detailed table of contents. Your journal entries should be easy to read and follow; illustrations should be carefully crafted.

Found Poetry	**The Work of a Poet**	**Figurative Language**
Take time to browse newspapers, magazines, and food container labels, and gather lots of words and phrases. Place the words and phrases in an envelope until you are ready to build your poem. Spread out the words and phrases and move them around to make the poem, then paste the words onto a page in your journal. Add an illustration.	Choose a poet and research his/her life. Choose a creative way to report your research facts. Be sure to include poetry from the poet you researched.	Browse a variety of poetry books and find examples of personification, simile, metaphor, and alliteration. Use your journal to record and explain the examples you have selected.
Date completed:	Date completed:	Date completed:
Haiku Poetry	**Poetry Performance**	**Limericks**
Participate in the introductory lessons on writing haiku poetry. Browse the book *Red Dragonfly on My Shoulder* to look at the materials used in creating the illustrations. Create your own nature scene, then write a haiku poem and place it in the scene.	Browse the poetry books in the media center and select one to share with the class. Give a booktalk and perform at least two poems from the book.	Edward Lear is famous for his limericks. Work with a partner and use the books in the class library to explore this verse form. Limericks have a definite rhyme pattern (aabba) and a distinctive rhythm. Practice reading them aloud until you are confident about writing one. Write one, then revise and edit it with the help of your partner.
Date completed:	Date completed:	Date completed:

Figure 5.6b Poetry Contract

www.ingramcontent.com/pod-product-compliance
Lightning Source LLC
Chambersburg PA
CBHW080411300426
44113CB00015B/2474